TO MY FAMILY – LYNNE, JC, AND NATALIE

EMBRACE THE STRUGGLE

THE ART OF CHRIS NAVARRO

BY CHRIS NAVARRO

20% CHANCE OF FLURRIES (2005)

Bronze, 36" x 30" x 14"

Monumental Bronze, 15' x 11' x 7'

20% Chance of Flurries was commissioned as a 15-foot tall monument by the Colorado Department of Agriculture. Placed at Colorado State University in Fort Collins, Colorado, the sculpture honors the dedication and hardships of the people who make their living through ranching and farming.

Guy and Vern Robinett, rancher friends of mine from Casper, Wyoming, modeled for the sculpture while we were riding out in their pasture to catch a young calf. As Vern put the calf across his saddle, he told me about the time a few years back when the weather forecast for that day was a twenty percent chance of flurries. The seemingly small storm turned out to be a severe spring blizzard that killed more than half of their herd! As I depict the rancher in the sculpture, his head is down against the wind, calf across the saddle, horse pulling through deep snow in the middle of a blizzard.

For me, this image of a cowboy on a horse saving a young calf embodies a test of endurance and highlights the best qualities of those who live in the West. They face hard conditions and take life as it comes.

WHEN EVERYTHING GOES TO HELL, THE PEOPLE WHO STAND BY YOU WITHOUT FLINCHING–THEY ARE YOUR FAMILY.
–JIM BUTCHER

First Printing, 2016

ISBN 978-0-692-69389-6
Printed in the United States of America
Bang Printing
3323 Oak Street
Brainerd, MN 56401

Edited by Robin Beaver
Design by Justin Pehrson

Contact information:
Navarro Studio
5231 Squaw Creek Road
Casper, WY 82604
307-259-7305
chrisnavarrostudio@gmail.com
chrisnavarro.com & cnavarroart.com

I would also like to thank all the collectors of my work for helping me to continue doing what I love. I would never have been able to follow my passions without your support.

WHEN YOU BUY FROM AN INDEPENDENT ARTIST YOU ARE BUYING MORE THAN JUST A PAINTING OR A NOVEL OR A SONG. YOU ARE BUYING HUNDREDS OF HOURS OF EXPERIMENTATION AND THOUSANDS OF FAILURES. YOU ARE BUYING DAYS, WEEKS, MONTHS, YEARS OF FRUSTRATION AND MOMENTS OF PURE JOY. YOU ARE BUYING NIGHTS OF WORRY ABOUT PAYING THE RENT, HAVING ENOUGH MONEY TO EAT, HAVING ENOUGH MONEY TO FEED THE CHILDREN, THE BIRDS, THE DOG. YOU AREN'T JUST BUYING A THING. YOU ARE BUYING A PIECE OF HEART, PART OF A SOUL, A PRIVATE MOMENT IN SOMEONE'S LIFE. MOST IMPORTANTLY, YOU ARE BUYING THAT ARTIST MORE TIME TO DO SOMETHING THEY ARE TRULY PASSIONATE ABOUT; SOMETHING THAT MAKES ALL OF THE ABOVE WORTH THE FEAR AND THE DOUBT; SOMETHING THAT PUTS THE LIFE INTO THE LIVING.

–REBEKAH JOY PLETT

FOREWORD

Embrace the struggle – it's a fairly innocuous line on the surface; sounds good rolling off the tongue... looks good on paper. But I must admit, it took me several attempts to really dig into that phrase. I was reluctant to address the kind of introspective questions that are provoked by such a loaded statement. "Why should I?" "How can I?" I mean, have I ever *truly* embraced anything that was a struggle in my life, or have I just simply endured?

A quick inventory of trying times, drove my initial impression to conclude that I struggle to embrace the struggle. However, exceptions surfaced after I dropped the negative connotation that I automatically assigned to the word. I embrace the challenges that involve someone or something that I have love for or have chosen to be a part of.

Alright then, *why* do I embrace the difficult aspects of the things I love? For me, the answer to that is beautifully captured in *Liberation,* one of my favorite works by Chris.

That is what Chris does so well time and time again with his art – speaking in simple truths, answers to questions or questions to answers are found through the narratives he creates.

Chris is constantly advising people to follow their passions, to really define a dream and go for it. Succeed or fail, 100% in, no regrets. This familiar tune, also found in pop songs and motivational posters, usually draws a rolling of the eyes. But I have learned that with Chris, it's not a cliché. He actually practices what he preaches and is living testament that with hard work and an unwavering constitution, a person really can adjust their reality to reflect their dreams.

So, how does a guy know that the right decision for himself and his young family is to quit a good paying job to become an artist? How does a guy break such a colorful assortment of bones and know that he has to get back in the saddle to rodeo on? How does anyone overcome tragedy, quiet the naysayers, and rise above doubt and fear?

You welcome those challenges with open arms. You always look for that silver lining and if nothing else, love the hard-earned lessons and experience gained from the trial. You do this because long after souvenirs lose their significance and said words have become forgotten, all we are really left with is how we felt at that moment in space and time. It's easy to feel good about good things in our past. It takes a bit more effort to recall positivity from the bad and I believe it's worth that extra effort to fill our buckets with as much happiness as possible. That is what I didn't know that I wanted to know. That is what Chris has taught me about embracing the struggle.

–JUSTIN PEHRSON
Photographer & Friend

MATTHEW H. MEAD
GOVERNOR

THE STATE OF WYOMING

STATE CAPITOL
CHEYENNE, WY 82002

Office of the Governor

December 10, 2015

Chris Navarro
5231 Squaw Creek Road
Casper, WY 82604

Dear Chris,

I am pleased to let you know that I have selected you to receive a Governor's Arts Award for 2015. This is a prestigious award which recognizes outstanding achievement in the arts in Wyoming. Since originating in 1982, the award has gone only to a select few each year.

Your monumental bronzes grace our University, our museums, and too many other places to enumerate. Everyone knows your work and marvels at it. It is indeed impressive. Along with talent, you have a generosity of spirit, giving back to the community in many ways. In a career spanning over 30 years, you have touched many lives in Wyoming, across the country, and around the world - and you continue to do so.

The 2015 Governor's Arts Award will be presented at a banquet and awards ceremony to be held in Cheyenne on the evening of February 26, 2016. You are one of six recipients I have chosen to be honored this year. Thank you for your commitment to the arts in Wyoming and congratulations!

Sincerely,

Matthew H. Mead
Governor

MHM:mdm

CONTENTS

MONUMENTS

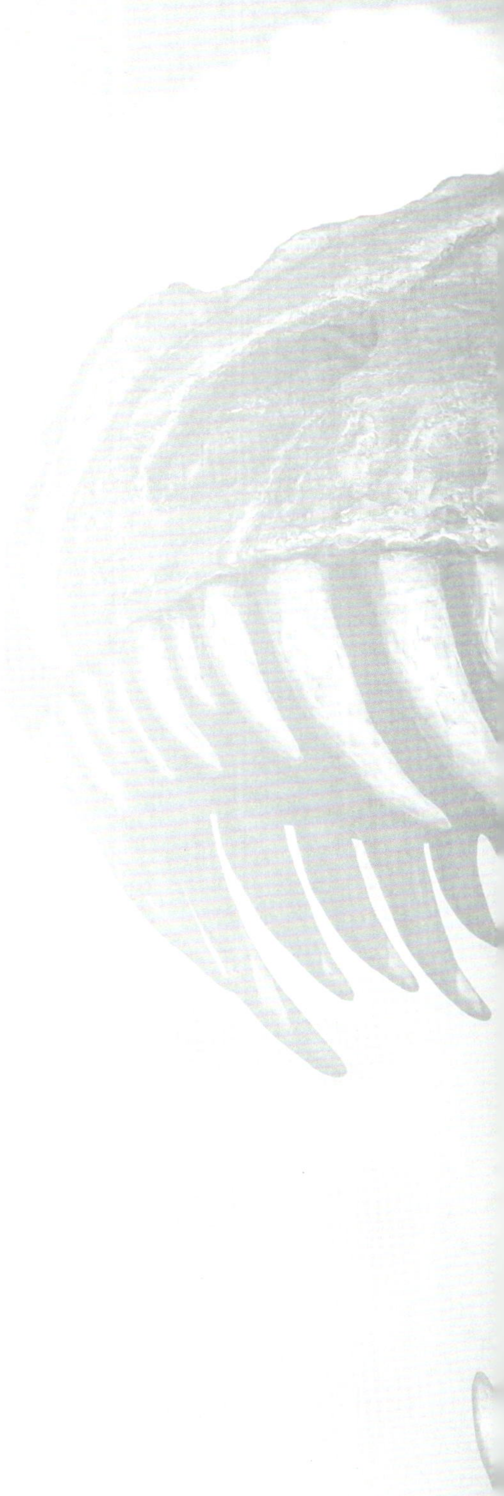

I KNOW IF I HAVE A TOOL IN MY HAND AND SPEND ENOUGH TIME AND EFFORT, NO PROJECT OR IDEA IS TOO BIG.
–CHRIS NAVARRO

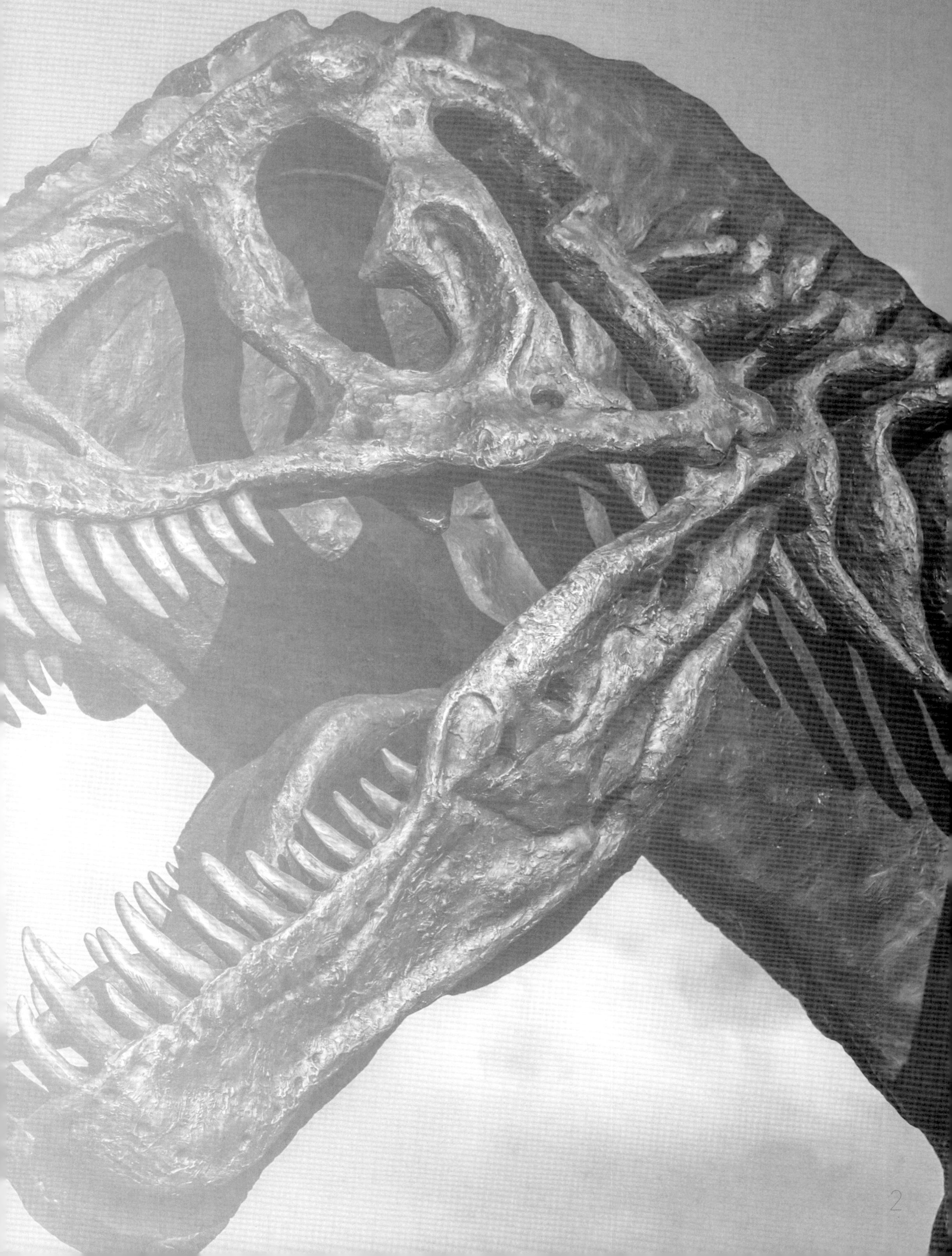

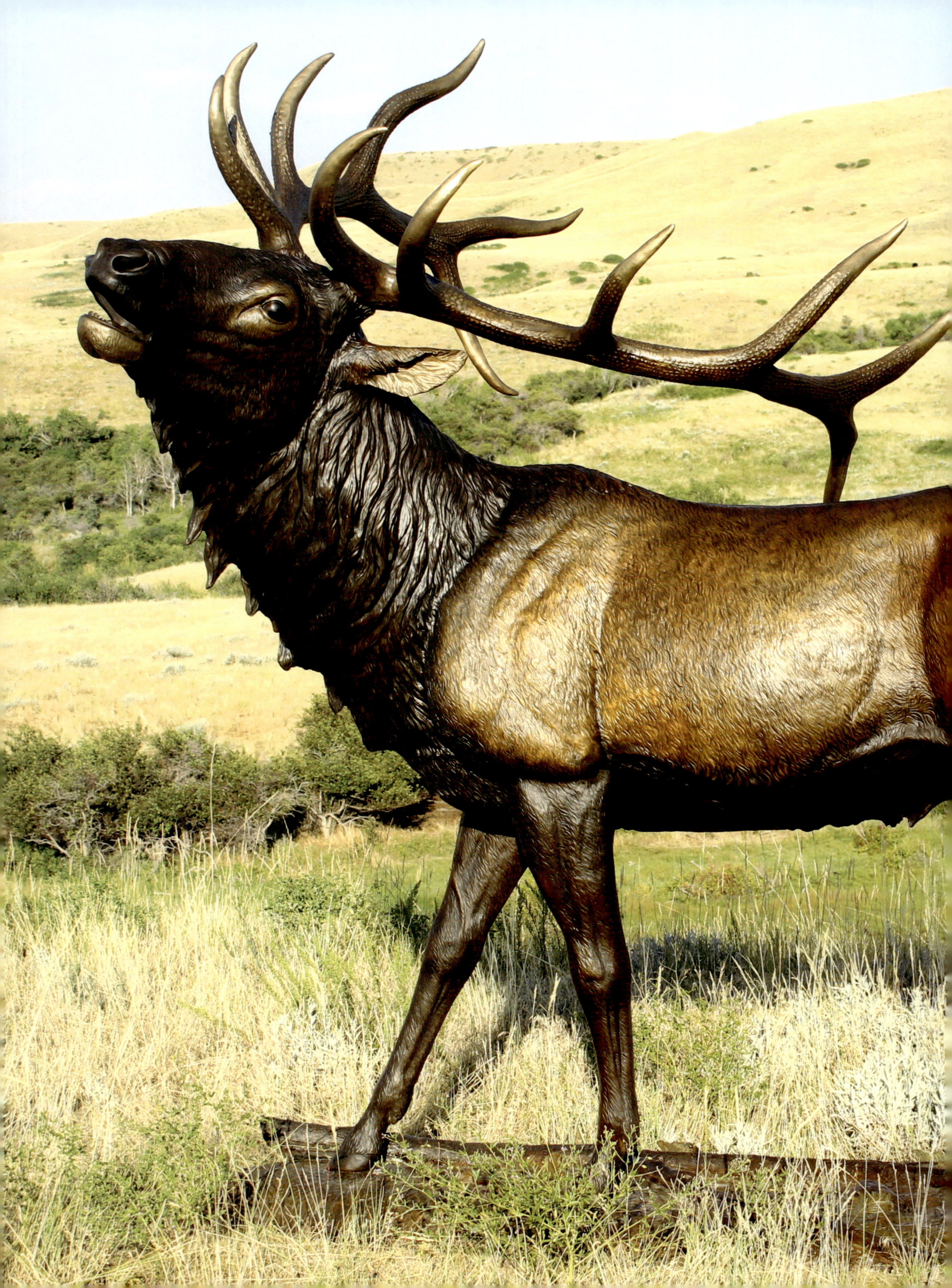

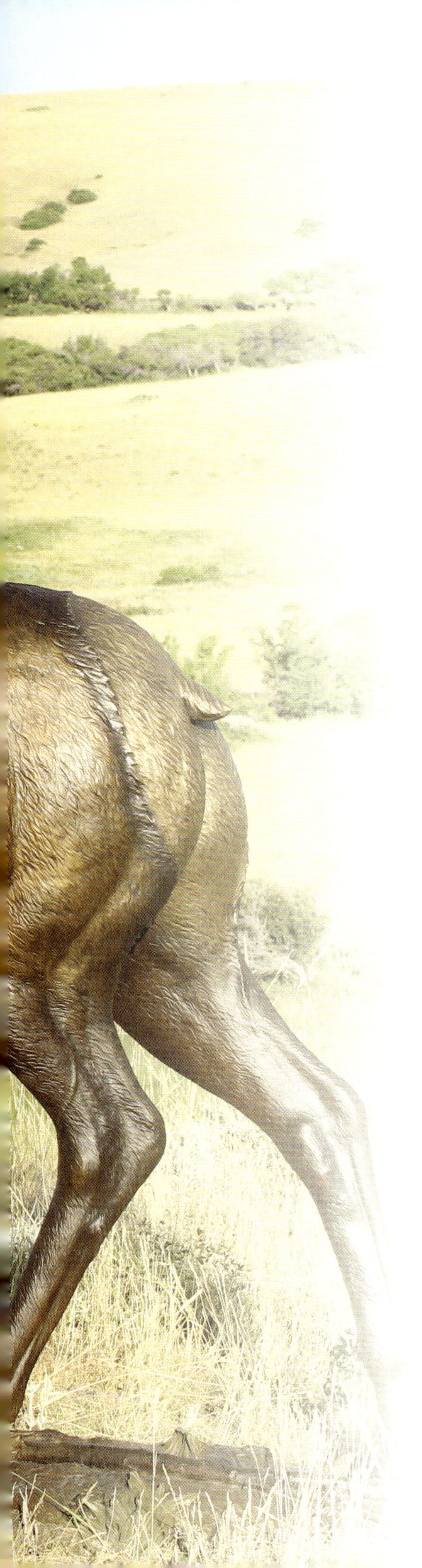

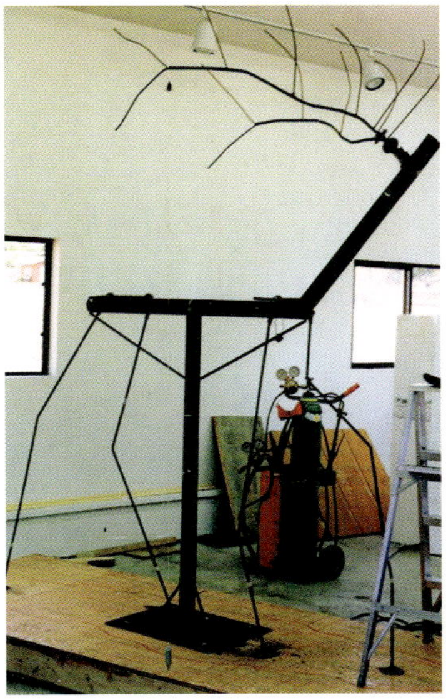

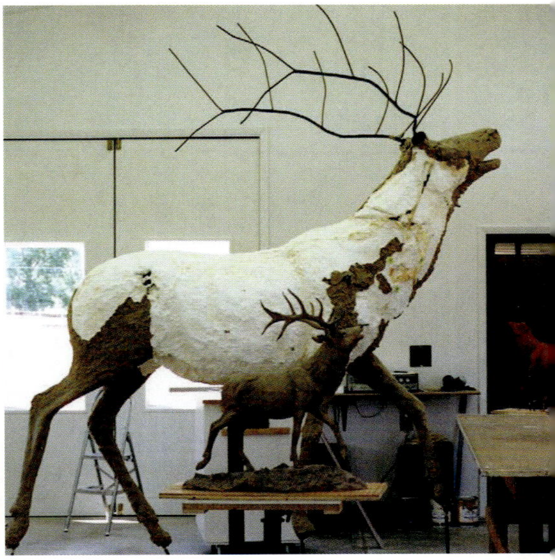

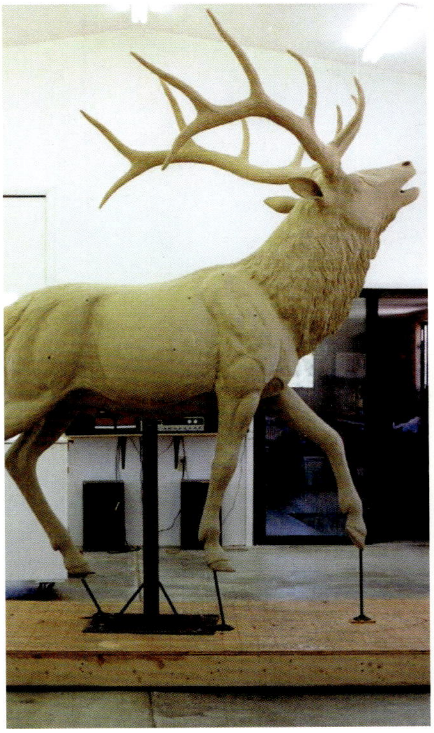

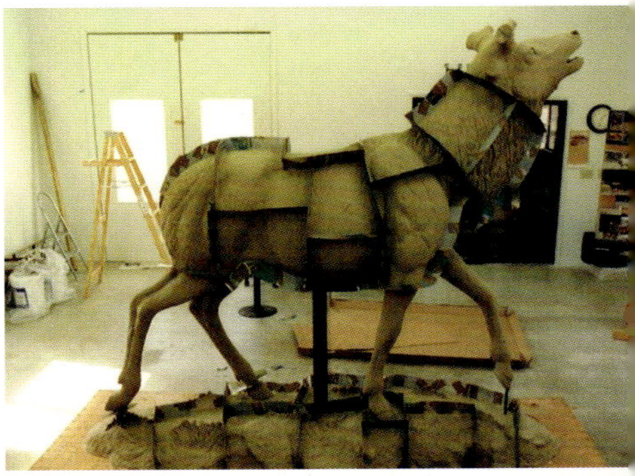

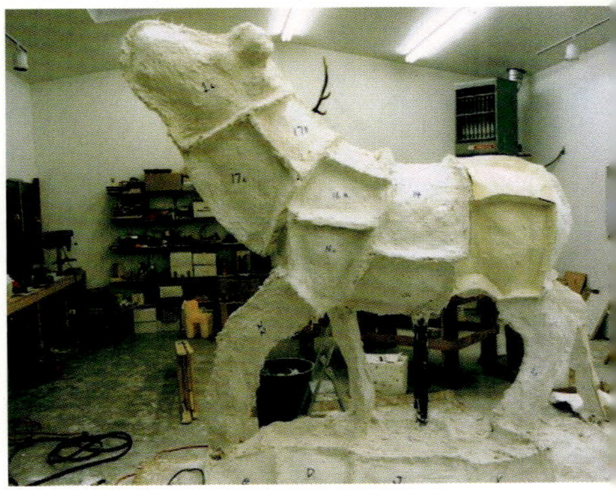

AUTUMN'S CHALLENGE (2004)

Bronze, 25.5'' x 25'' x 10''

Monumental Bronze, 9' x 9.5' x 9'

Bull elk will sound their bugle or whistle call during the rutting season. It begins with a low bellow and changes almost immediately to a high-pitched noise that can be described only as a whistle or scream. The bugle serves as a challenge to other bulls and the signal of domination over cows.

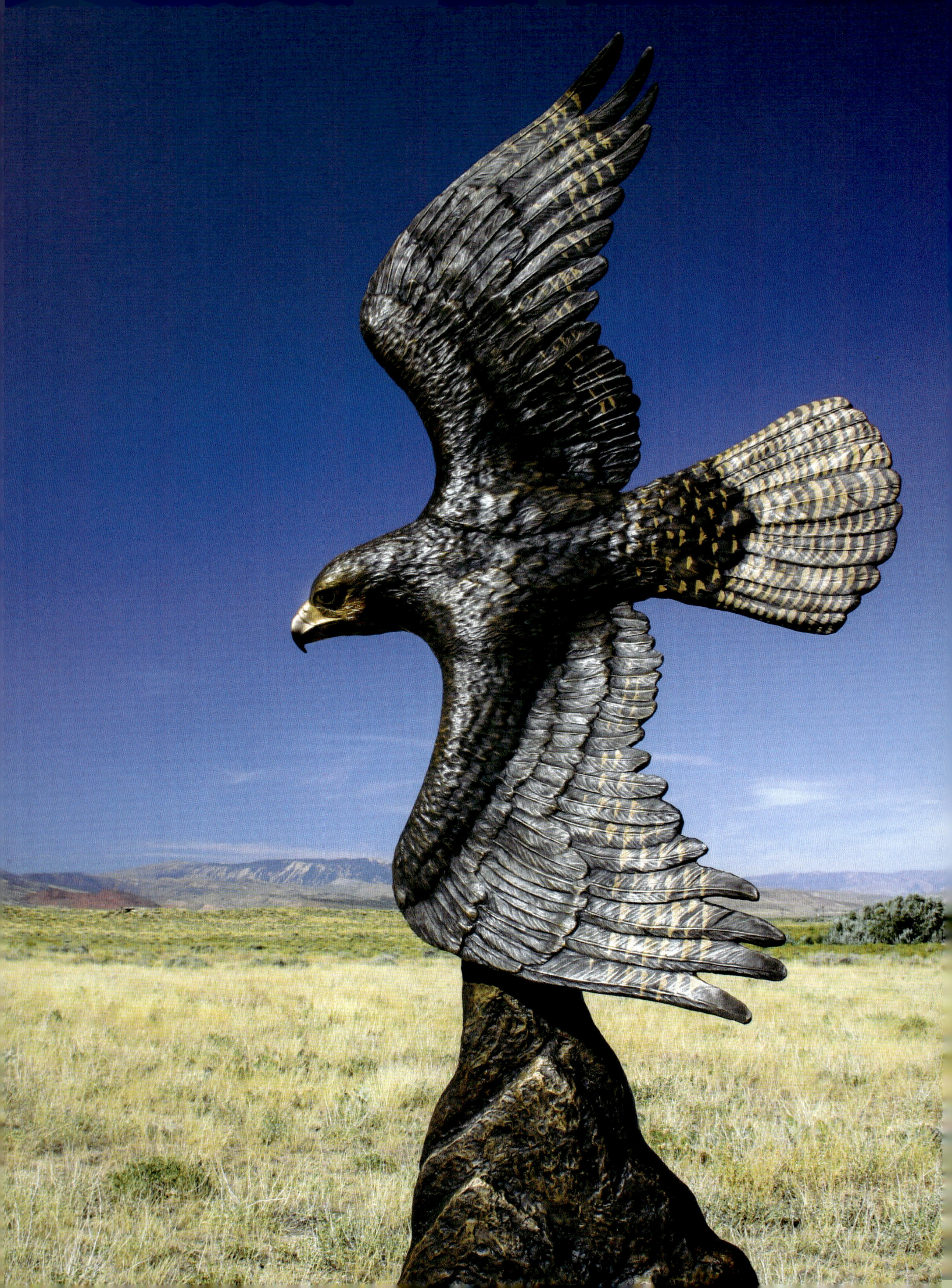

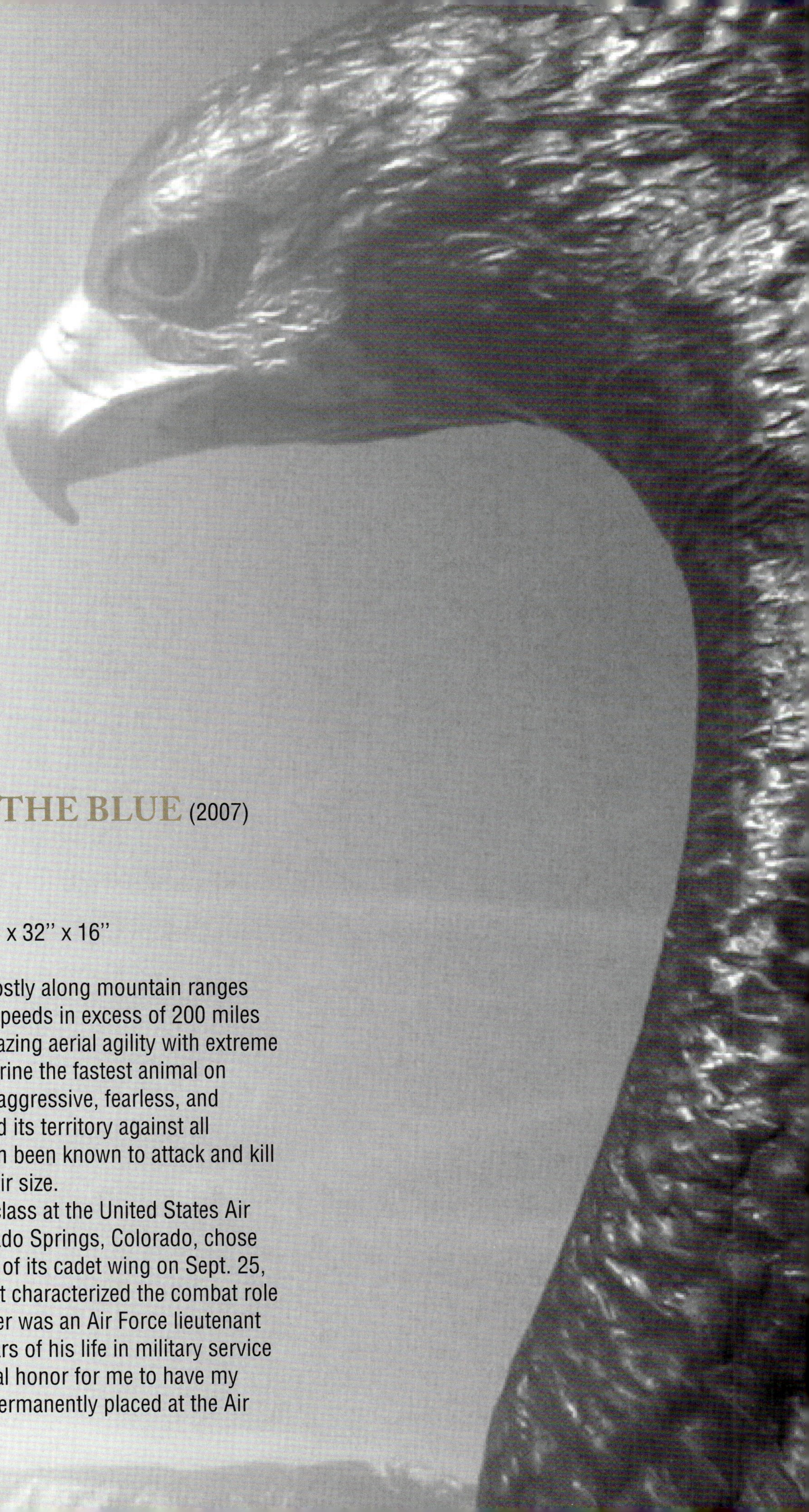

BOLT FROM THE BLUE (2007)

Bronze, 20" x 9" x 5"

Monumental Bronze, 72" x 32" x 16"

Peregrine falcons live mostly along mountain ranges and are known to clock speeds in excess of 200 miles per hour. Combining amazing aerial agility with extreme velocity makes the peregrine the fastest animal on the planet! Known to be aggressive, fearless, and courageous, it will defend its territory against all intruders. They have even been known to attack and kill prey more than twice their size.
Members from the first class at the United States Air Force Academy in Colorado Springs, Colorado, chose the falcon as the mascot of its cadet wing on Sept. 25, 1955, in belief that it best characterized the combat role of the Air Force. My father was an Air Force lieutenant colonel and spent 30 years of his life in military service for his country. It is a real honor for me to have my monumental sculpture permanently placed at the Air Force Academy.

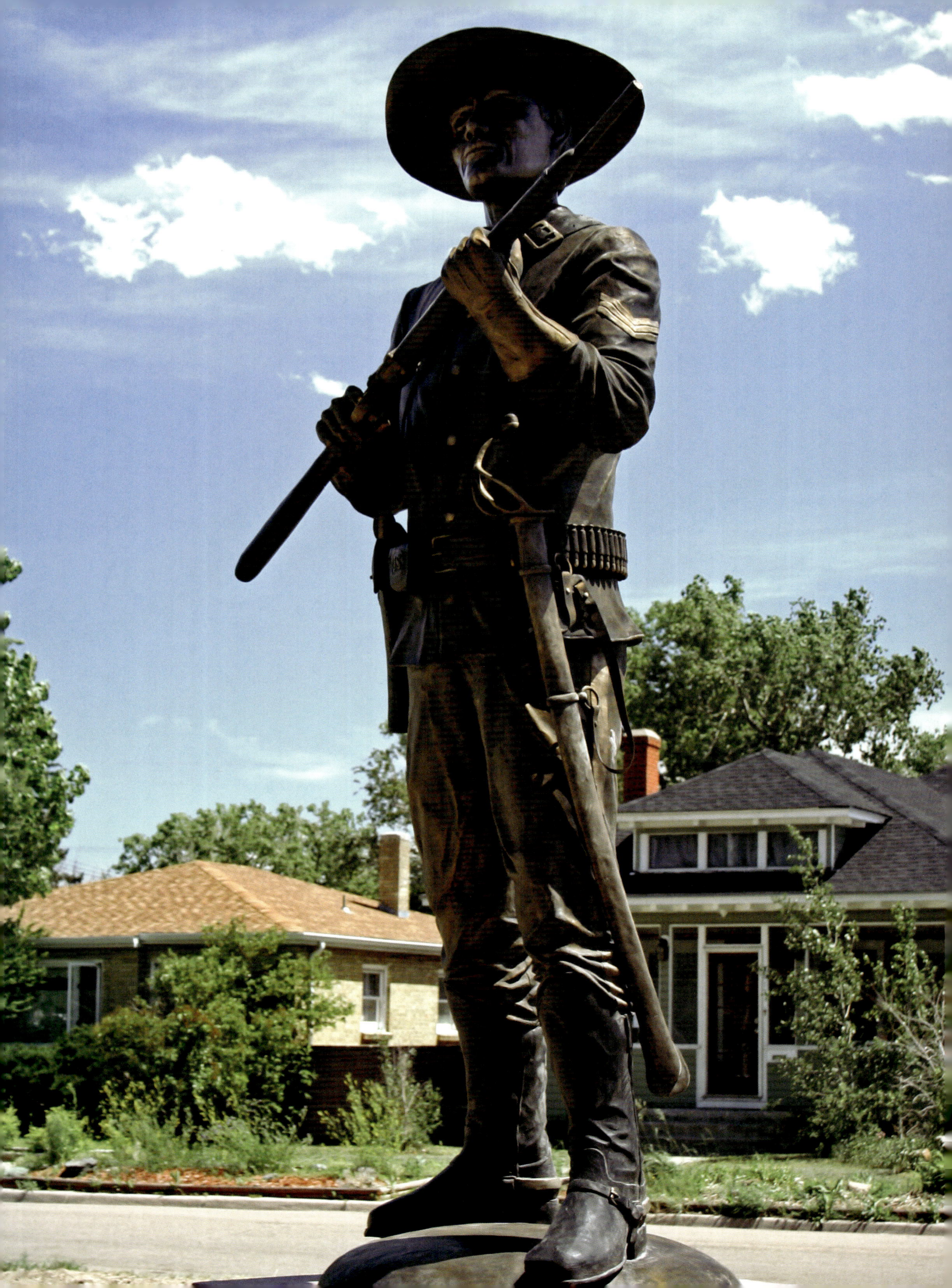

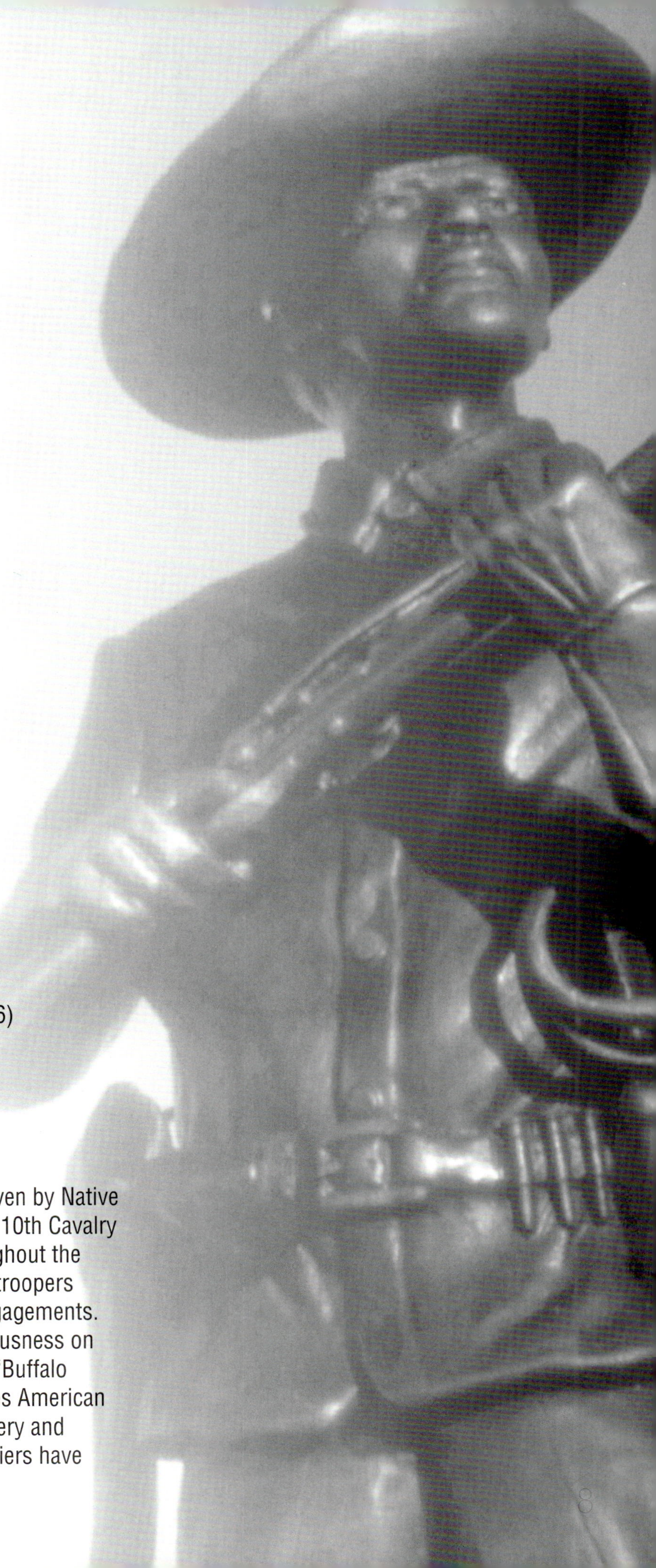

BUFFALO SOLDIER (2006)

Bronze, 14.5" x 5" x 5"

Monumental Bronze, 10' x 50' x 40"

"Buffalo Soldier" is a nickname originally given by Native American tribes to the members of the U.S. 10th Cavalry Regiment of the United States Army. Throughout the Indian wars, 20 percent of the U.S. Cavalry troopers were black and fought in more than 177 engagements. Their combat prowess, bravery, and tenaciousness on the battlefield inspired Indians to call them "Buffalo Soldiers." Many believe the name symbolizes American Indian respect for the Buffalo Soldiers' bravery and valor. Down through the years, Buffalo Soldiers have worn the name with pride.

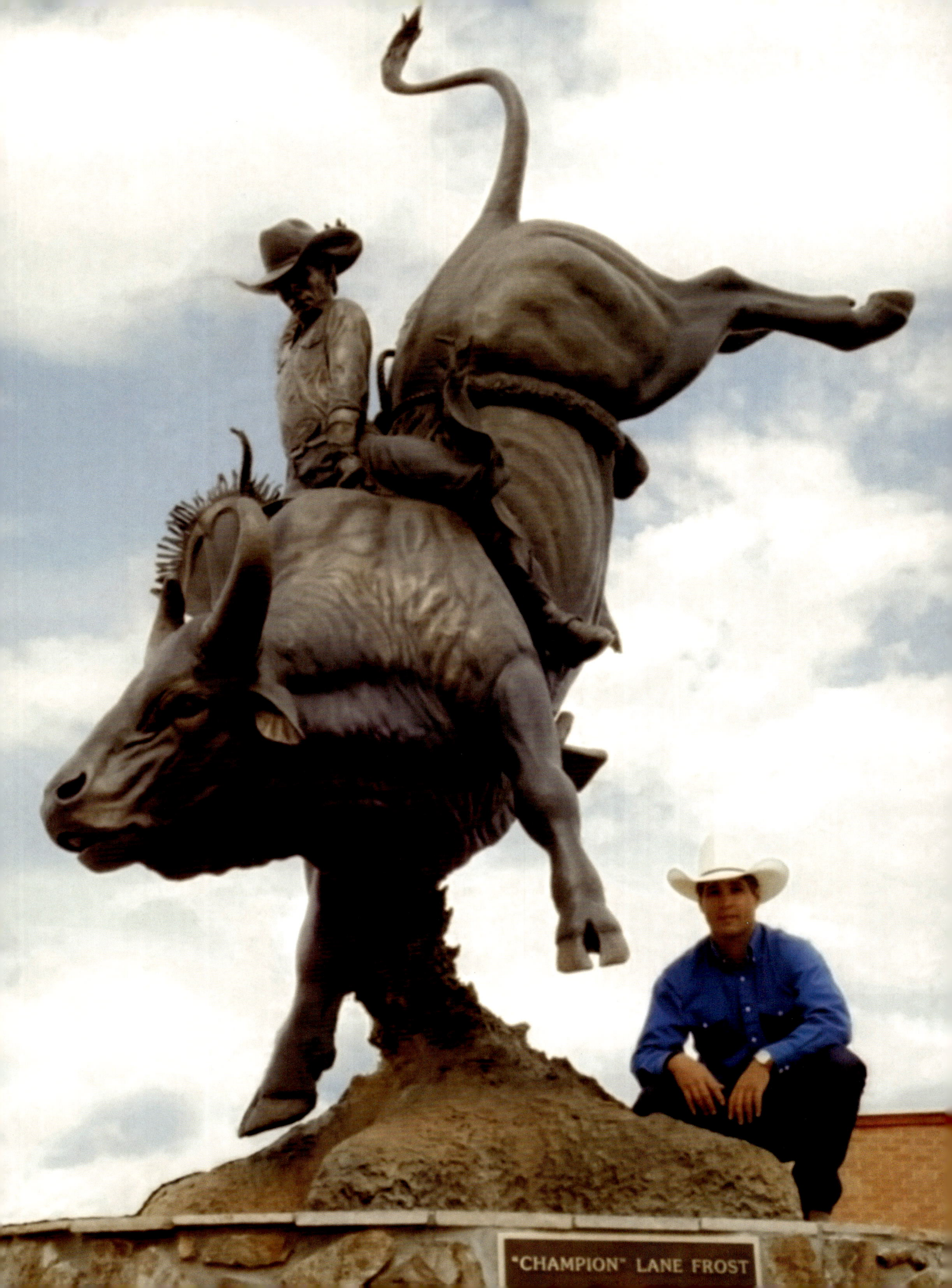
"CHAMPION" LANE FROST

LANE KNEW THE BULL THAT KILLED HIM. HE HAD BUCKED HIM OFF ABOUT A MONTH AGO AT SAN ANGELO. IT'S A BAD DEAL. HE WAS WANTING TO RIDE HIM. AND HE GOT IT DONE.
–JIM SHARP

CHAMPION LANE FROST (1993)

Bronze, 38'' x 15'' x 15''

Monumental Bronze, 15' x 11' x 9'

World Champion bull rider Lane Frost lost his life at age 25 competing in the 1989 Cheyenne Frontier Days rodeo. Lane was one of those individuals that never let success go to his head. He was a champion in both skill and his treatment of his fellow man. One night after I drove past Cheyenne Frontier Park, Frost's image wouldn't leave me. I knew I had to create a monument that would capture his image and his spirit. And the monument needed to be in Cheyenne, where he died doing what he loved. So I decided to commission myself as the artist. *Champion Lane Frost* is always going to be one of my favorite sculptures because of all of the difficulties and challenges it took to complete it.

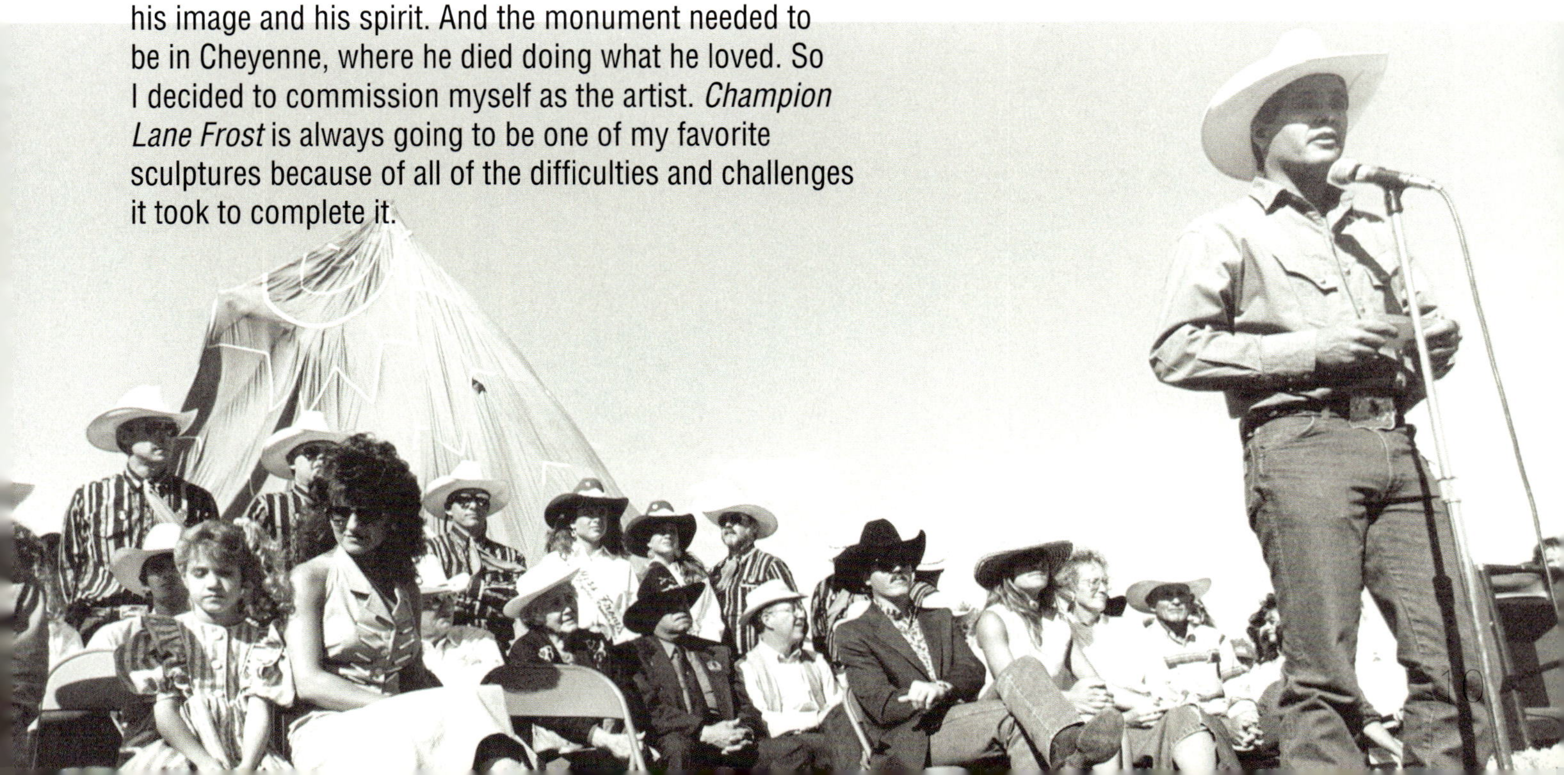

Every time I started feeling good about the project, something would come along and knock me on my ass. Right out of the gate, the Cheyenne Frontier Days Rodeo Committee turned me down, saying I would have to raise all of the funds on my own. My father suffered a stroke just as I was starting the monument. He died on Nov. 8, 1992. When I was nearly finished with the clay original, it burned up in a fire at Caleco Foundry in Cody, Wyoming, on March 6, 1993.

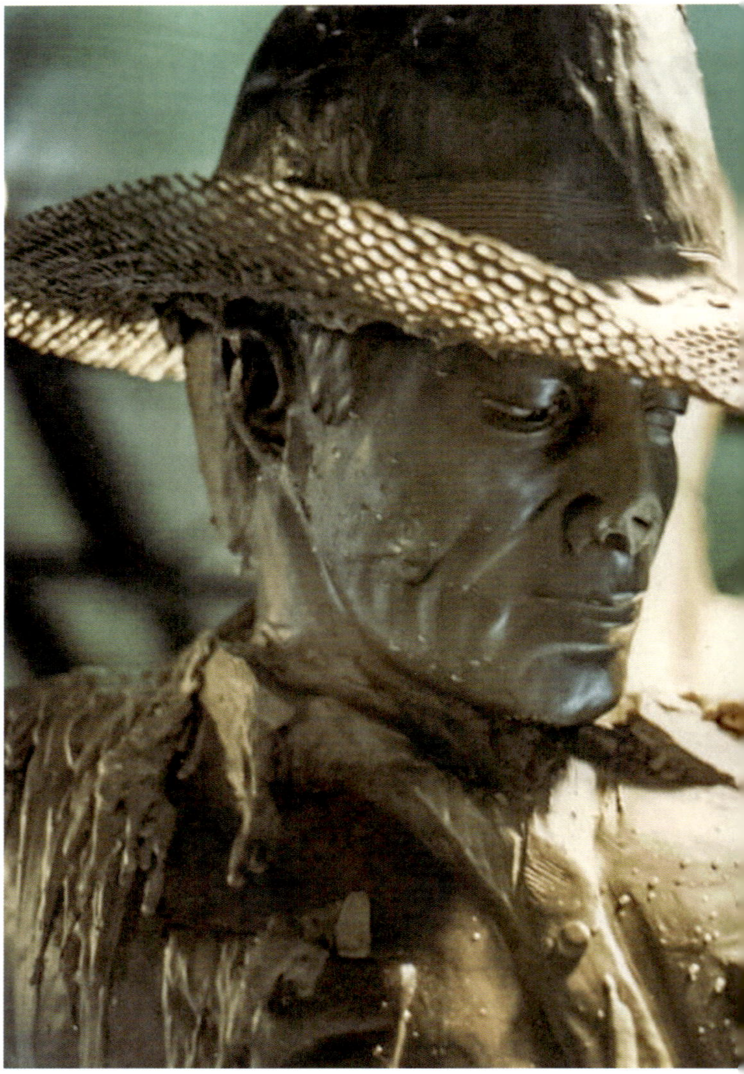

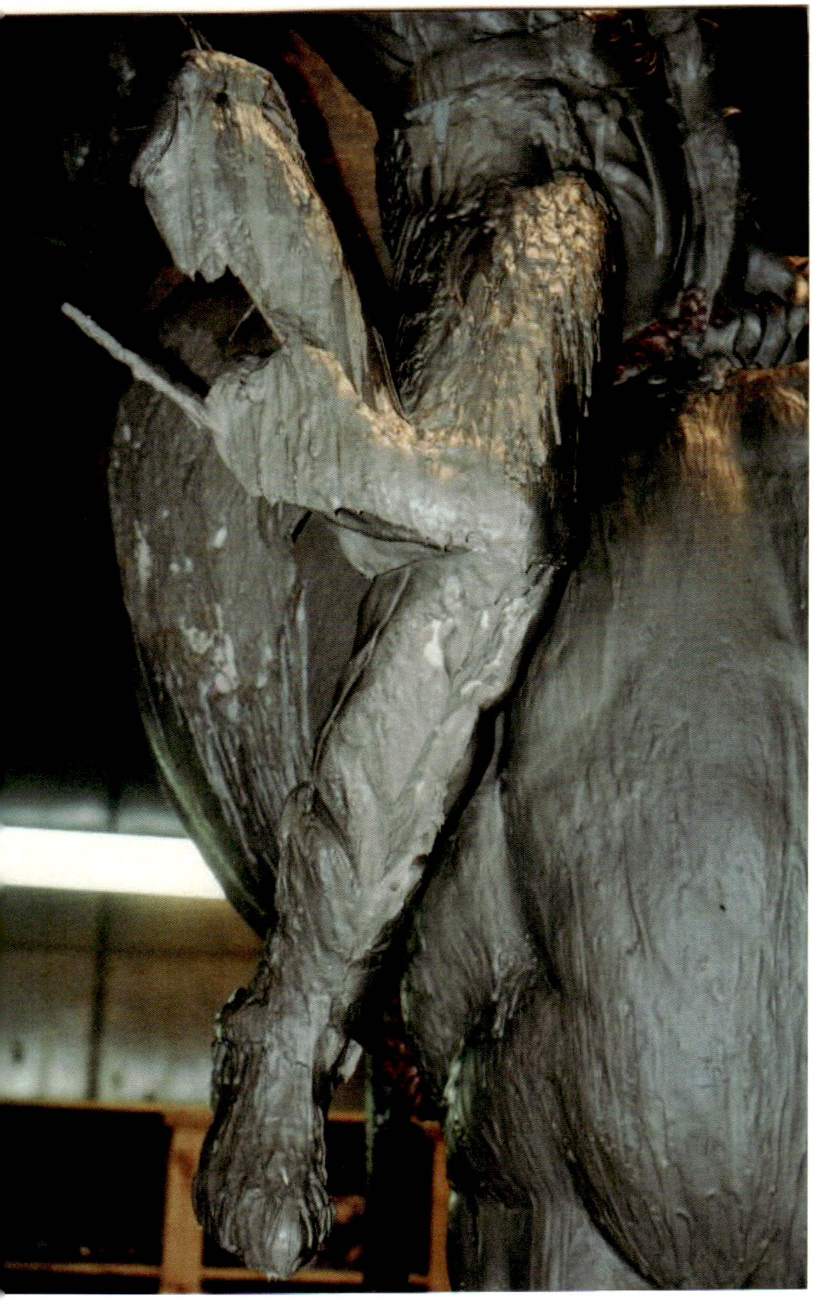

I was living in the foundry when an electric heater warming the clay shorted out and started a fire in the building. I awoke at 3 a.m. to find my room filled with smoke and called 911 before jumping out of the second story window. The volunteer fire department arrived and extinguished the fire, but not before the surface of the clay sculpture and most of my tools had been destroyed. I ordered new tools and clay that very day and began working long hours to repair the damage. I was able to finish the monument and delivered it just days before the dedication on July 26, 1993. This was my first large public monument and it will always have a special place in my heart. *Champion Lane Frost* is located at Cheyenne Frontier Days Old West Museum in Cheyenne, Wyoming.

DON'T BE AFRAID TO GO AFTER WHAT YOU WANT TO DO AND WHAT YOU WANT TO BE. BUT DON'T BE AFRAID TO BE WILLING TO PAY THE PRICE.

—LANE FROST

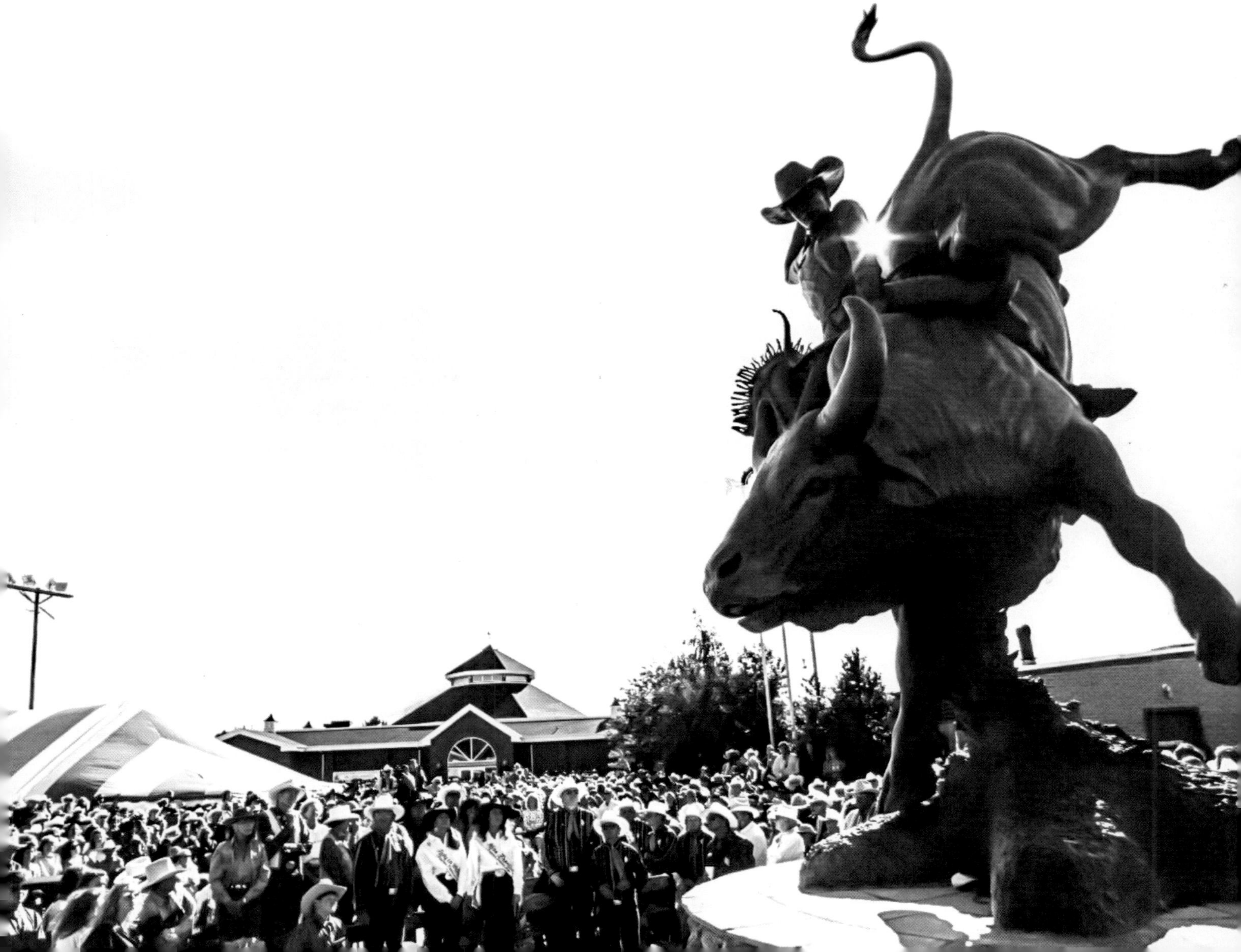

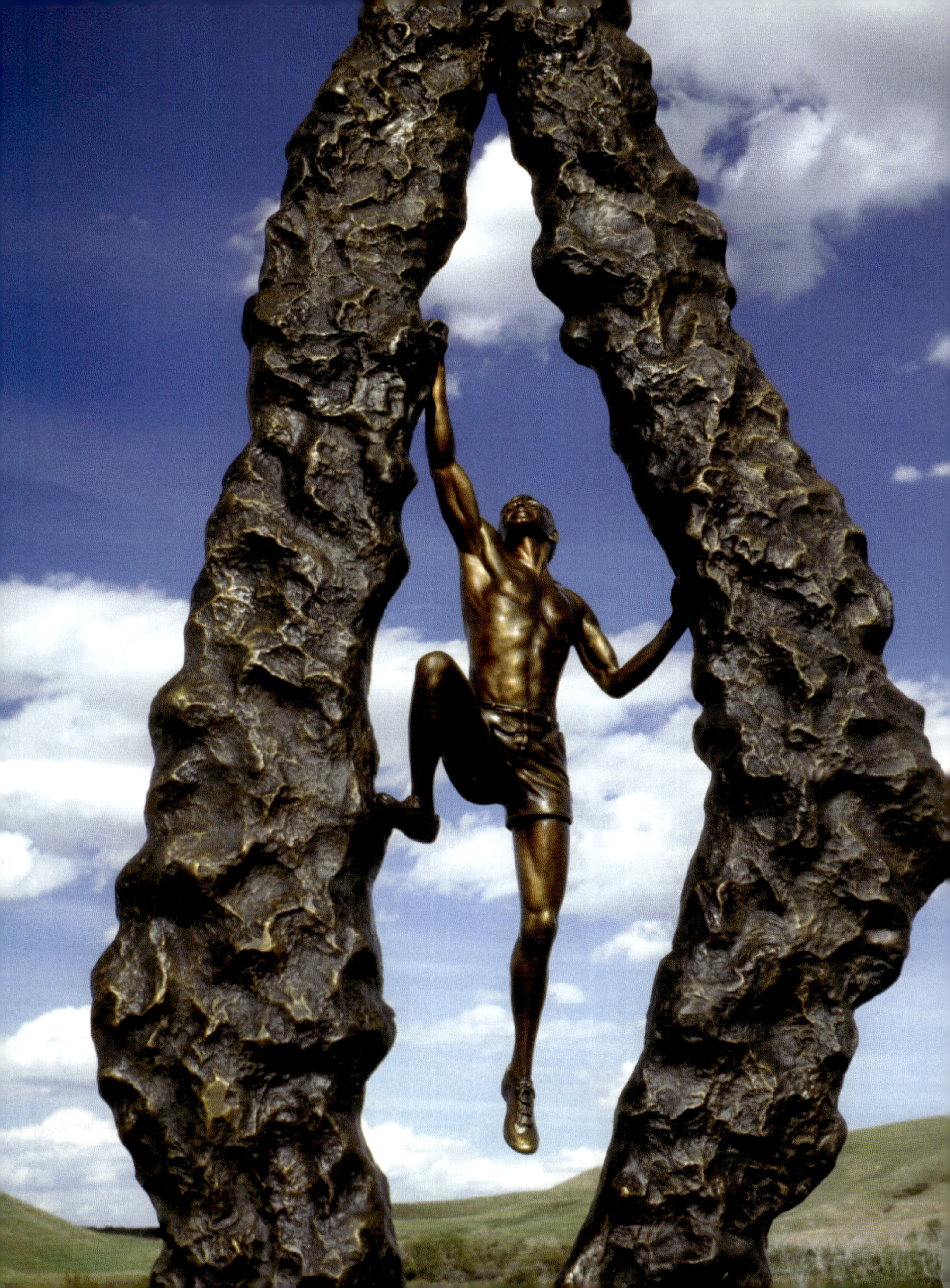

YOUR ATTITUDE WILL DETERMINE
YOUR ALTITUDE IN LIFE.
–JOHN C. MAXWELL

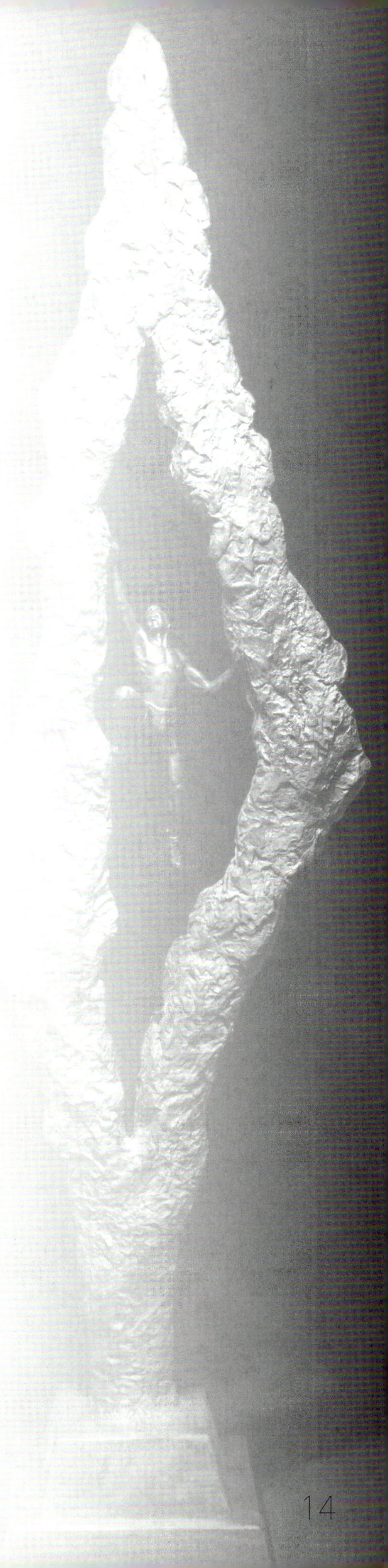

CLIMB AS HIGH AS YOUR DREAMS (relief) (2008)

Bronze, 36" x 10" x 1.5"

Monumental Bronze, 109" x 32" x 32"

The difference between the ground and the heights one achieves will only be limited by one's desire, for nothing in this world is impossible to a willing heart.

The overall abstract design of this sculpture is in the shape of a flame, which represents the desire that burns in man. Inside the rock crevice, a man, strong in mind and body with determination, struggles to pull himself up through a difficult passage in order to reach the top. He is alone, free climbing without the security of ropes. At this point in his life, his fate is literally in his own hands. He must trust in his ability to climb higher, because only with self-discipline and belief will he be able to reach the top.

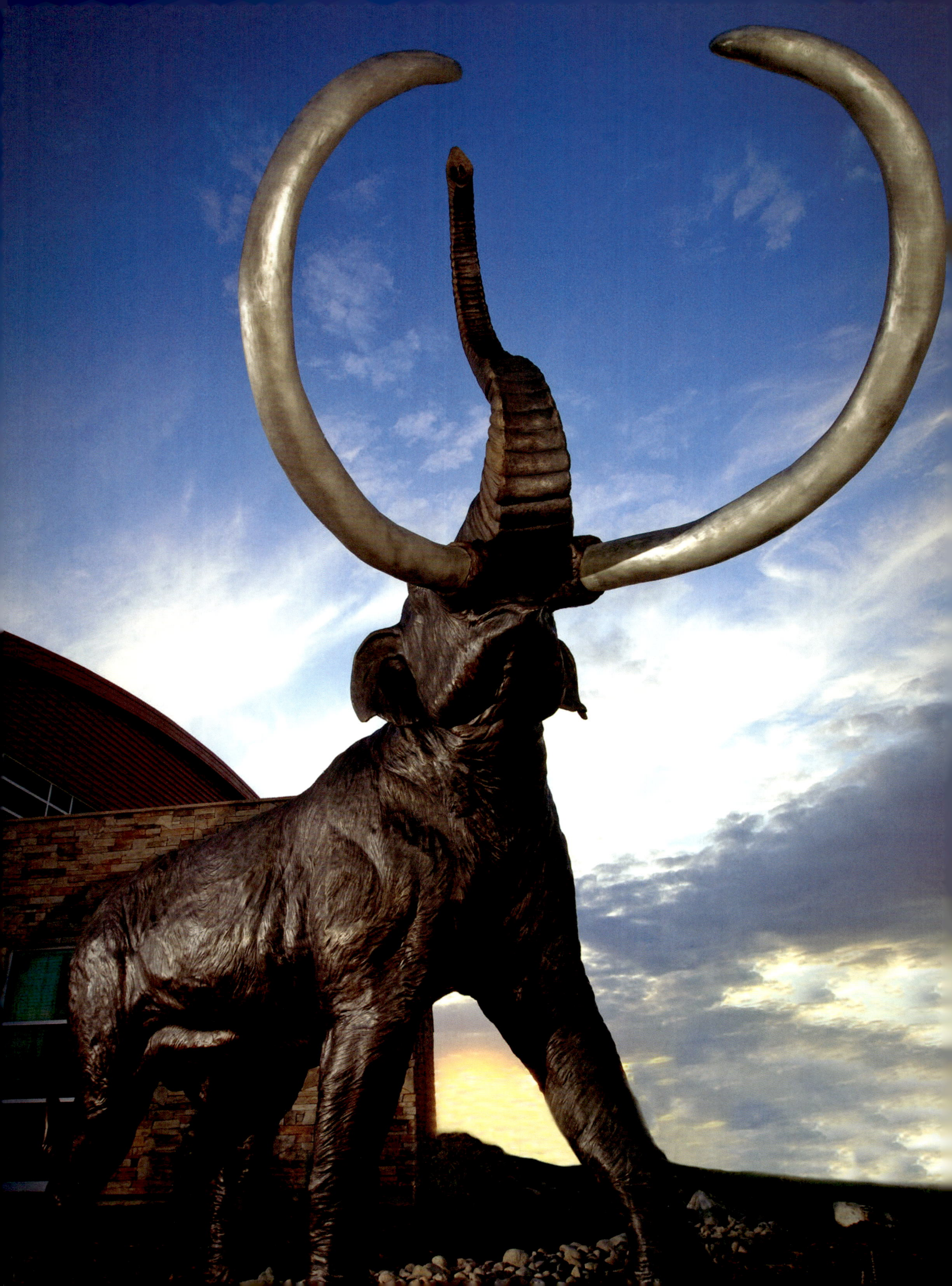

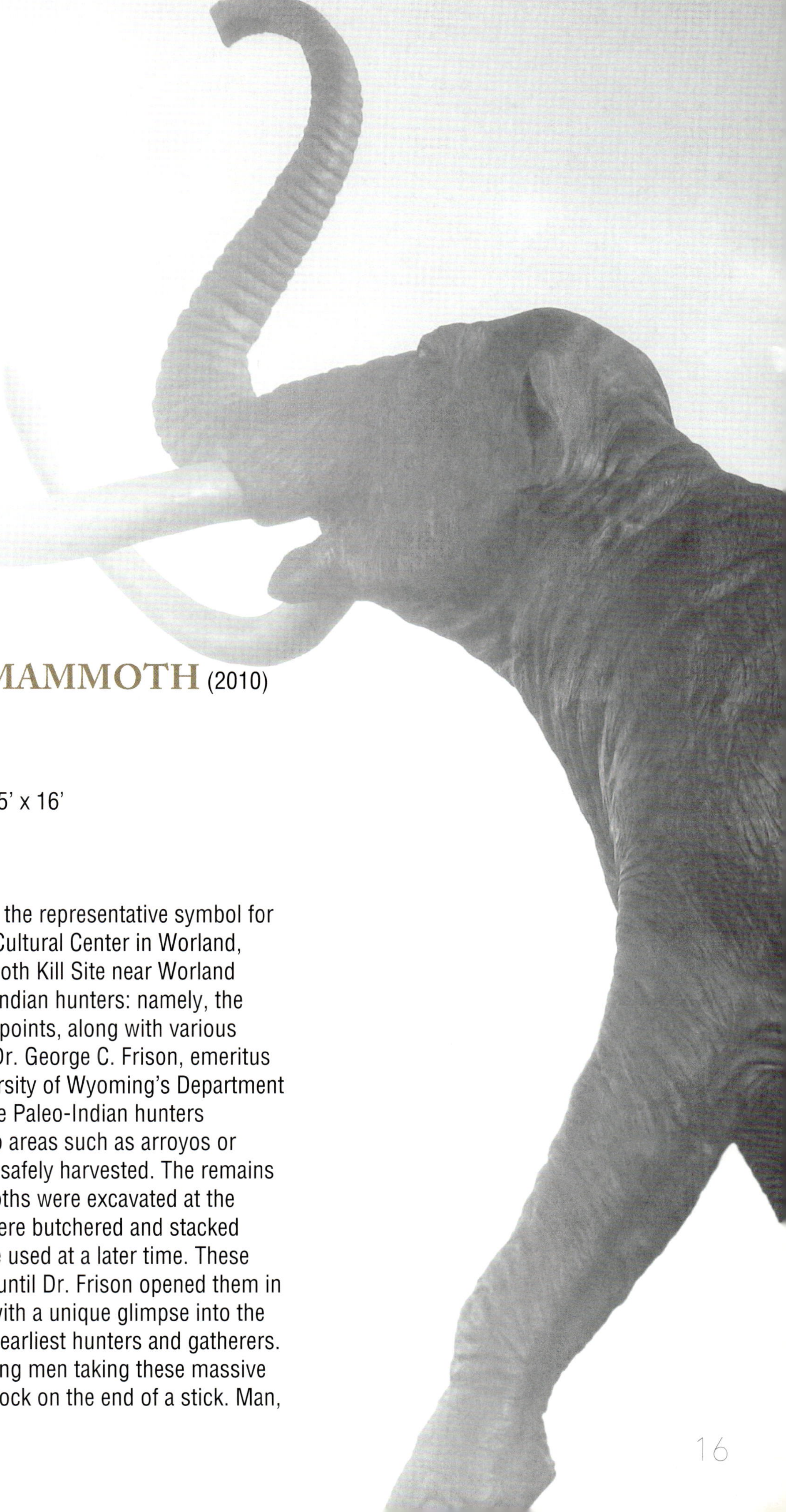

COLUMBIAN MAMMOTH (2010)

Bronze, 25" x 33" x 16"

Monumental Bronze, 20' x 25' x 16'

Photo by David Huber

The *Columbian Mammoth* is the representative symbol for the Washakie Museum and Cultural Center in Worland, Wyoming. The Colby Mammoth Kill Site near Worland provides evidence of Paleo-Indian hunters: namely, the recovery of Clovis projectile points, along with various stone fragments and tools. Dr. George C. Frison, emeritus faculty member at the University of Wyoming's Department of Anthropology, believes the Paleo-Indian hunters maneuvered mammoths into areas such as arroyos or gullies, where they could be safely harvested. The remains of seven prehistoric mammoths were excavated at the Colby Site, where animals were butchered and stacked in meat caches or piles to be used at a later time. These caches remained unopened until Dr. Frison opened them in 1973. The site provides us with a unique glimpse into the lives of some of Wyoming's earliest hunters and gatherers. I am amazed at early Wyoming men taking these massive animals down with a sharp rock on the end of a stick. Man, they had to be tough!

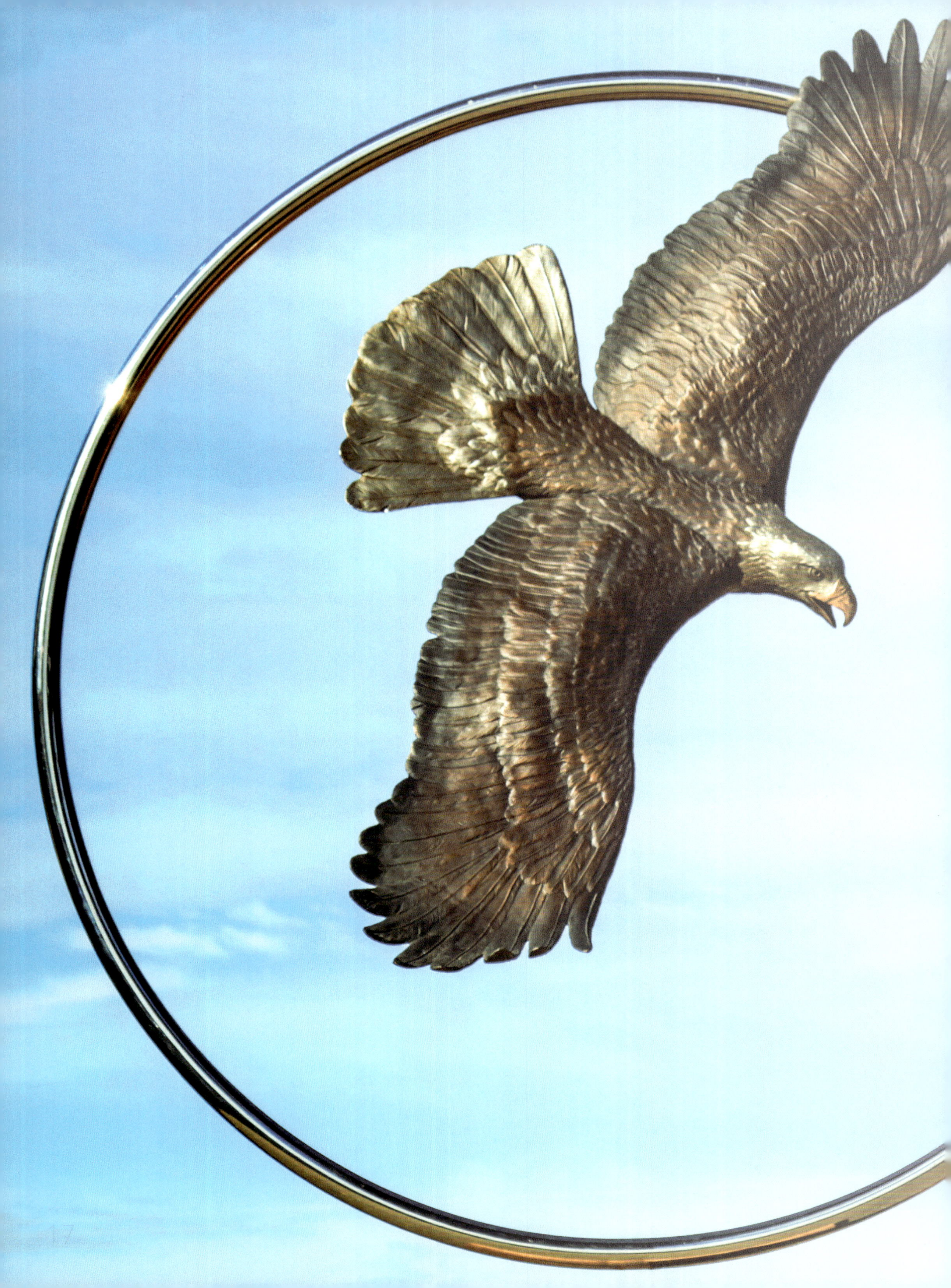

EAGLE, SPREAD YOUR WINGS
WIDE AND RISE.
CATCH THE WIND AND SOAR
TO YOUR KINGDOM IN THE SKY.
CIRCLE THE AIR BETWEEN
HEAVEN AND EARTH
KNOWING THE FREEDOM TO
SOAR AGAINST THE SUN.
–CHRIS NAVARRO

EAGLE AGAINST THE SUN (1999)

Bronze and Stainless Steel, 18.5'' x 10'' x 6''

Monumental Bronze and Stainless Steel, 10' x 6' x 3'

A polished stainless steel ring represents the sun. Attaching the Eagle's upper wing to the top of the ring allows the lower wing to be surrounded by negative space, creating a stronger sense of flight.

ESSENCE OF REX (2013)

Bronze, 17.5'' x 34'' x 11''

Monumental Bronze, 13.5' x 28' x 7'

Essence of Rex is a life-size Tyrannosaurus rex. One side is skeletal while the other side is "fleshed out." LED lights illuminate the piece from within, and the light radiating outward gives the sculpture a special effect. To bring it to life and to create that "wow" factor, I had to inject emotion into *Rex*. The sculpture is located at the entrance to the Tate Geological Museum in Casper, Wyoming.

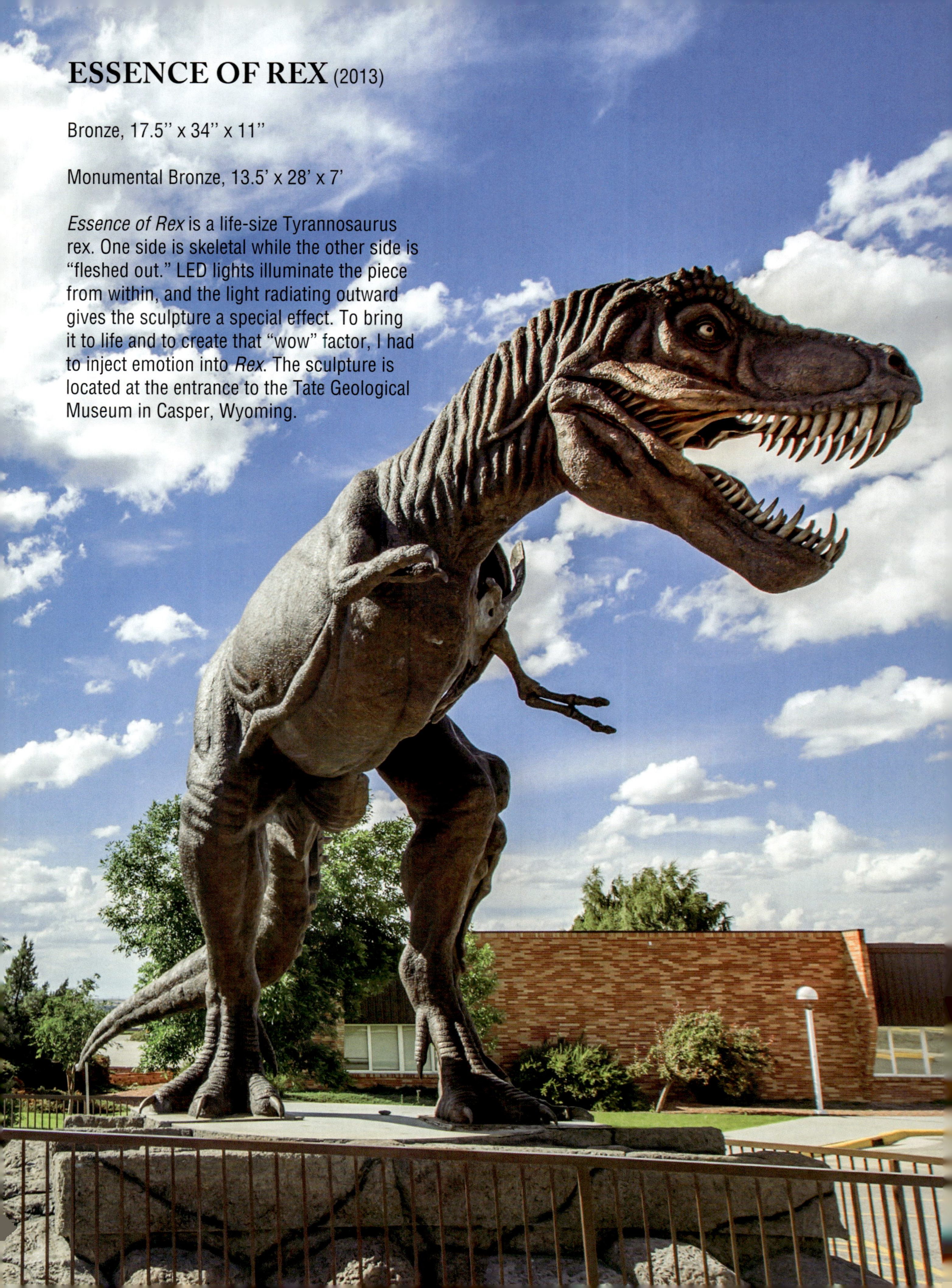

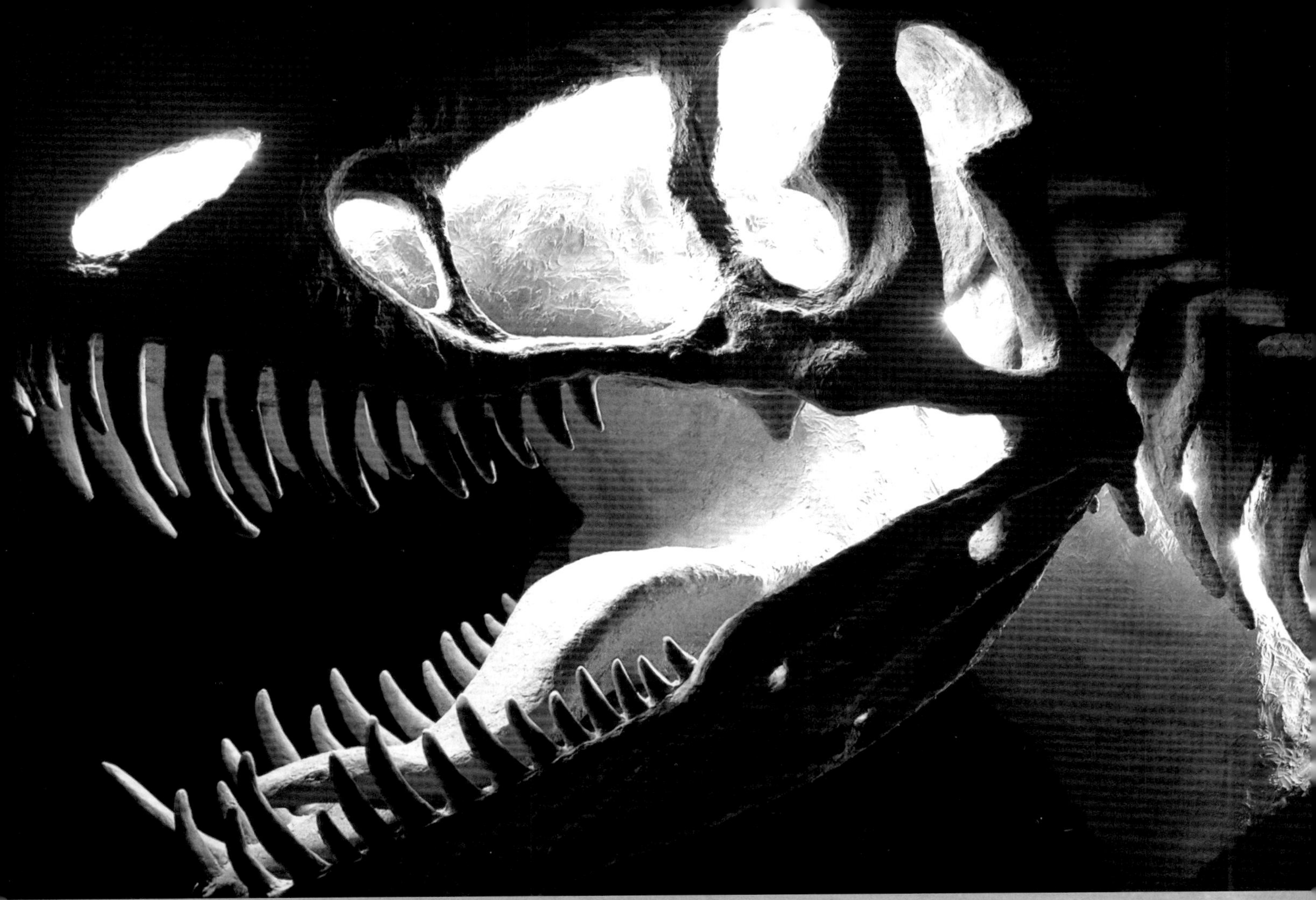

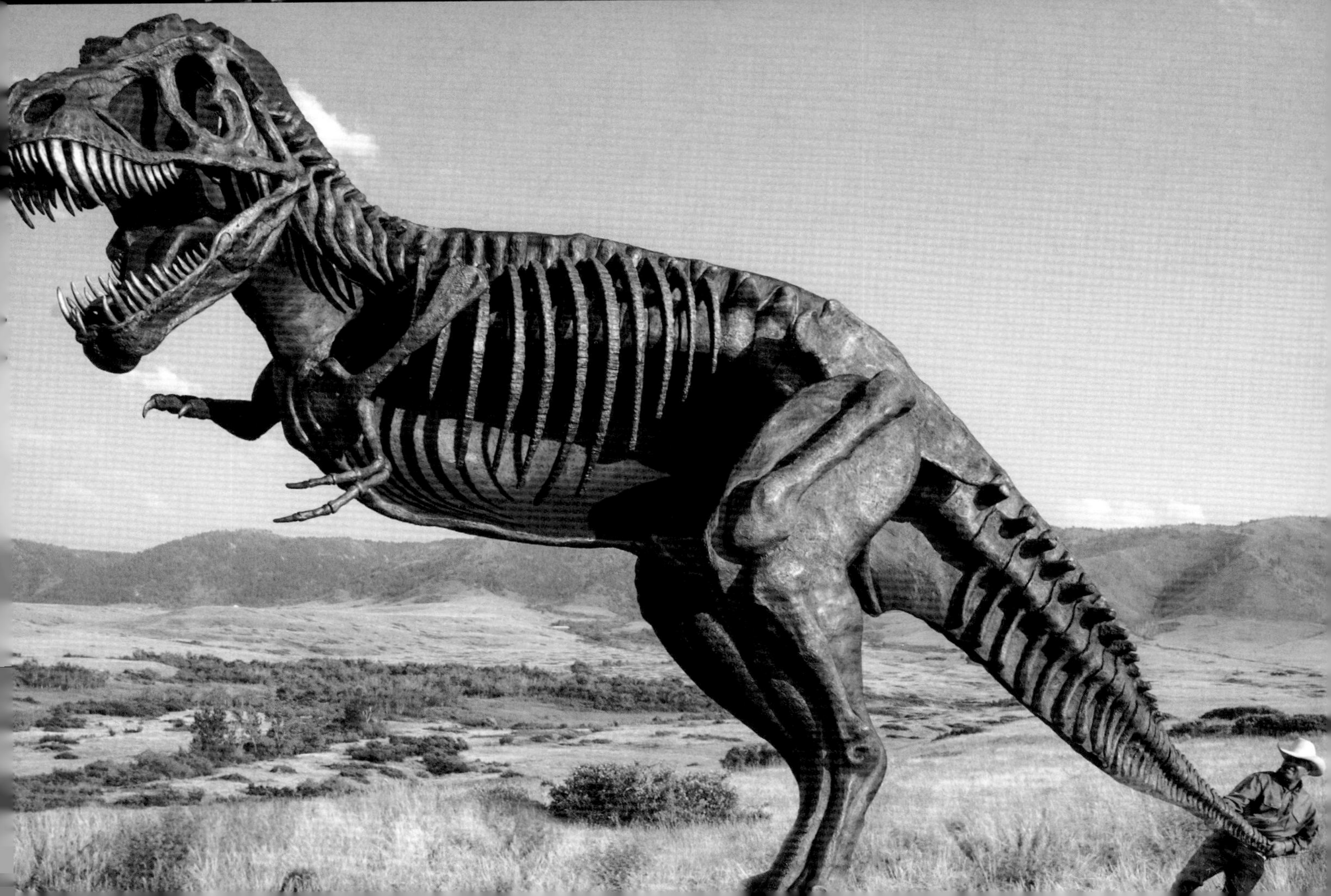

JOY OF LIFE (2007)

Bronze, 12.5" x 19" x 6"

Monumental Bronze, 9' x 14' x 4'

Whenever I see a mare with a young colt running and playing in a pasture, it never fails to bring pleasure to my heart and a smile on my face. To me, it expresses the real joy of living and the pure happiness of being alive.

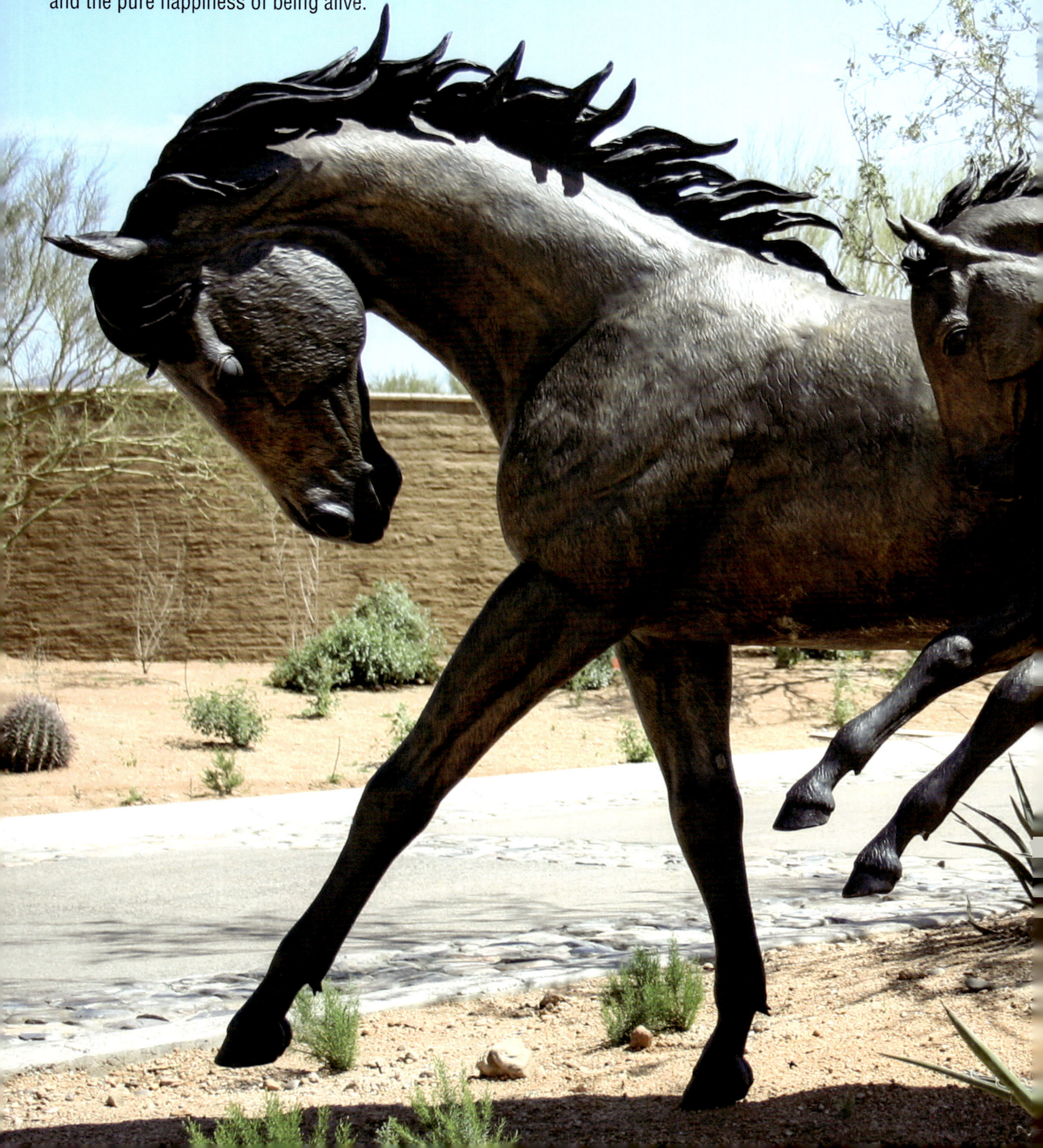

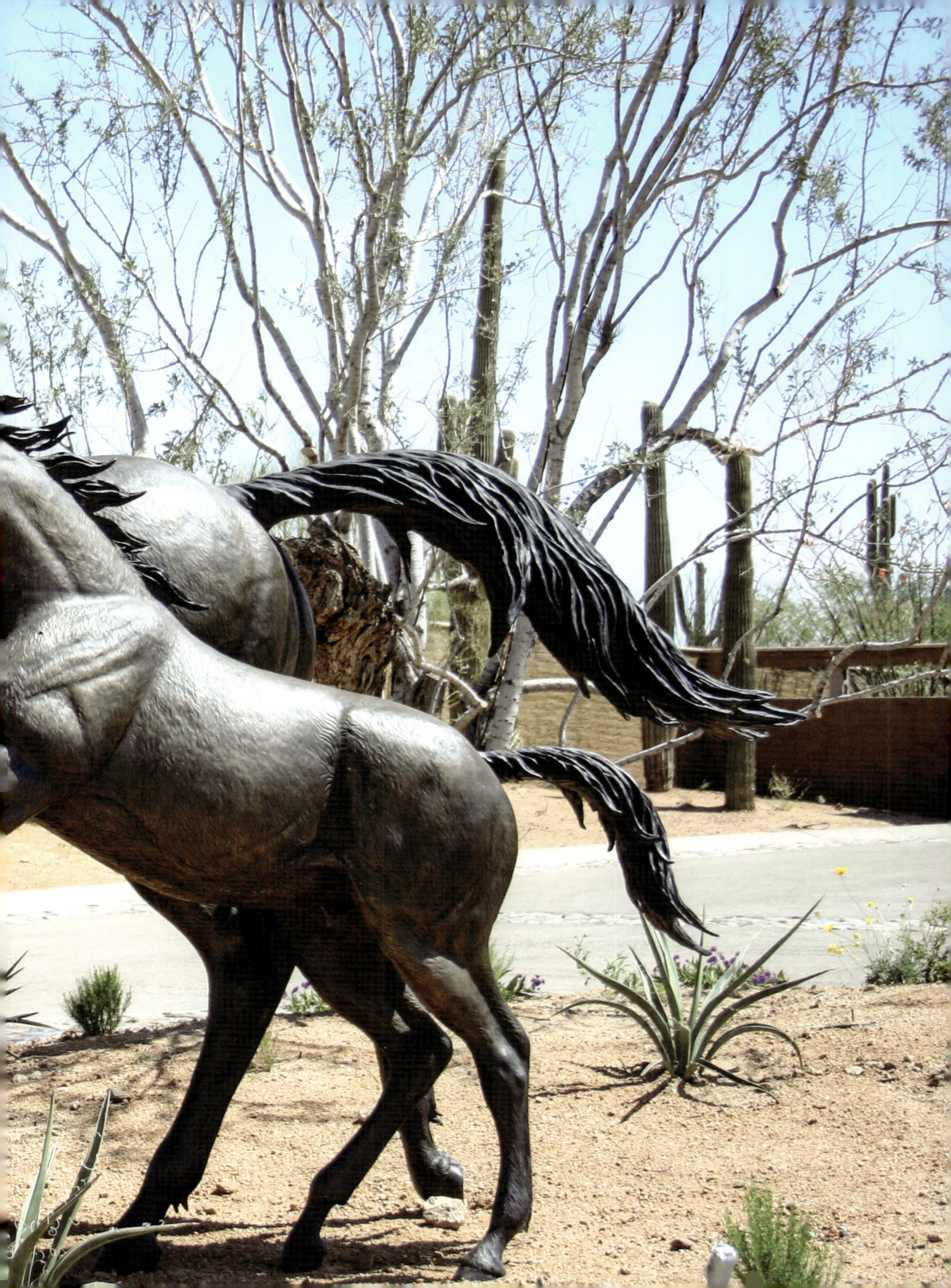

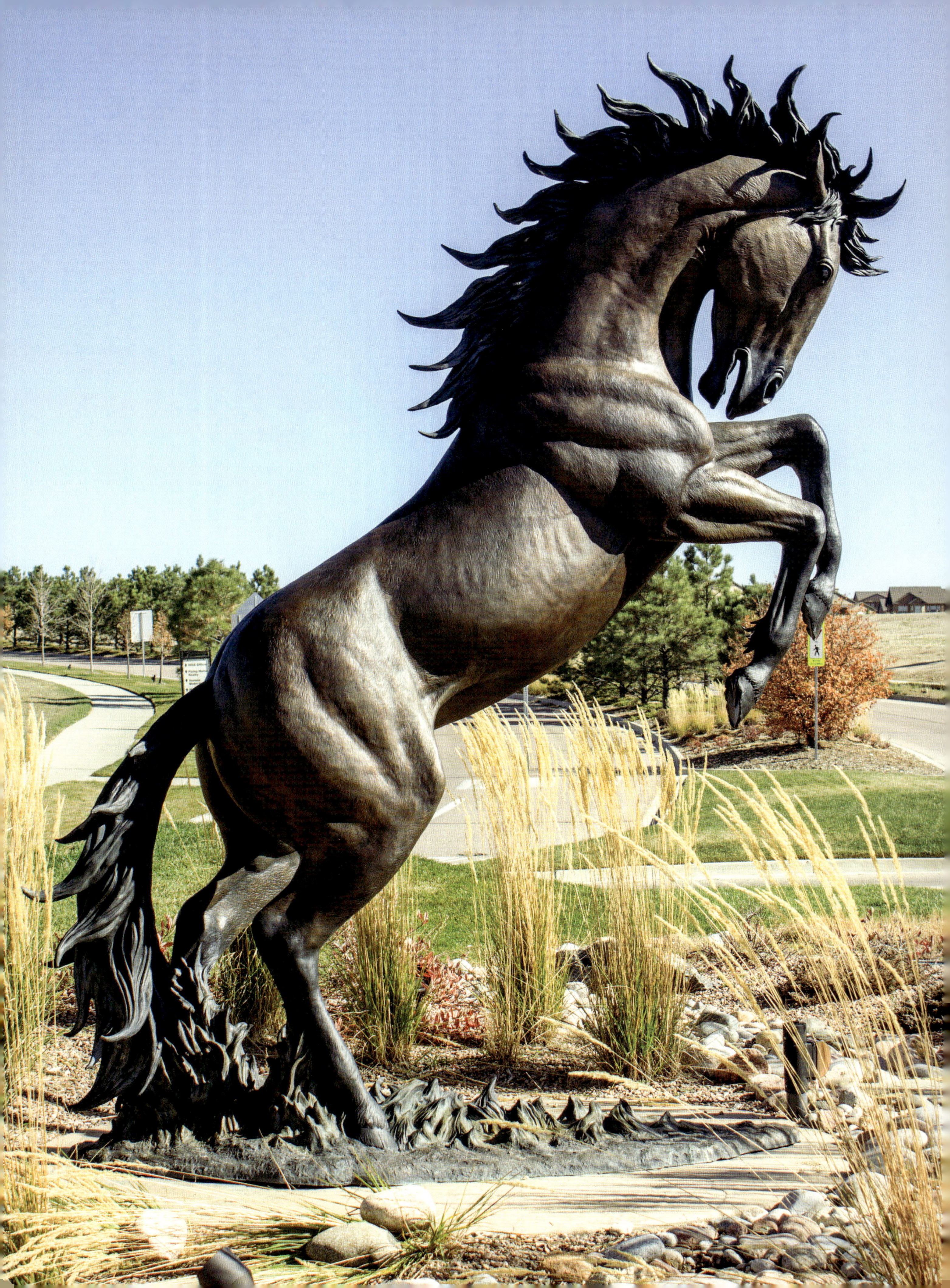

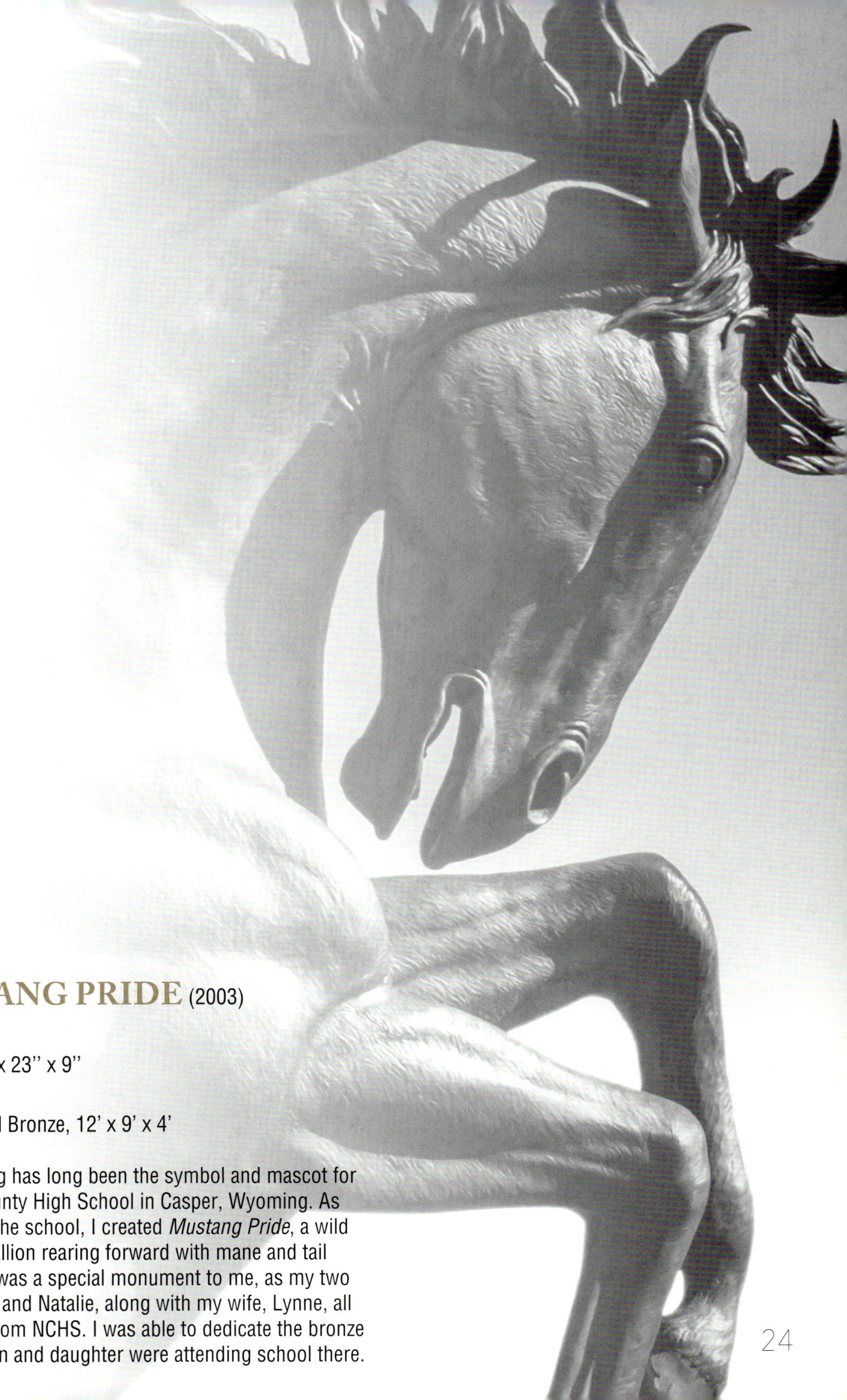

MUSTANG PRIDE (2003)

Bronze 16'' x 23'' x 9''

Monumental Bronze, 12' x 9' x 4'

The mustang has long been the symbol and mascot for Natrona County High School in Casper, Wyoming. As a tribute to the school, I created *Mustang Pride*, a wild mustang stallion rearing forward with mane and tail flying. This was a special monument to me, as my two children, JC and Natalie, along with my wife, Lynne, all graduated from NCHS. I was able to dedicate the bronze while my son and daughter were attending school there.

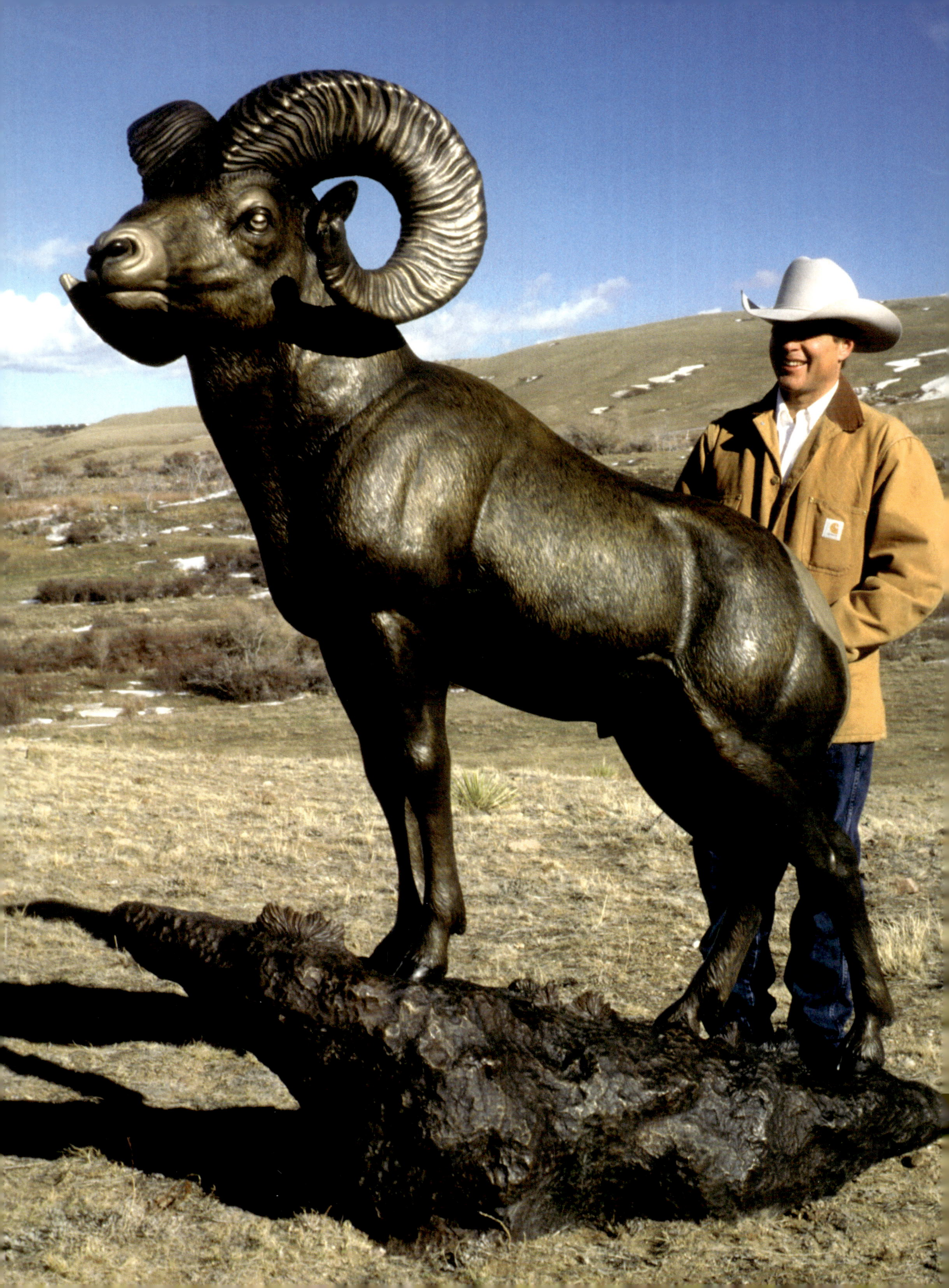

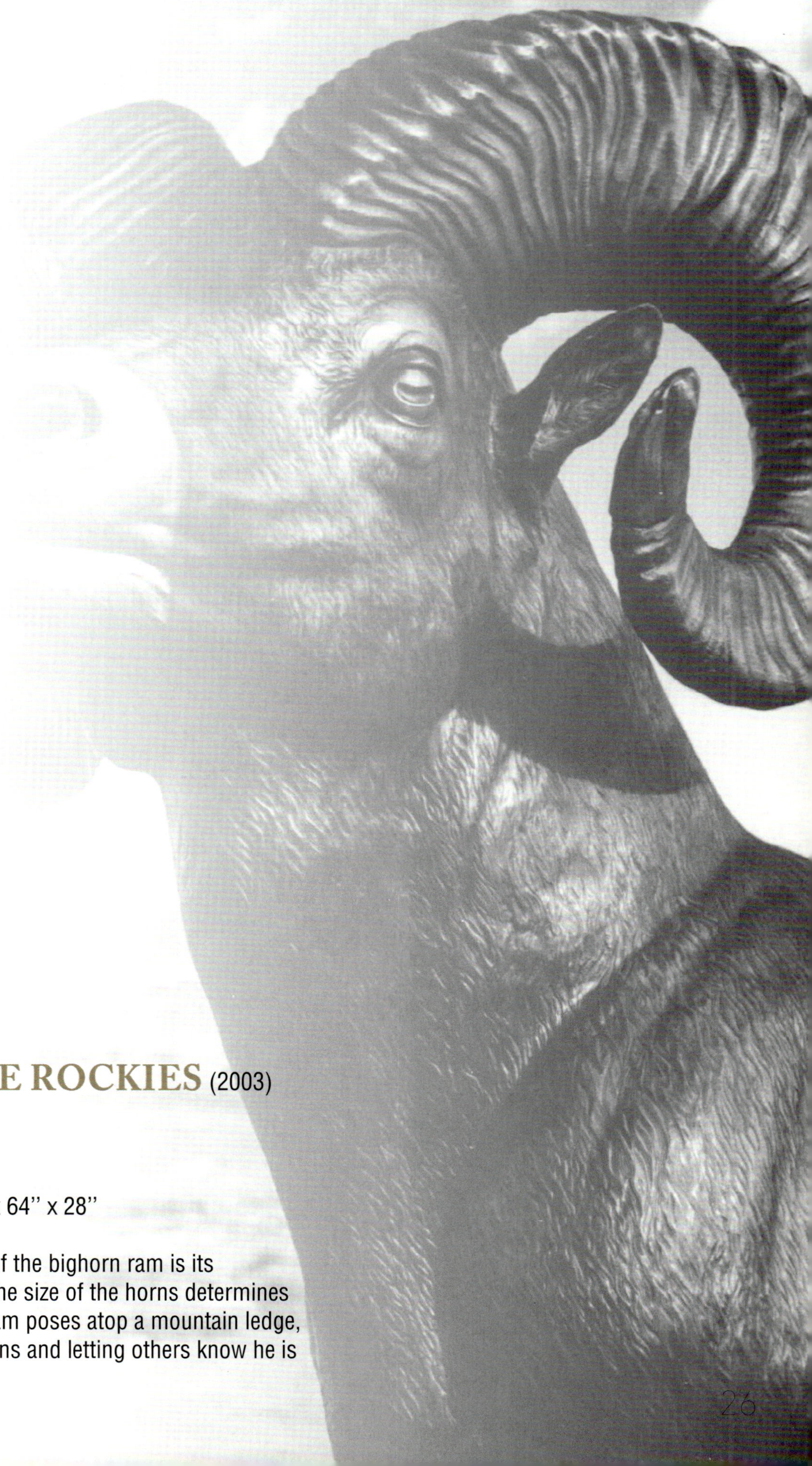

PRIDE OF THE ROCKIES (2003)

Bronze, 16" x 11.5" x 5"

Monumental Bronze, 81" x 64" x 28"

The most notable feature of the bighorn ram is its massively curved horns. The size of the horns determines the animal's status. This ram poses atop a mountain ledge, displaying his massive horns and letting others know he is king of the mountain.

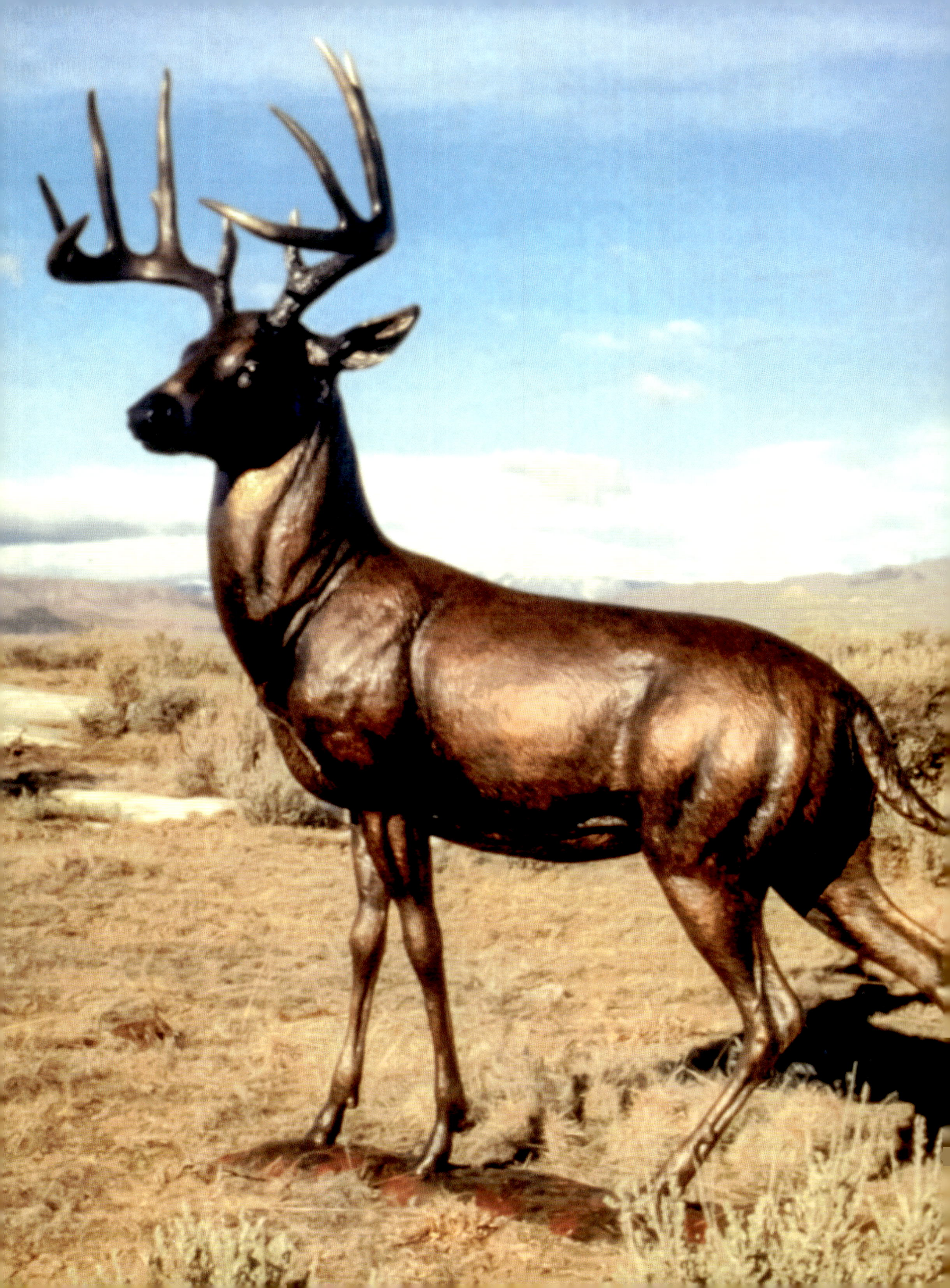

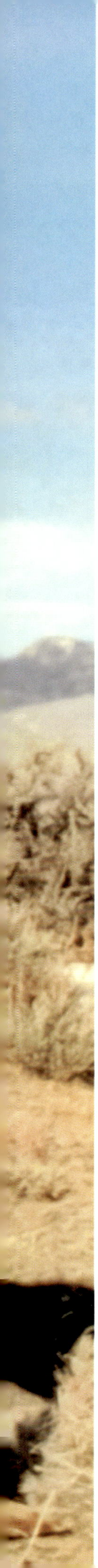

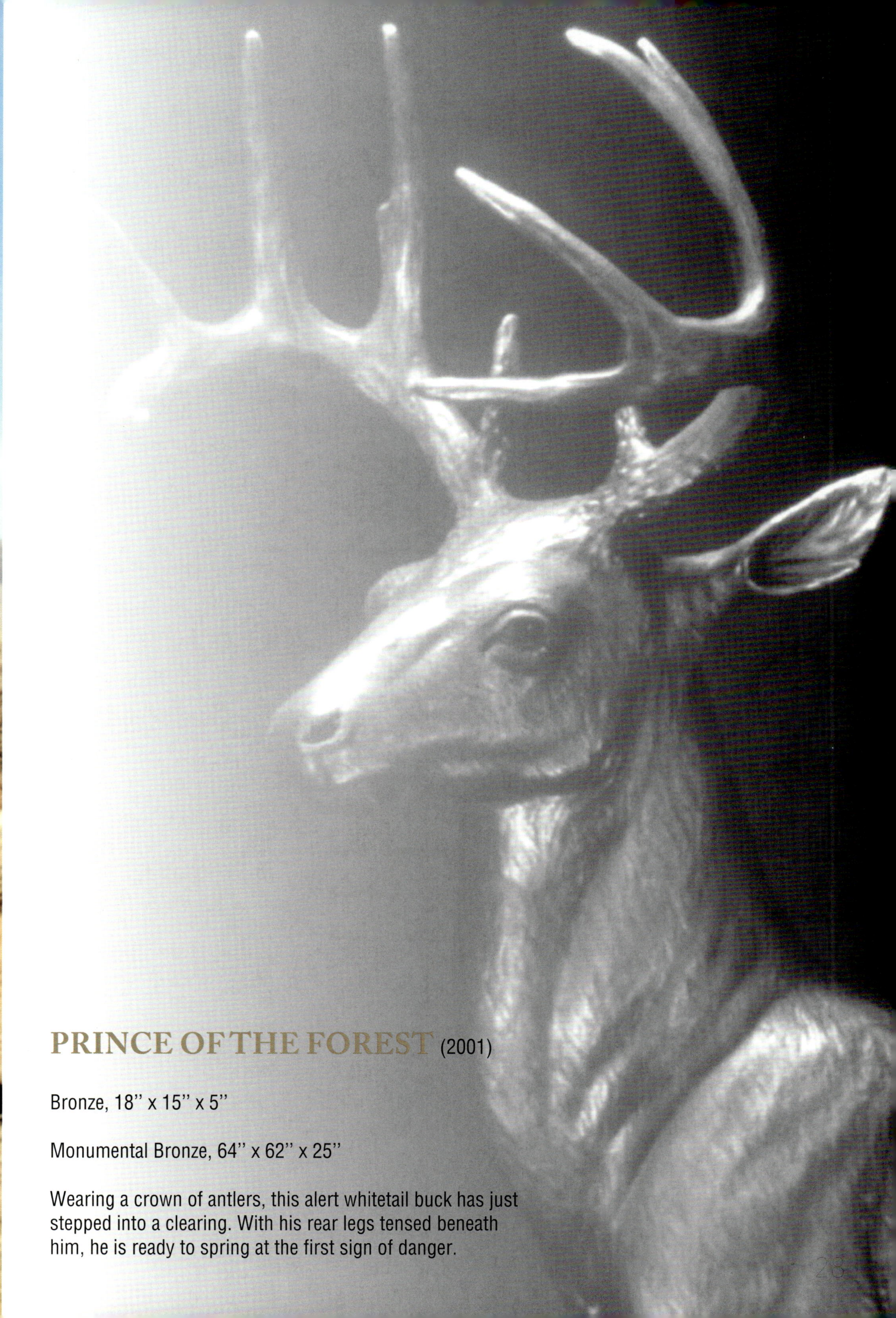

PRINCE OF THE FOREST (2001)

Bronze, 18" x 15" x 5"

Monumental Bronze, 64" x 62" x 25"

Wearing a crown of antlers, this alert whitetail buck has just stepped into a clearing. With his rear legs tensed beneath him, he is ready to spring at the first sign of danger.

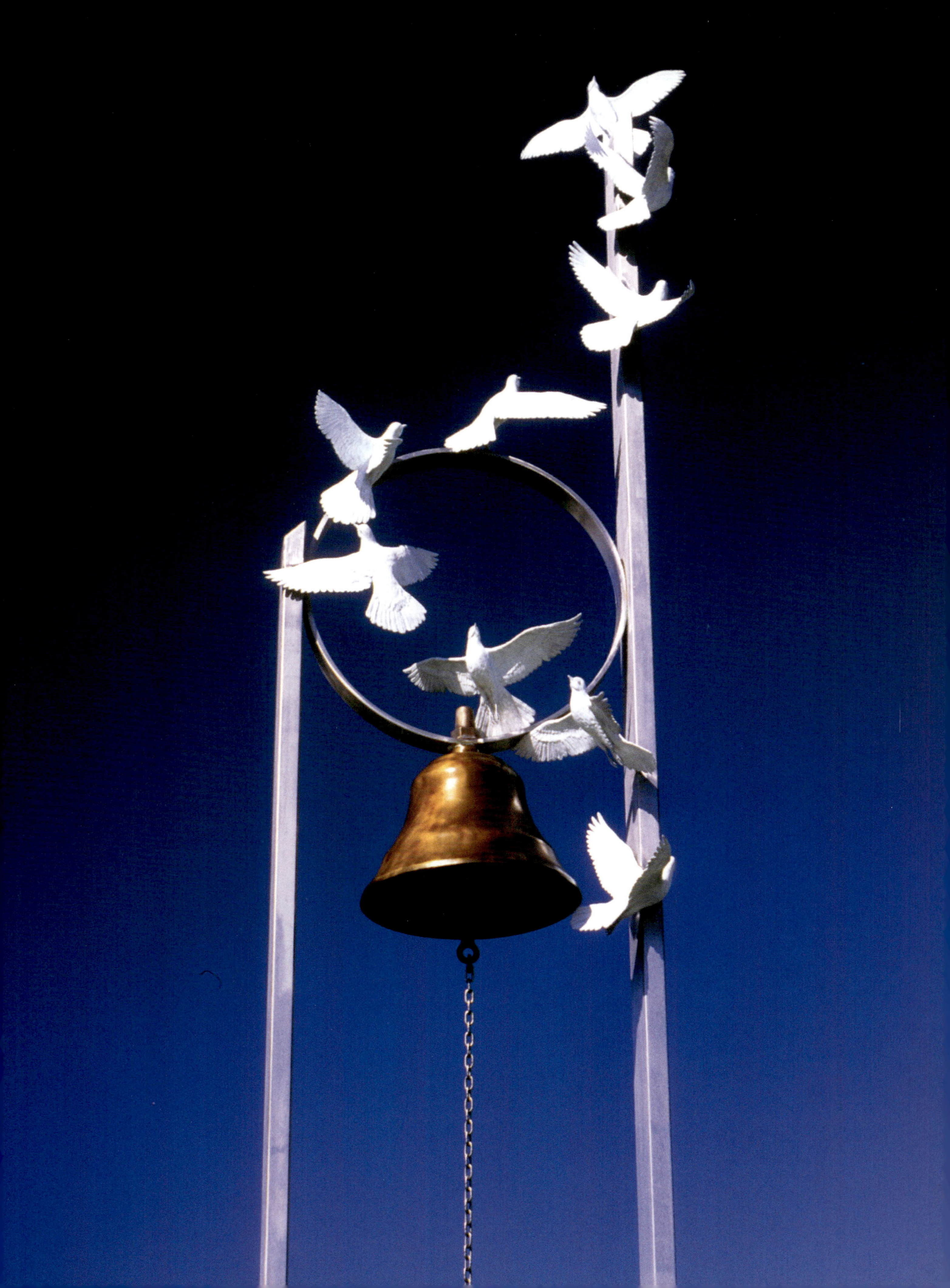

THE RING OF PEACE

IF YOU BELIEVE IN HOPE

AND THE NEED FOR PEACE,

STEP UP AND RING THE BELL,

SO IT WILL SING

FOR THE PROMISE OF TOMORROW.

–CHRIS NAVARRO

RING OF PEACE (1999)

Bronze and Stainless Steel, 41" x 9.5" x 6"

Monumental Bronze, 19' x 4' x 3.5'

I created this sculpture in memory of Matthew Shepard, the University of Wyoming student who was murdered in 1998. The 19-foot tall memorial is located in Casper, Wyoming. I was driving home to Wyoming from Texas in 1998 after delivering a monument when my wife called to tell me that Judy Shepard, Matthew's mother, wanted to talk to me about a memorial to her son. Later, from my motel room, I awoke at 3 a.m. I have a habit of keeping a pen and paper next to my bed, so I quickly made note of my thoughts before falling back to sleep. The next morning, I noticed my sketch and the accompanying poem that had come to me as a dream. As I looked at it, I knew I would create this sculpture.

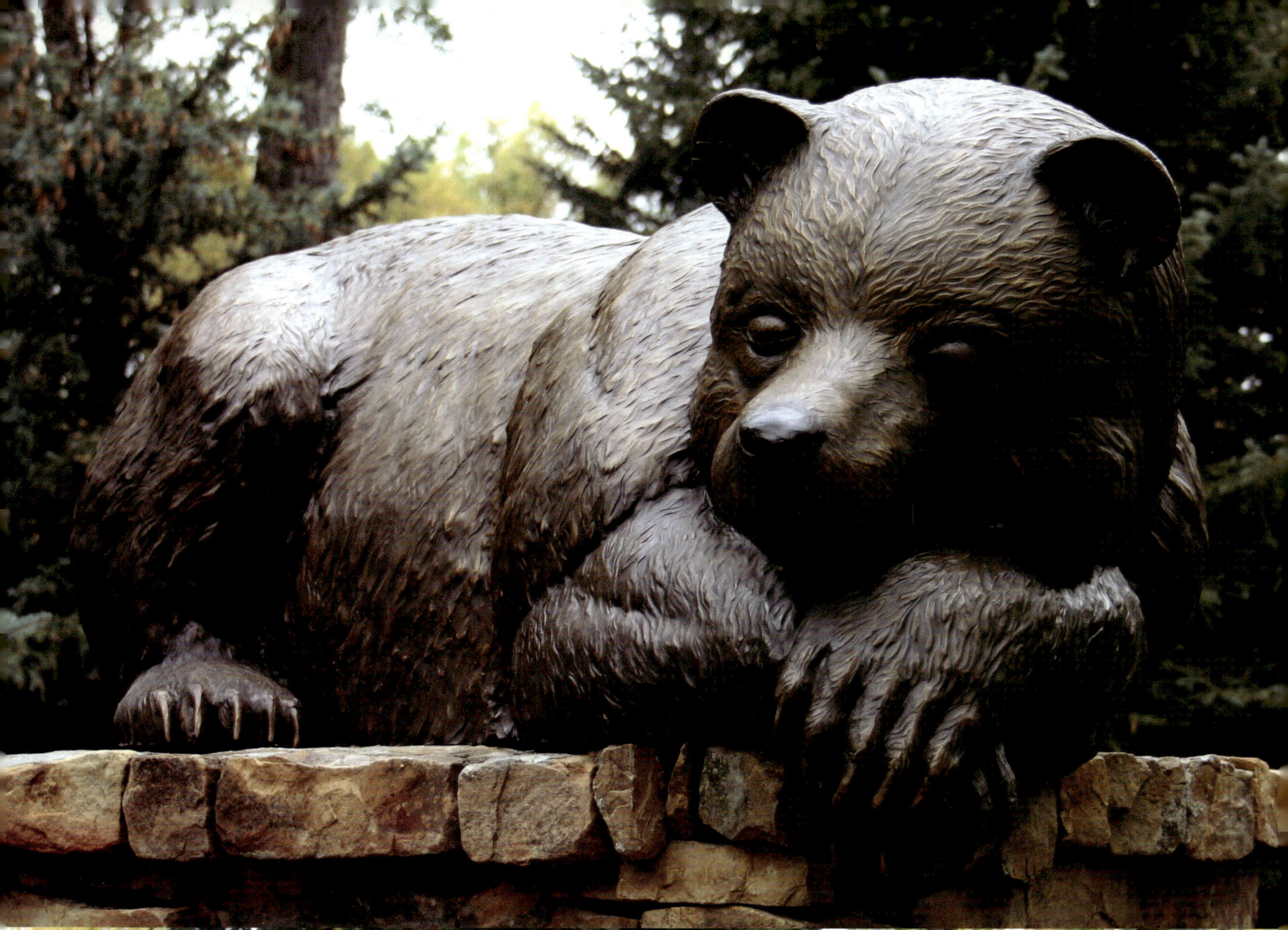

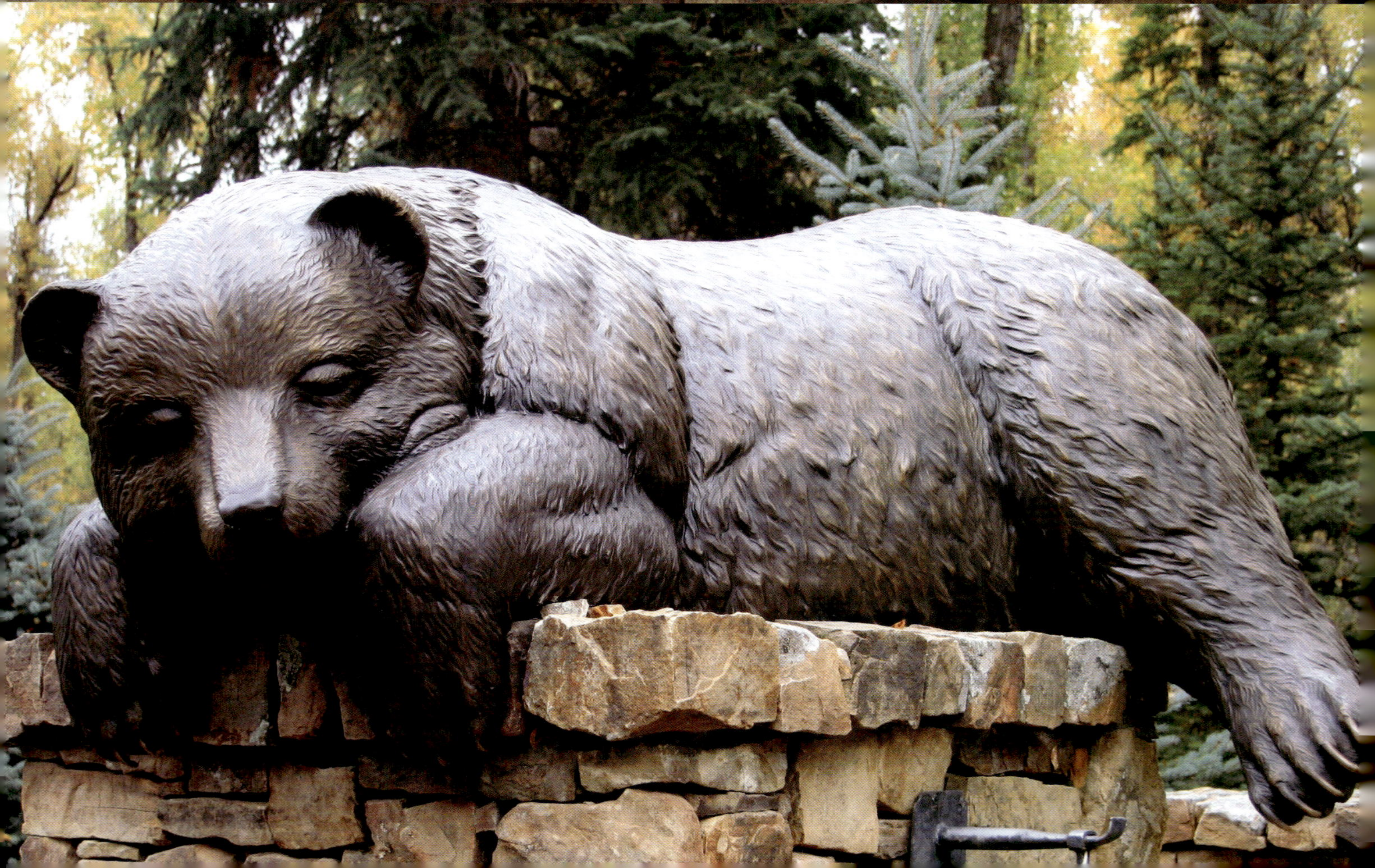

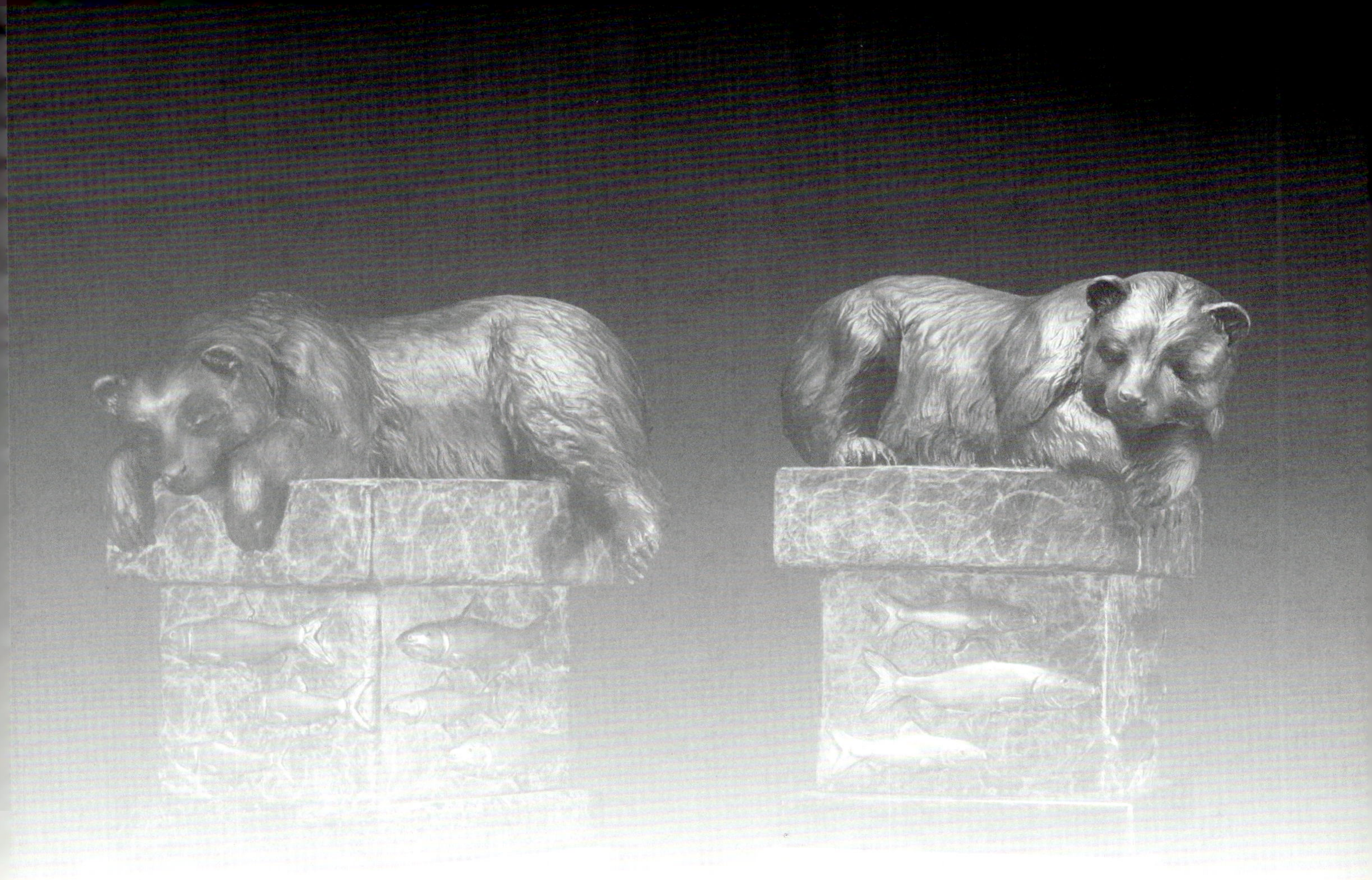

SALMON DREAMS (2006)

Bronze, 9" x 5" x 5"

Monumental Bronze, 32" x 70" x 38"

Salmon Dreams is a special commission for a collector who has a beautiful gated entry to his home, and he wanted two grizzly bears guarding his property. However, the bears have fallen asleep on the job. I always create a maquette of the monument to first work out my design and composition. In the small-scale model, I chose to tell the story of the bears in a dream state. I wondered, what do bears dream of? Why not salmon, one of their favorite foods? So, I placed salmon, swimming, around the square sculpture base, giving it a surrealistic quality.

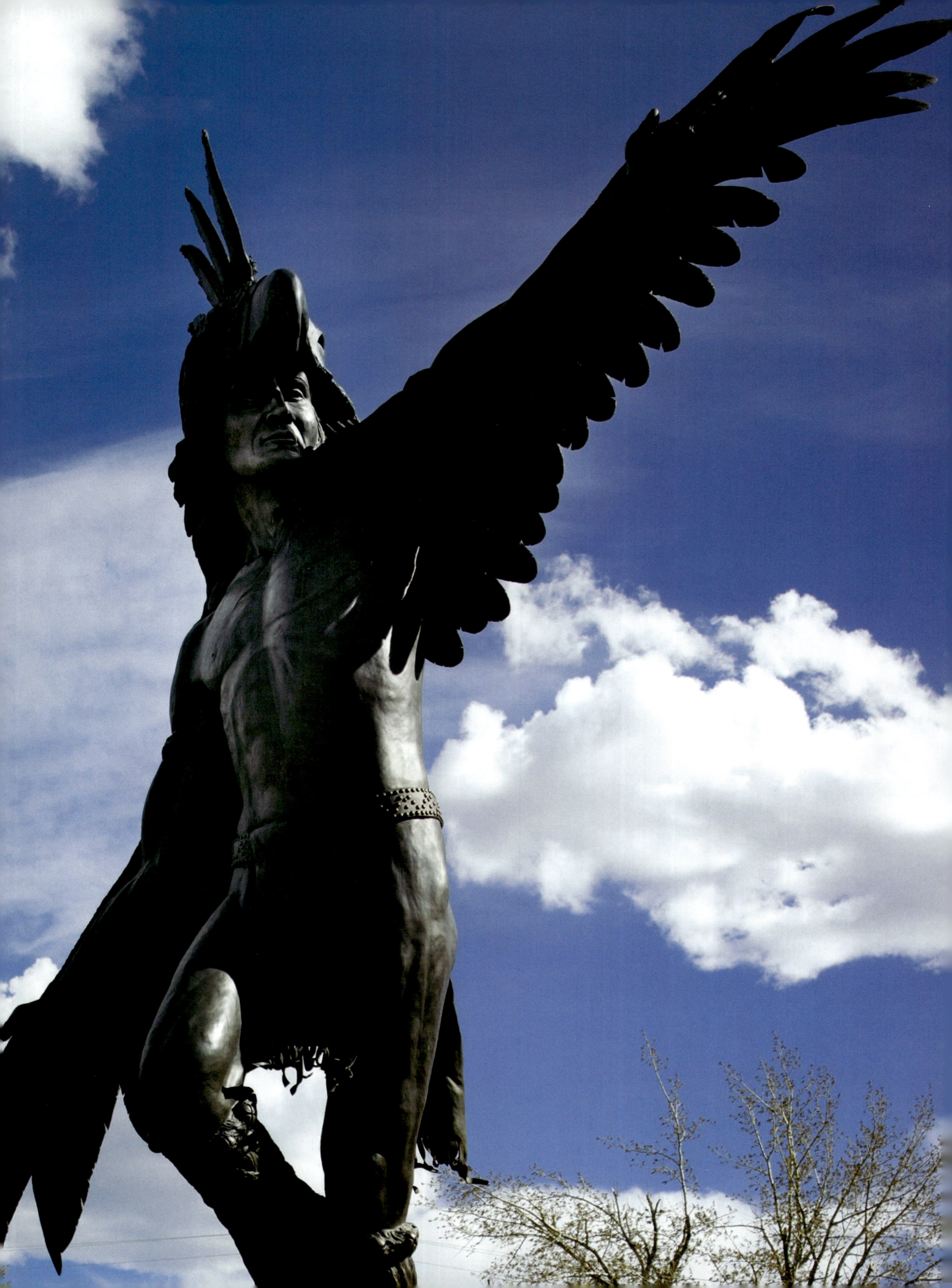

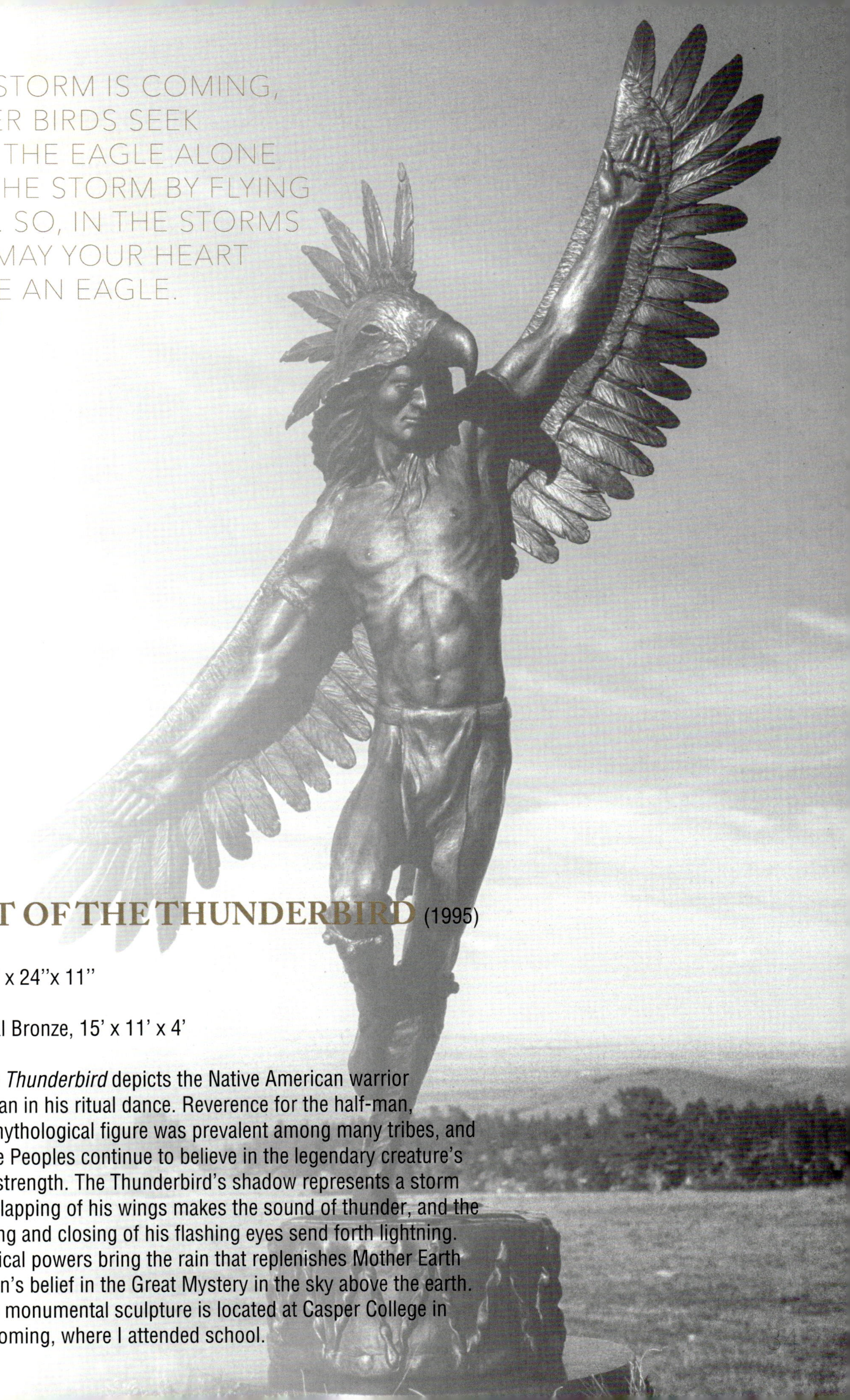

WHEN A STORM IS COMING, ALL OTHER BIRDS SEEK SHELTER. THE EAGLE ALONE AVOIDS THE STORM BY FLYING ABOVE IT. SO, IN THE STORMS OF LIFE, MAY YOUR HEART SOAR LIKE AN EAGLE.
—UNKNOWN

SPIRIT OF THE THUNDERBIRD (1995)

Bronze, 41" x 24"x 11"

Monumental Bronze, 15' x 11' x 4'

Spirit of the Thunderbird depicts the Native American warrior medicine man in his ritual dance. Reverence for the half-man, half-eagle mythological figure was prevalent among many tribes, and some Native Peoples continue to believe in the legendary creature's power and strength. The Thunderbird's shadow represents a storm cloud. The flapping of his wings makes the sound of thunder, and the rapid opening and closing of his flashing eyes send forth lightning. These mystical powers bring the rain that replenishes Mother Earth and test man's belief in the Great Mystery in the sky above the earth. This bronze monumental sculpture is located at Casper College in Casper, Wyoming, where I attended school.

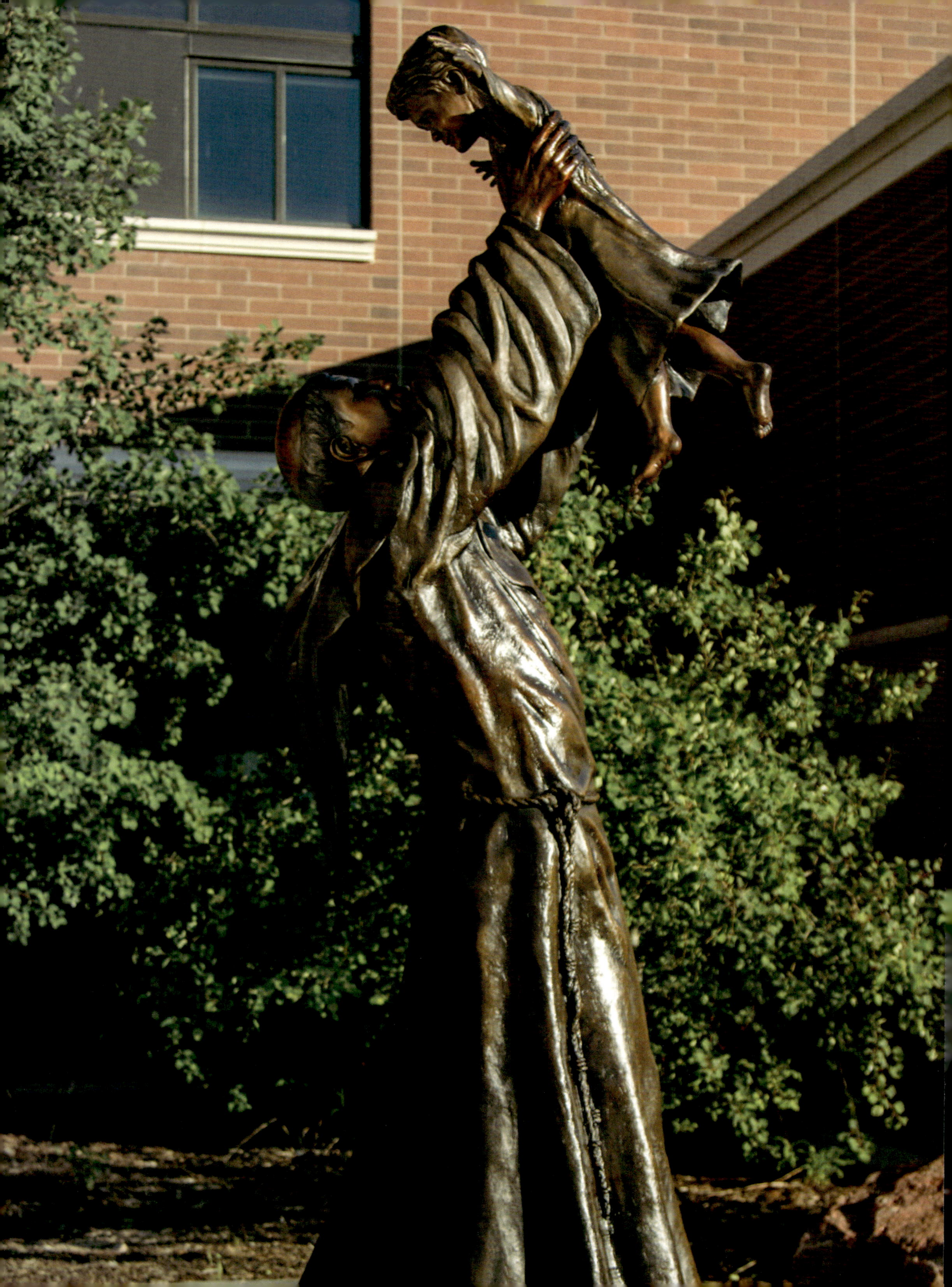

ST. ANTHONY'S JOY (2011)

Bronze, 15.5" x 7" x 7"

Monumental Bronze, 96" x 44" x 38.5"

I created this sculpture for Saint Anthony's School and Parish in Casper, Wyoming. When I researched the artists that had depicted St. Anthony in the past, they always portrayed him holding baby Jesus, the bible, and white lilies in his arms. I wanted my interpretation of St. Anthony with the Christ-child to reflect one of the simple pleasures in life that I have shared with my children. Nothing is more heartwarming than watching a smile grow into an expression of pure joy as a child is tossed into the air. St. Anthony, the patron saint for lost articles, is credited with many miracles involving lost people, lost things, and even lost spiritual goods.

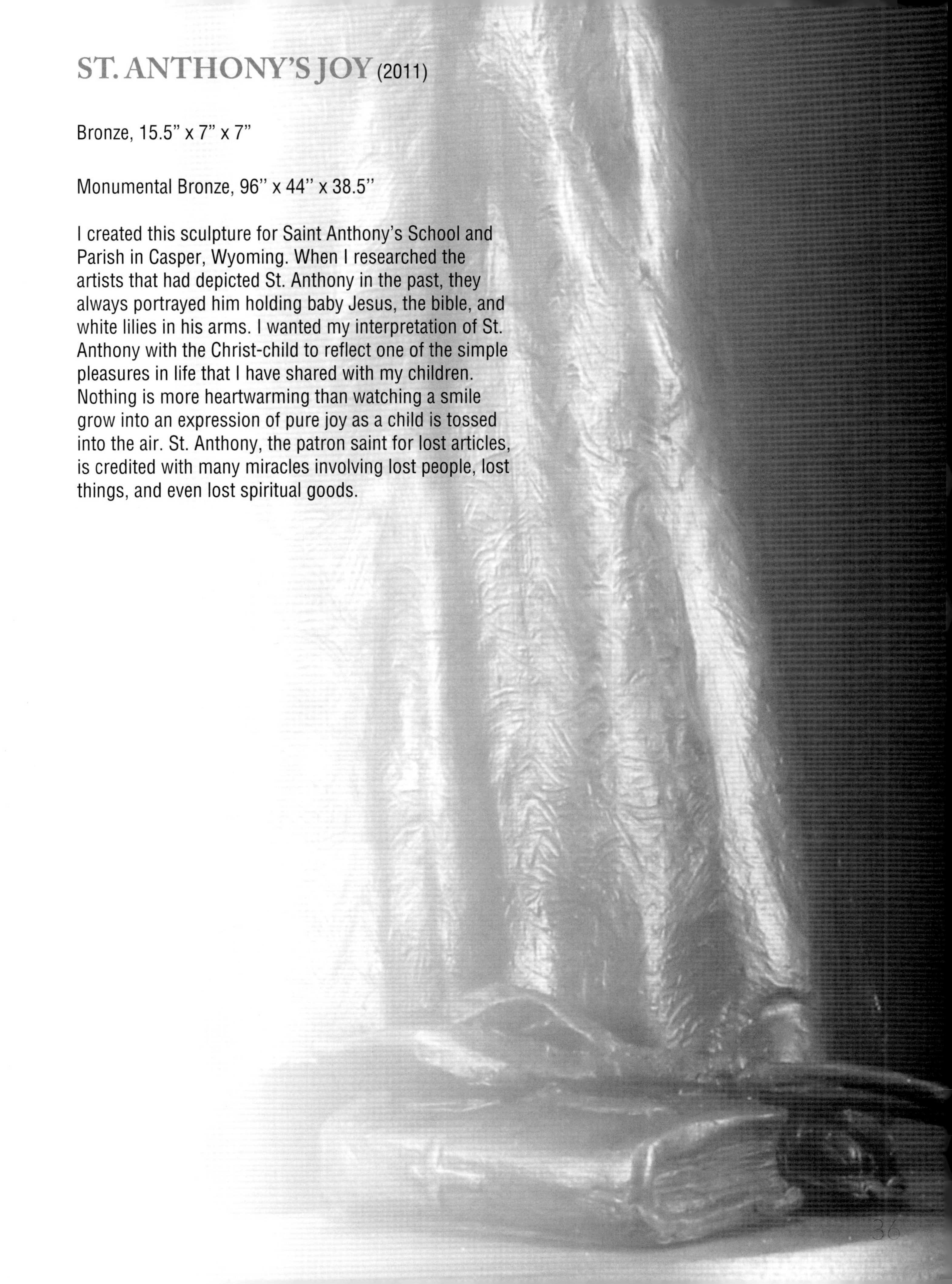

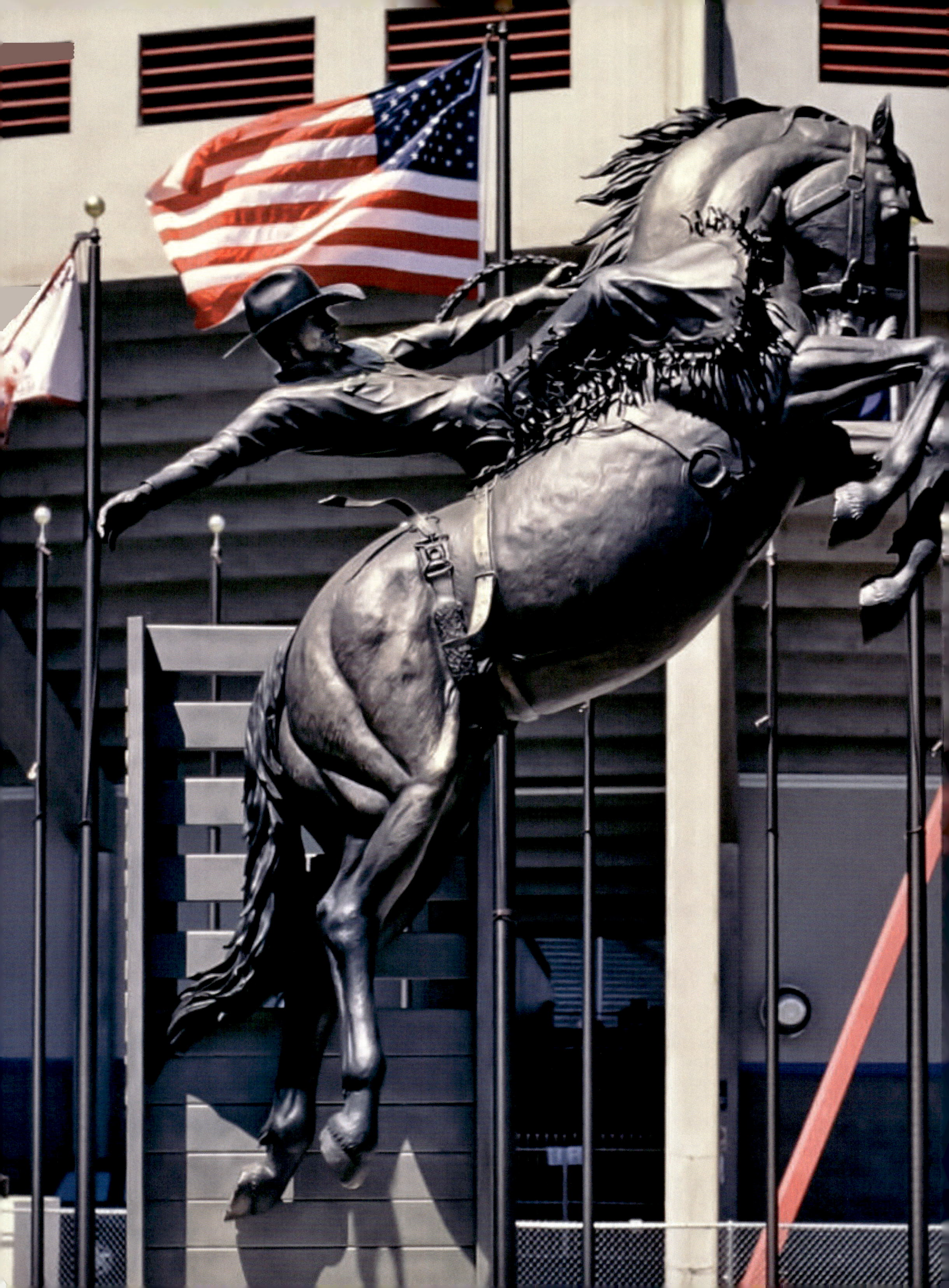

THEY SAY I'VE DRAWN A
CHAMPION BRONC THAT
NO ONE CAN RIDE.

WELL, I'M A CHAMPION,
TOO, AND I'VE GOT JUST
AS MUCH PRIDE.

SO I GUESS I'LL TAKE MY
CHANCES AND NOD FOR
THE GATE,

'CAUSE IT GIVES MY LIFE
MEANING, BEING IN THIS
WILD DANCE WITH FATE.

–CHRIS NAVARRO

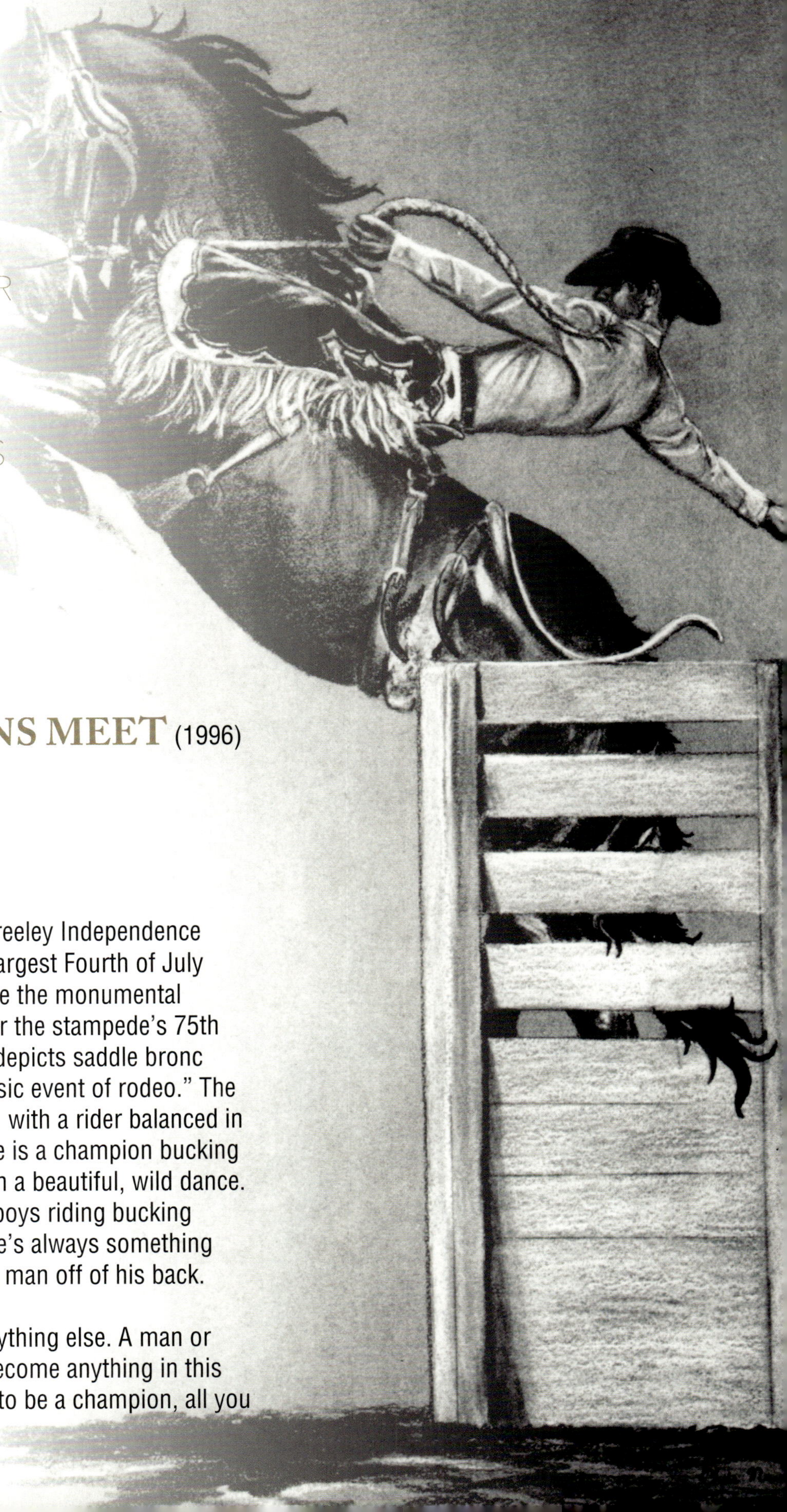

WHEN CHAMPIONS MEET (1996)

Bronze, 38'' x 23.5'' x 15''

Monumental Bronze, 15' x 11' x 7'

Located in Greeley, Colorado, the Greeley Independence Stampede is known as the world's largest Fourth of July rodeo. I was commissioned to create the monumental sculpture *When Champions Meet* for the stampede's 75th anniversary in 1997. The sculpture depicts saddle bronc riding, often referred to as "the classic event of rodeo." The horse is rocketing out of the chutes, with a rider balanced in the mark-out position. What you see is a champion bucking horse against a champion cowboy in a beautiful, wild dance. I have probably sculpted more cowboys riding bucking horses than any other subject. There's always something epic about a horse trying to throw a man off of his back.

Rodeo is more about trying than anything else. A man or a woman with guts and heart can become anything in this world they want or desire, because to be a champion, all you have to give is all you got.

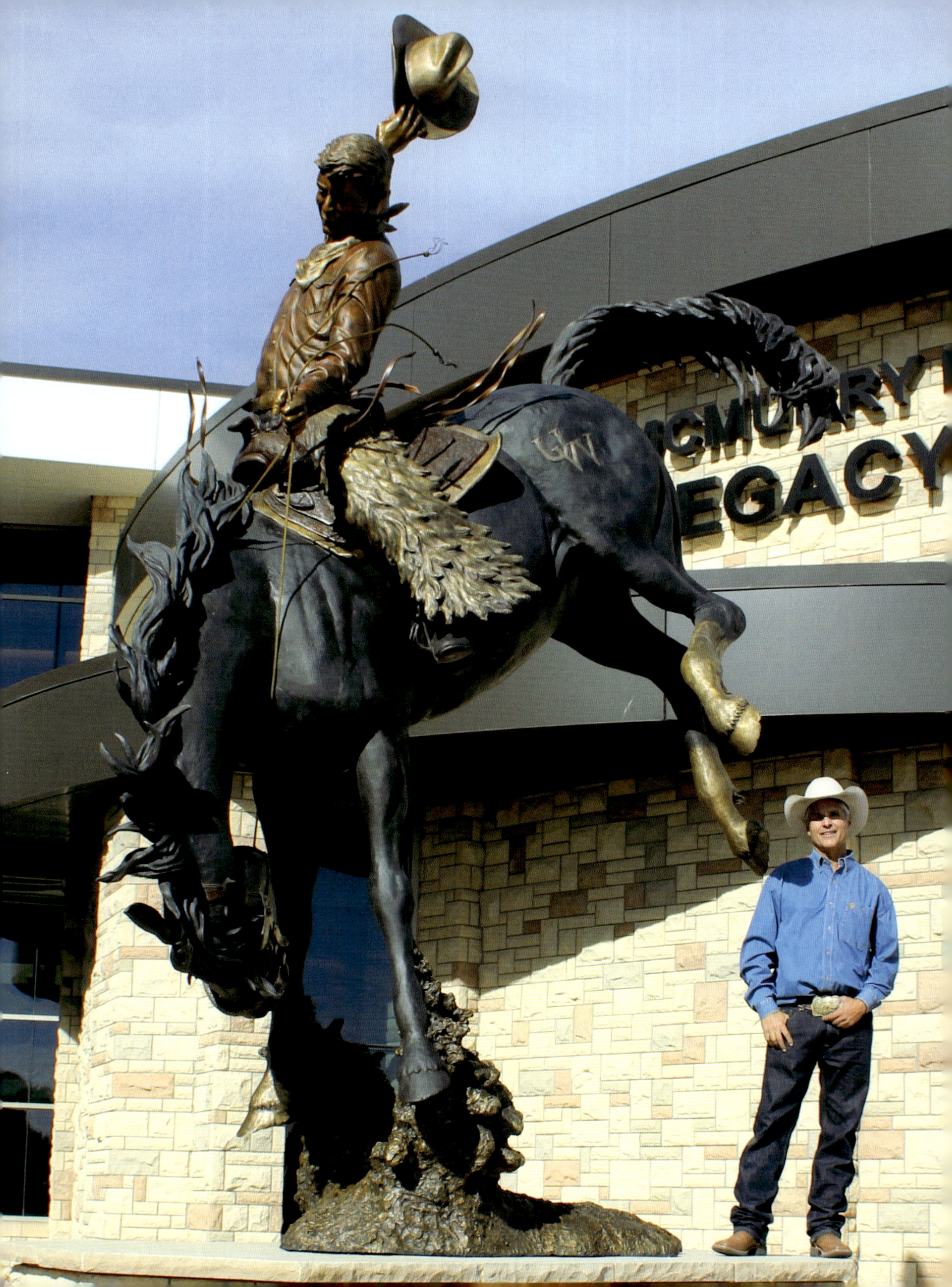

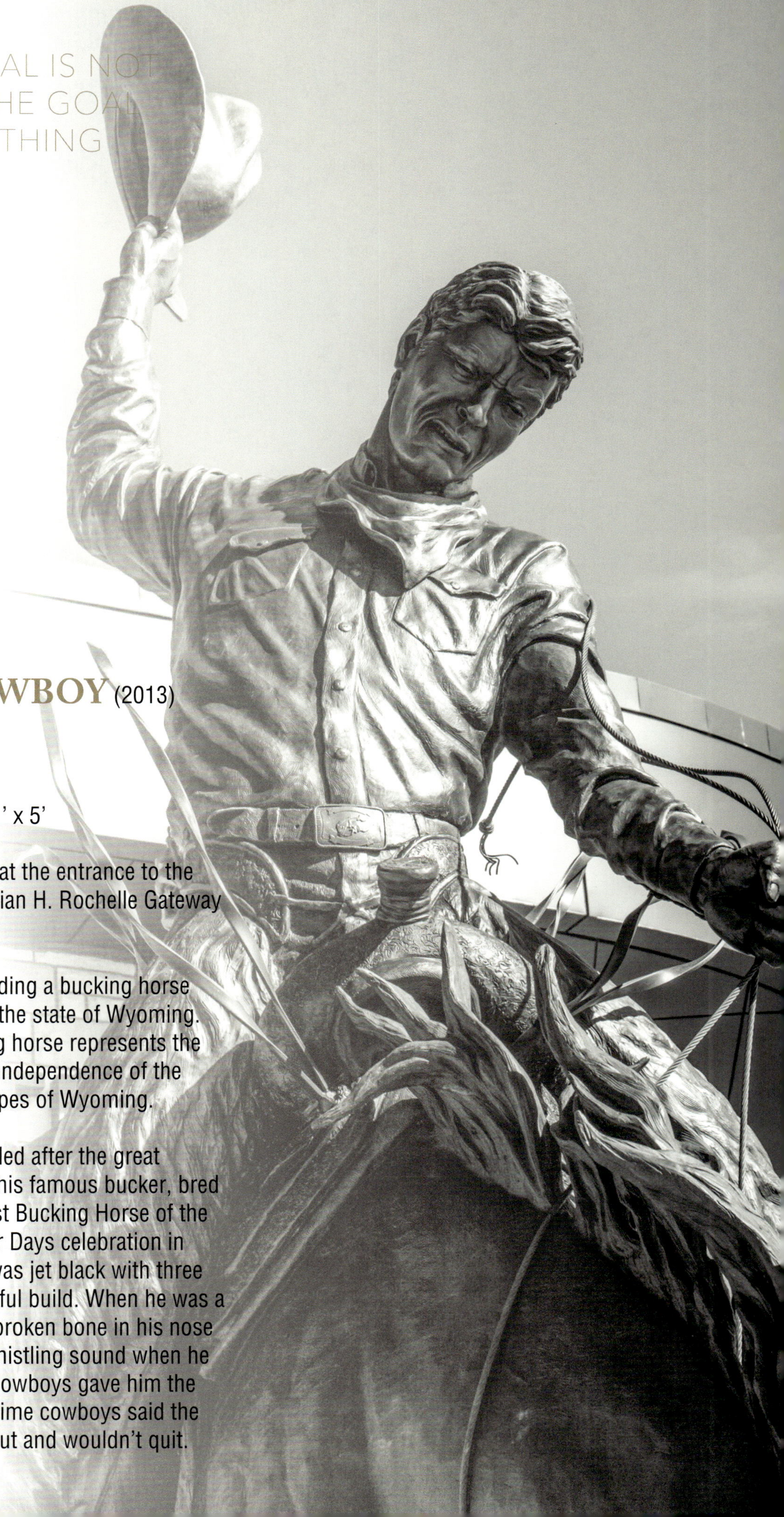

WE ALL DIE. THE GOAL IS NOT TO LIVE FOREVER. THE GOAL IS TO CREATE SOMETHING THAT WILL.
—CHUCK PALAHNIUK

WYOMING COWBOY (2013)

Bronze, 30" x 18" x 9"

Monumental Bronze, 16' x 11' x 5'

Wyoming Cowboy is located at the entrance to the University of Wyoming's Marian H. Rochelle Gateway Center in Laramie.

The silhouette of a cowboy riding a bucking horse has long been the symbol of the state of Wyoming. The cowboy astride a bucking horse represents the toughness, pride, spirit, and independence of the people, animals, and landscapes of Wyoming.

My sculpture has been modeled after the great bucking horse, Steamboat. This famous bucker, bred in Wyoming, was voted Worst Bucking Horse of the Year at the Cheyenne Frontier Days celebration in 1906 and 1907. Steamboat was jet black with three white socks and had a powerful build. When he was a colt, Steamboat sustained a broken bone in his nose that caused him to make a whistling sound when he bucked, and that is why the cowboys gave him the name "Steamboat." The old-time cowboys said the horse would buck his heart out and wouldn't quit.

THERE IS NOTHING IN A CATERPILLAR
THAT TELLS YOU IT'S GOING TO BECOME
A BUTTERFLY.
–R. BUCKMINSTER FULLER

EVERY LIFE HAS A STORY

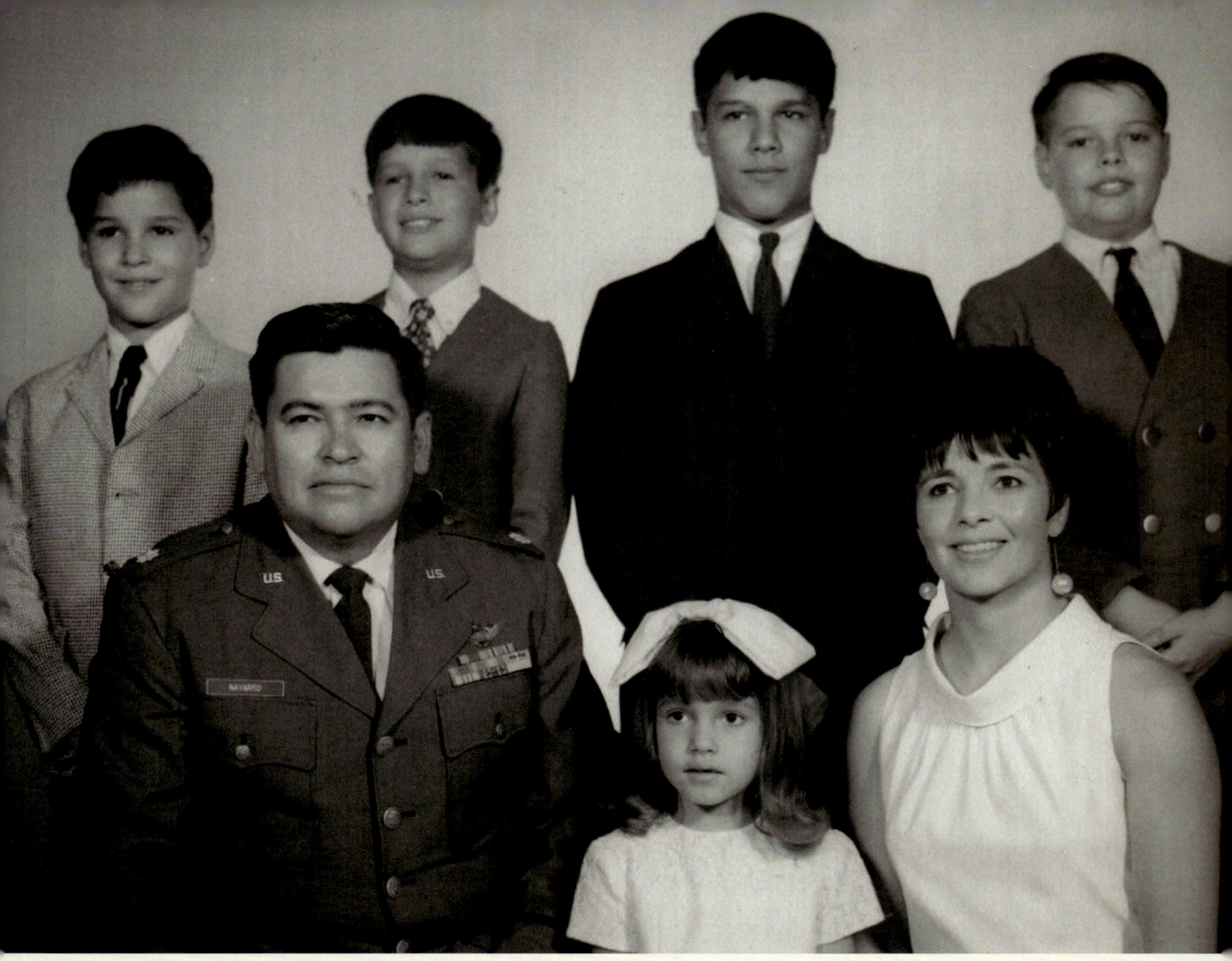
From left: Chris, Herbert, Rick, Mark, Herbert, Eve, and Mary, 1966.

FAMILY

We all have a worthwhile story to tell about the path that brought us to a certain point in existence. However, sometimes when we glance over our past, our first instinct is to say, "Nothing has happened in my life that would interest others." I have found that a fascinating narrative develops if we take a deeper look into the collection of circumstances and choices that helped shape who we are.

My story begins growing up in a family of military aviators. My father, Herbert Navarro, was born in Del Rio, Texas, on Feb. 11, 1926, and grew up as one of 13 children in San Antonio, Texas. There wasn't much money, and my grandfather was not one for sticking around. In 1941, at 15, he began working for The Western Union Company as a bicycle delivery boy to help support his family. He said that the most difficult aspect of this job was delivering the military death notice telegrams to the families of soldiers fighting in World War II.

Herbert enlisted in the U.S. Army in February 1944, after turning 18. When he completed boot camp, he was given the assignment of a POW guard for German prisoners who were relocated to Louisiana. At the end of the war, he went to college on the G.I. Bill as an ROTC cadet. He graduated in 1950 with a degree in physics and was sent to the Korean War as a second lieutenant in the U.S. Army 1st Field Artillery. He told me that after his tour in Korea, he would see military planes flying overhead and decided right then that he would "rather be up in the sky than down here on the ground." This led to his transfer into the U.S. Air Force in 1952. He completed flight navigation school and received a bachelor's degree in electrical engineering. He did a tour in Vietnam in 1970, where he developed night vision imagery systems on the gunship Puff the Magic Dragon. Our family was transferred to Torrejón Air Base in Madrid, Spain, in 1972. By then, Herbert was a lieutenant colonel and fluent in Spanish. He was put in charge of Combat Grande, the installation of the defense radar for Spain. My father joined the Army as a private in 1944 and retired at age 48 as a lieutenant colonel, with 30 years of military service. He was a veteran of World War II, the Korean, and Vietnam wars. My dad suffered a massive stroke and died Nov. 8, 1992, at 66. He was buried with full military honors at Fort Sam Houston in San Antonio, Texas.

My mother, Mary Louise Brown, was born Nov. 12, 1933, in San Antonio, Texas. She also had an extremely difficult childhood when she was orphaned at age 5, following her mother's death. She married young, and at age 22, she brought me into this world as her fourth child on Jan. 23, 1956. My mother has always been the backbone of our family. There were many times when my father was gone six months or more on deployment, and it was up to my mom to keep everything together. She basically raised us alone. The quality I most admire about my mom is her dedication to education. While rearing five children, she began college and completed her bachelor's, master's, and doctoral degrees in English literature. In 1999, she retired from college teaching as Professor emeritus and Director of Honors at Sinclair Community College in Dayton, Ohio.

I was the youngest of four boys with a younger sister, named Eve. My three older brothers all became military aviators. The oldest, Rick, graduated from the Naval Academy and flew P-3 Orions. He later became a flight captain for Delta Airlines. The next brother, Mark, was a naval mission commander on an ES-3. Herbert, the third brother, was a helicopter pilot with the 101st Airborne Division and an emergency medical service captain flying PC-12s. I was the only male in my family who did not go into military aviation. My first solo flight occurred when I was 20. I later owned several airplanes, but my first love and passion was horses.

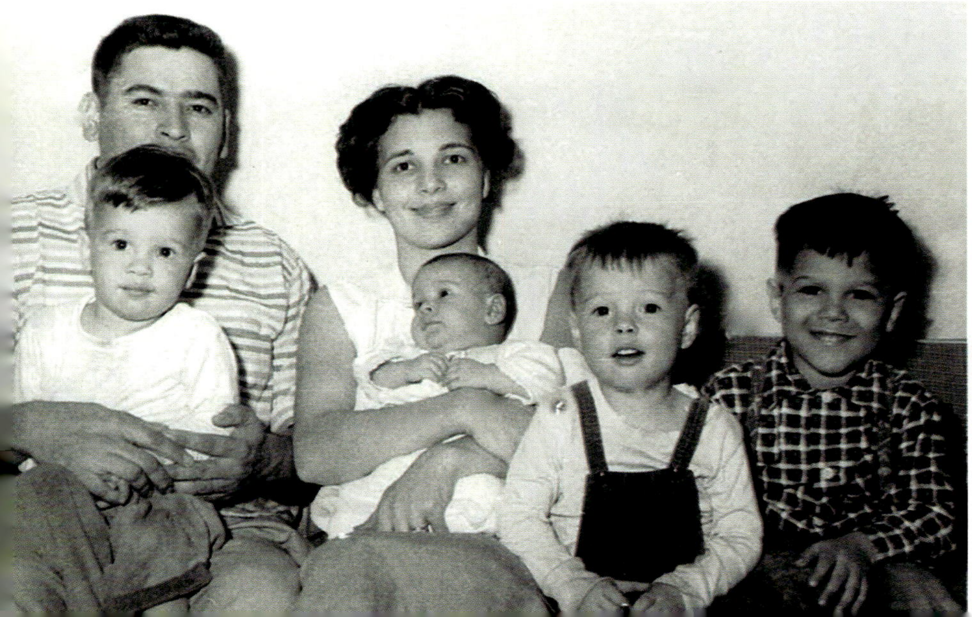

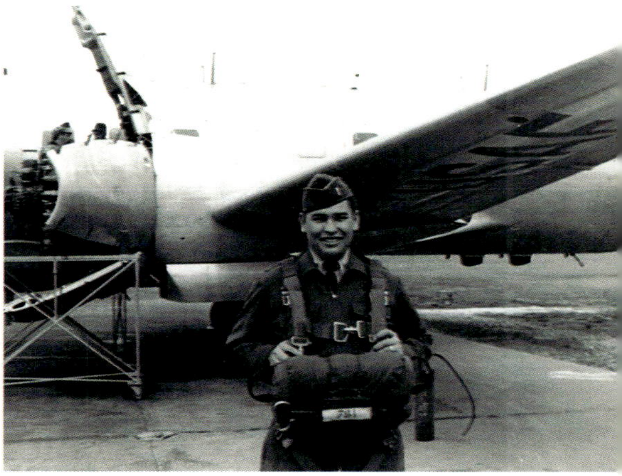

Left: Family photo 1956. Above: Herbert Navarro at U.S.A.F. navigation school, 1952.

NOTHING DOES MORE FOR THE INSIDE OF A MAN THAN THE OUTSIDE OF A HORSE.
—WILL ROGERS

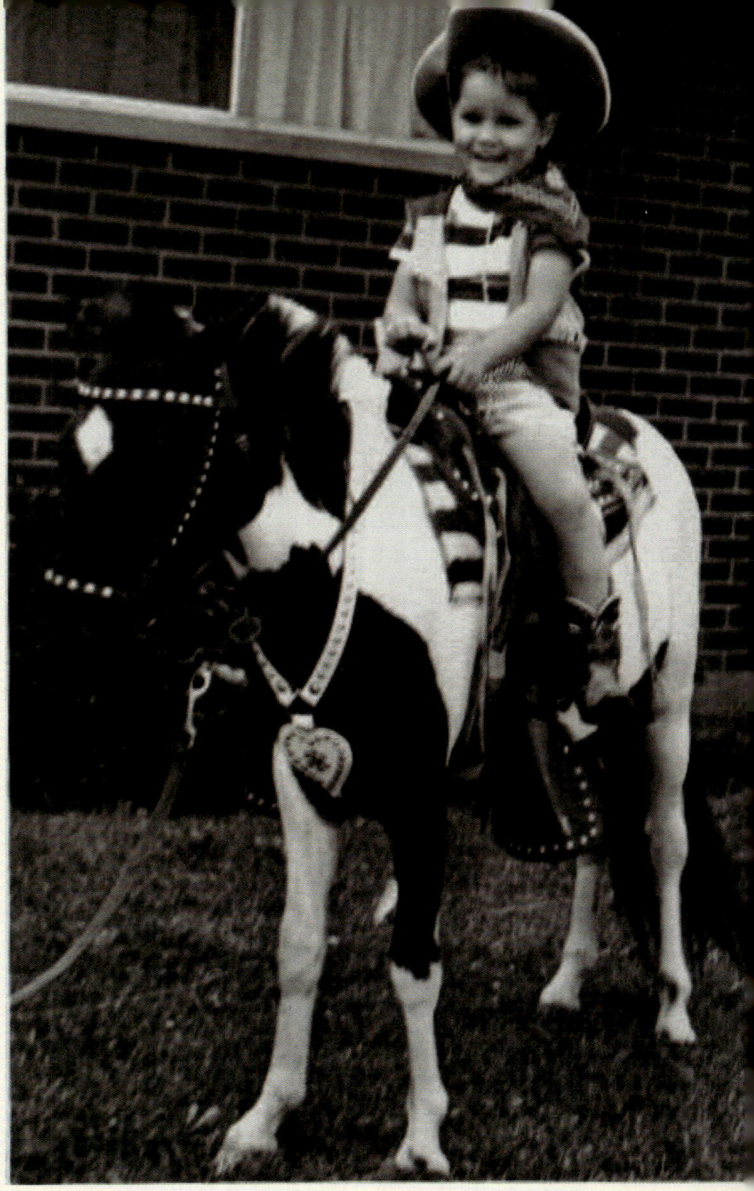

Chris's first pony ride in Albuquerque, New Mexico, 1959.

A BOY'S DREAM

My love of horses and respect for the cowboy way of life has been my entire focus since boyhood. There is something magical about the way God created horses so that they fit a person and feel good under a rider. My first horse, Grome, was given to me by a military family, also stationed at Wright Patterson in Ohio, when they went overseas. Most kids at 12 preferred riding their bikes, but I rode with Grome wherever I ventured. We went everywhere together, bareback, because I didn't have a saddle. A few other kids my age had horses and we'd race, take them swimming, and spend whole days at the riding stables. I spent so much time at Joseph's Stables, that a few trainers asked me to ride young horses for them.

When you grow up in a military family, you never really put down permanent roots. It's always difficult to make long-lasting relationships, because you're expecting to be transferred every two or three years. I joined 4-H and started showing horses in halter, pleasure, and gymkhana events. Since horses were my big passion in life, I thought being a professional horse trainer would be a great way to make a living. I did that until I was 16, when my father received orders to transfer to Torrejón Air Force Base in Madrid. My parents told me I'd have to sell my horse. As sad as I was about this, I really had no choice in the matter. Moving always meant starting over in a new school and making new friends. That's just the way it is when your father is a soldier. We packed up and moved to Spain in 1972. My parents did not want us to live on the base, so we moved into an apartment less than one mile away from Plaza de Toros (bull fighting ring). Spain has a strong horse society, historically, and bull fighting is embedded in their culture. One of the most beautiful things I have ever witnessed at Plaza de Toros is a bullfight from horseback. Imagine the graceful movements of the pair: a costumed matador and beautiful grey Andalusian. It is spectacular to watch, as horse and rider charge the bull, only to dodge out of its way at the last instant.

My father had promised that I'd get a new horse in Madrid, and he kept his word. He helped me buy a 5-year-old registered bay thoroughbred racehorse right off of the racetrack for $400. Her name was Yucatan. I kept her at the air base riding stables, and I remember vividly our first day together. I took Yucatan to a big open field. Riding bareback, I wanted to see how fast she was. Well, that mare could fly! She did not have much of a stop, but she sure could run. She was easily the fastest horse at the stables.

One fateful day, my parents and I traveled to the naval base in Rota, Spain, where they had a Rodeo association. I was captivated, watching the military cowboys riding bulls and broncs. It looked like a lot of fun and something I wanted to try. I was only 16 and talked my parents into signing the consent form to permit me to ride. All the time I had spent bareback riding was good training for riding rough stock. I really took to it and started making qualified rides fairly quickly. But more importantly, I loved it.

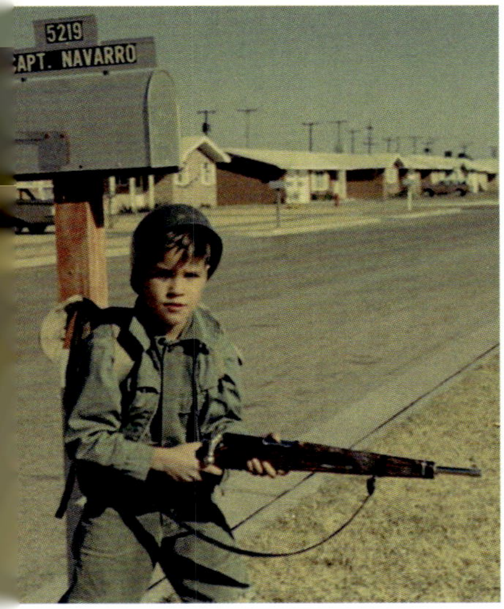

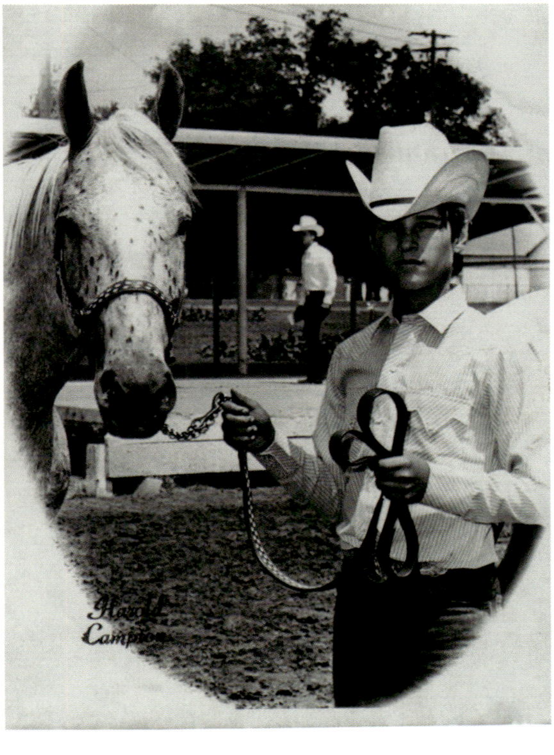

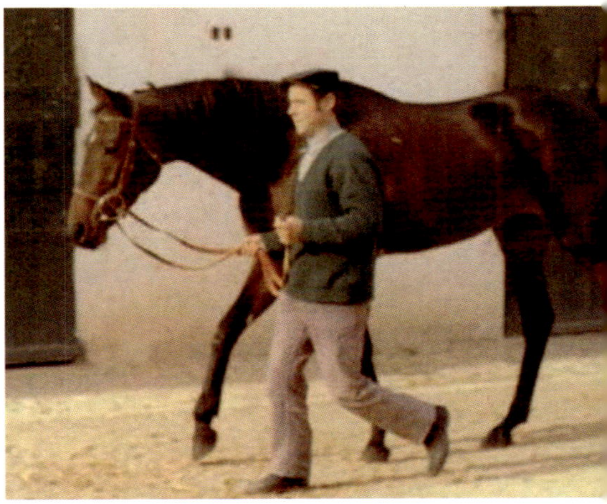

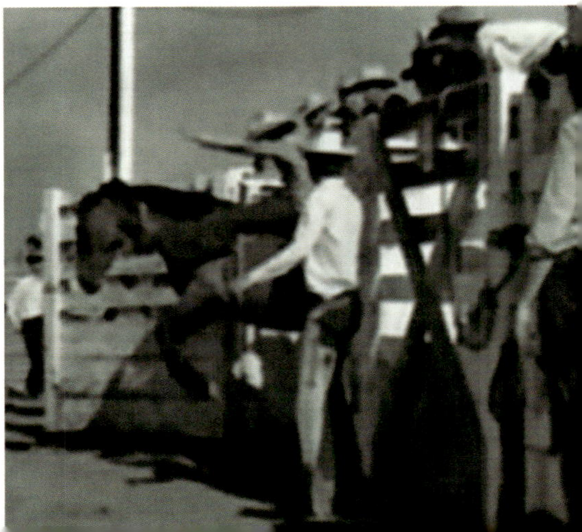

From left:
Chris, age 5, Lubbock, Texas.
Chris, age 14 showing horses in 4-H halter class, Dayton, Ohio.
Yucatan, English-registered thoroughbred.
Chris rides Easy Lovin' in Rota, Spain, 1972.

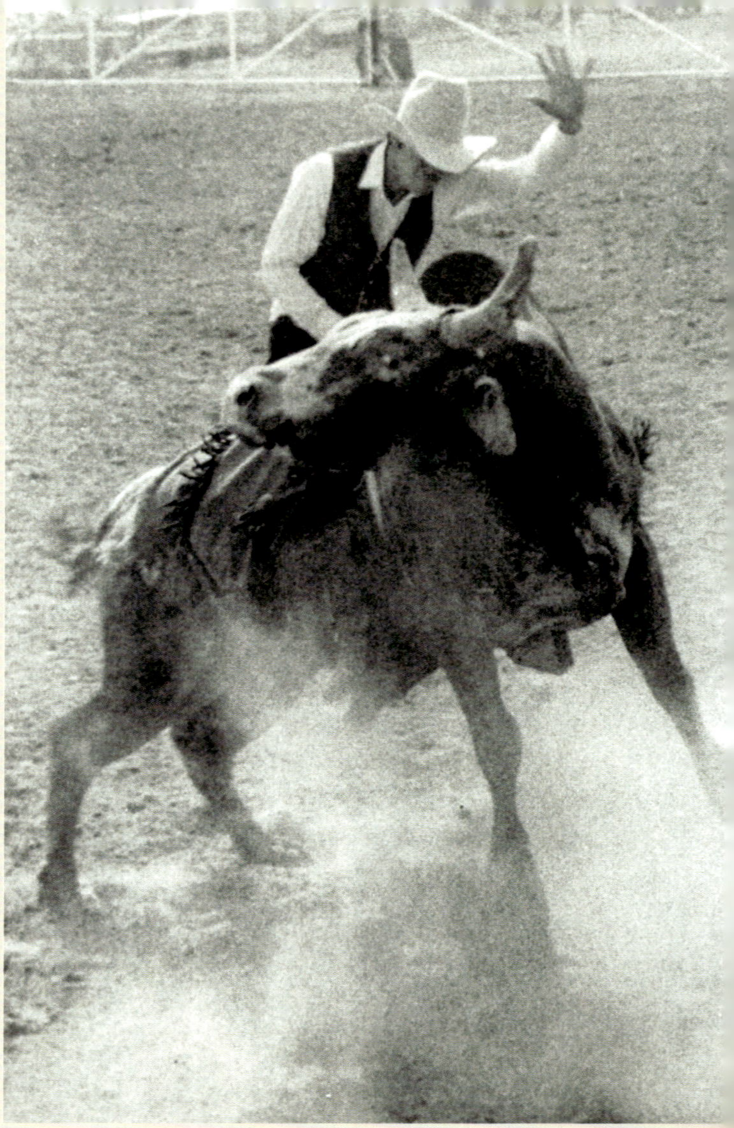
Chris, wearing a Casper College vest at the Ropin' and Riggin' Days Rodeo, rides a Vold bull. Photo by Bill Landen, 1976.

RODEO RUSH

The two events in which I competed were bareback broncs and bulls. Bull riding may be the most dangerous event, but bareback bronc is the most physically demanding. The bareback rider uses rigging that is made of leather and rawhide, often compared to a suitcase handle. The rigging is placed just behind the horse's withers. The rider leans back and spurs with an up-and-down motion from the horse's point of shoulder toward the rigging handle, spurring at each jump and buck in rhythm with the motion of the horse. Bull riding, on the other hand, is not that complicated. The rider holds onto a flat, braided rope; he can use only one hand to ride, and he must not touch the bull or himself with his free hand. He uses spurs with locked rows, having at least a quarter turn, and the bull must be wearing a flank strap. The rider is required to stay on for eight seconds. The performance of both the bull and rider are scored by two judges who give up to 50 points for the rider and 50 points for the bull, with a total possible score of 100.

WHEN YOU LOVE WHAT YOU ARE DOING THE REAL REWARD IS IN THE EXPERIENCE OF DOING IT.
—CHRIS NAVARRO

I rode in the military rodeo association until I graduated from high school in Madrid in 1974. I then traveled back to the United States to live with my Uncle Leo and Aunt Dot in San Antonio, Texas, where I rodeoed throughout the summer. My parents were still stationed in Spain and wanted me to go to college. I thought about an article that I had read in Western Horseman Magazine about the champion Casper College Rodeo Team in Casper, Wyoming. I talked to the counselor at my high school, and she informed me that Wyoming was known as "The Cowboy State." That sold it for me. I decided that's where I was going to college and rodeo, too.

The minimum driving age in Spain was 18, so during my first week in Texas, I obtained a driver's license and purchased my first car all in the same day. It was a 1966 Plymouth for $250. She was a two-door with a 318 v8 and a 3-speed column shifter. She had a few miles on her and went through a quart of oil with every tank of gas, but she was all mine; a four-wheeled horse that could take me anywhere I wanted to go. At the end of summer, I loaded everything I owned into that old Plymouth and headed out on a 1,250-mile road trip to Casper. I had never been to Wyoming and did not know anyone there when I moved into the Bailey Hall dorms on the Casper College campus in the fall of 1974.

Bull riding is a dangerous ballet of brutal beauty. Rodeo has always been a passion in my life. Doing something that both scares and thrills me makes me feel more alive. There is an excitement in uncertainty, and one gets that in spades with rodeo. I rode bulls for five years, and my son, JC, rode bulls professionally in the PBR. The most obvious downside of bull riding is that it is an extremely dangerous sport. Serious injuries occur more often in bull riding than in any other rodeo event. Bad things have a way of happening any time a man gets on an unpredictable animal weighing close to a ton. Bulls usually have a mean disposition, and some only want to get a hoof or horn into you. The one constant fact of bull riding is not if you are going to get hurt. It's *when* and *how bad* you'll get hurt. I became addicted to the risk. There is an enjoyment that comes not so much from the danger itself, but from the ability to move through it. You are so focused and concentrated in the

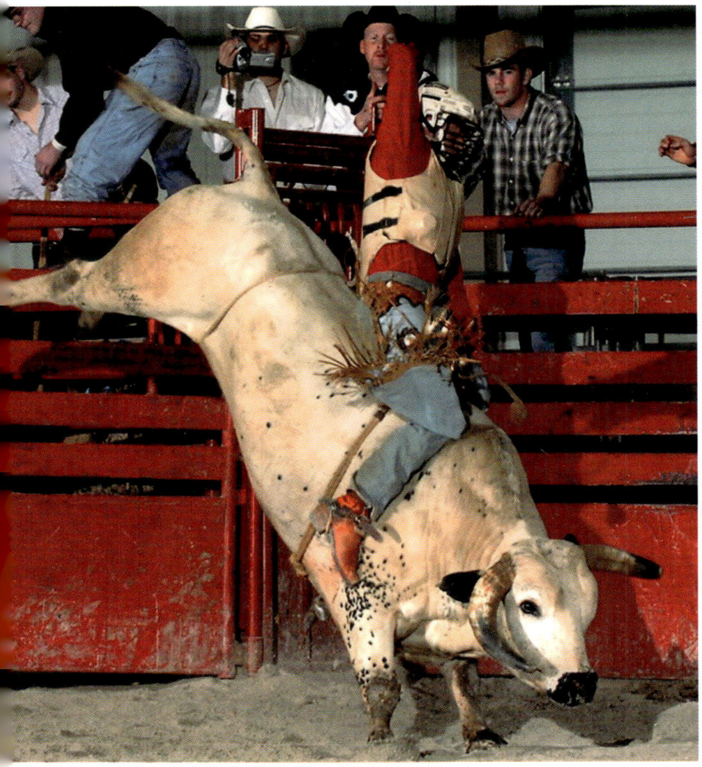

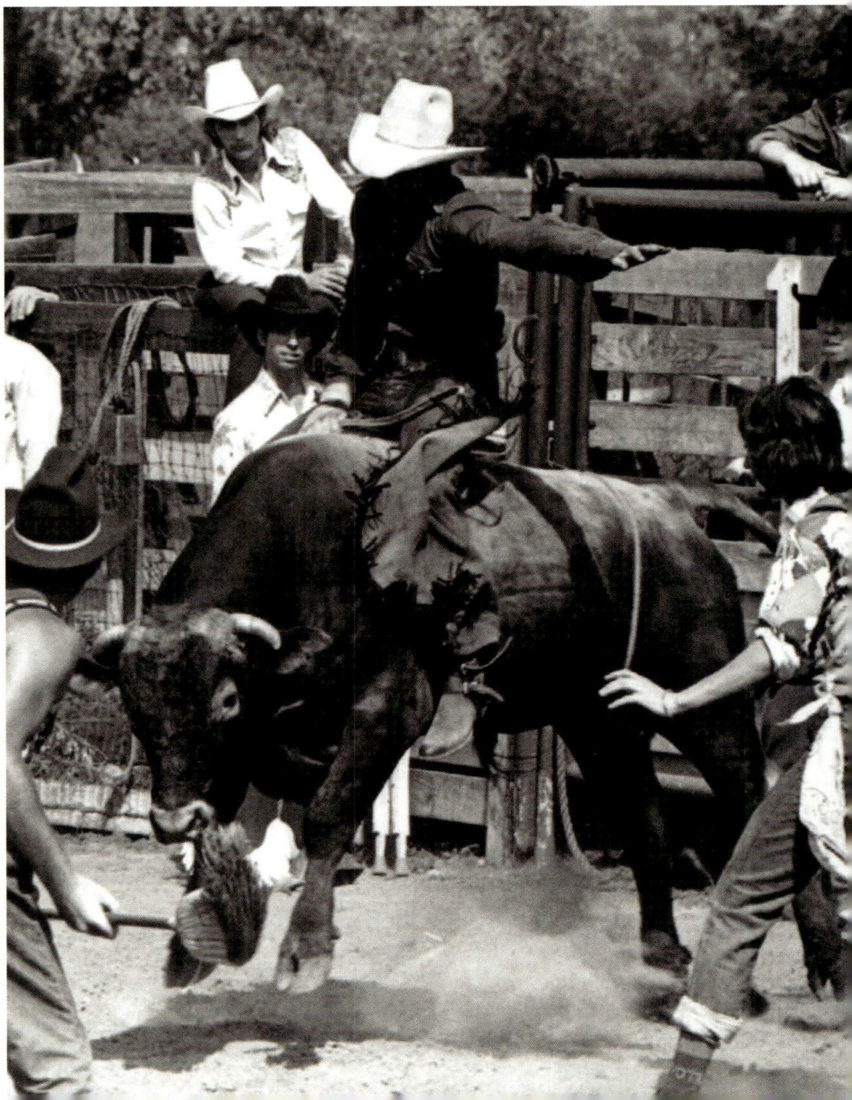

Above: JC, riding in the PBR.
Right: Chris, riding Lil' Brown Jug in San Antonio, Texas, 1974.

IN BULL RIDING, YOU NEED CONFIDENCE AND IGNORANCE. THE SAME TWO THINGS YOU NEED TO BE AN ARTIST.
–CHRIS NAVARRO

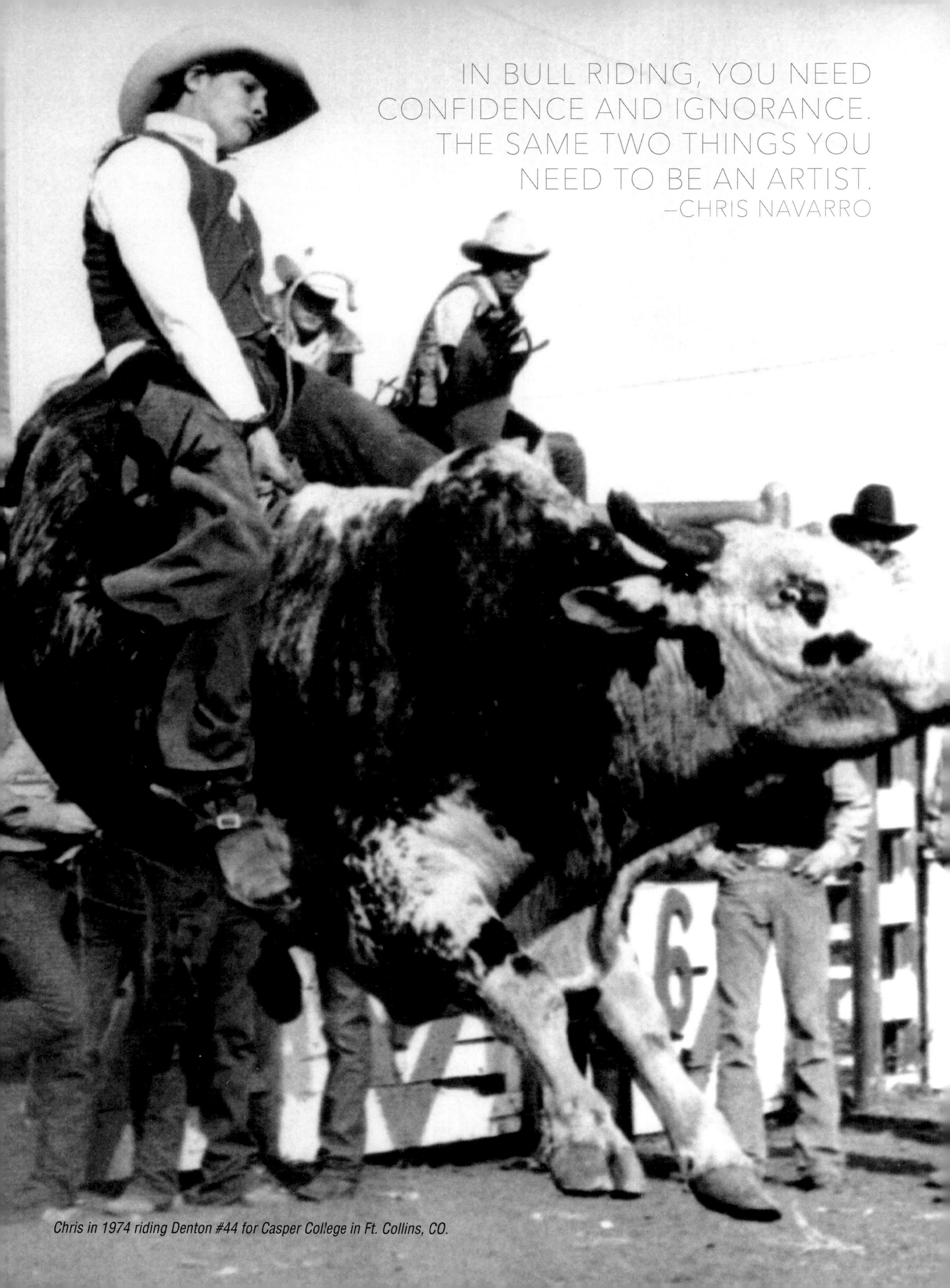

Chris in 1974 riding Denton #44 for Casper College in Ft. Collins, CO.

moment that nothing else matters except the sensation of the experience. Riding bulls is a high-stakes game of chance. If you want to play, you have to be willing to use your physical health for chips. People who have never been on a bull often ask, "What is the reason for competing in such a dangerous sport?" It is difficult to put into words, but for me, it's about getting into a mental state where I am so involved in the "moment of now" that nothing else seems to matter. The experience is so intense that you do it whatever the cost. Mixing adrenaline with joy is an addictive cocktail that keeps you coming back for another taste. The best moments occur when my body and mind are stretched to its limits in an effort to accomplish something difficult but worthwhile. No doubt about it, rodeo takes its toll on the body. Getting injured, hospital bills, and lack of money are the main reasons most bull riders give up the sport. It was no different for me. I tell people that when I quit riding bulls, I was so poor that I couldn't afford to pay attention! I started rodeo when I was 16, competing on bulls and broncs. I later switched to team roping, the sport in which I still compete. To date, I have had my front teeth knocked out; dislocated my left and right shoulders; broke my right and left collarbone; suffered 12 broken ribs and a collapsed left lung; busted my left thumb and right hand; broke my left shoulder blade; and had five concussions. I have had three surgeries to repair my left shoulder, left collarbone, and my right hand. Not all of my injuries were rodeo related, however. Skiing and hang gliding also have caused a fair share of injuries! I was 21 when I quit riding bulls. With no money in my pocket, I thought it best to get what my dad called a "real job" in the Wyoming oil fields.

AMF-Tuboscope hired me as a hard-hat, steel-toe-wearing jack hand to work on a pipe inspection truck. This meant going out to the drilling rigs to inspect the drill pipe. It was dirty work with long, physically demanding hours working outside in the elements. It wasn't my dream job, but I earned good money. I remember working on a rig in the Red Desert of Wyoming, where I had accumulated 72 hours of overtime in one week. The company had a high turnover rate, but I stuck with the job. As the years went by, AMF promoted me to an operator, inspector, and field superintendent. I wasn't competing in rodeo at the time, and I felt as though something was missing in my life.

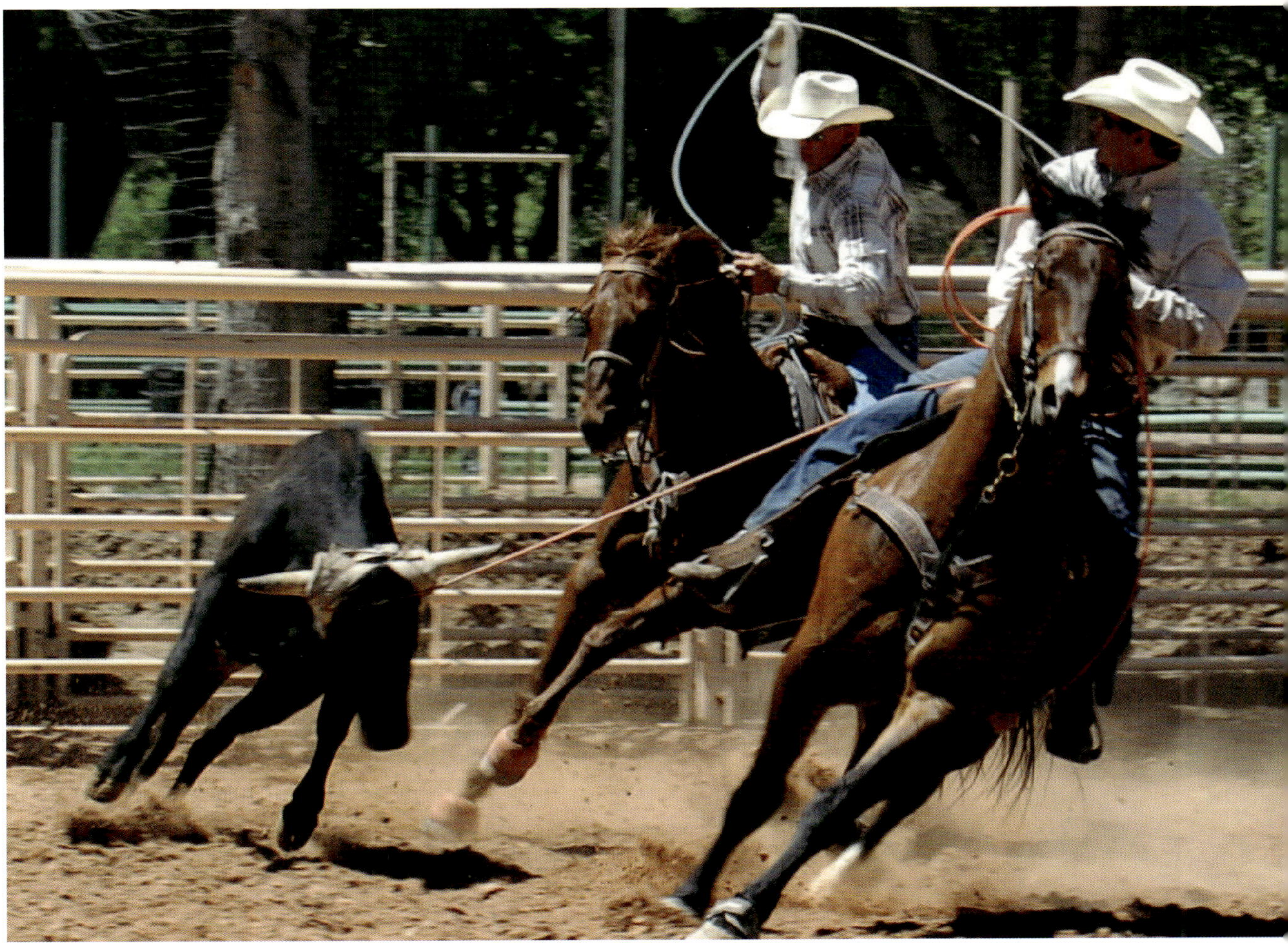

Roping with Buddy Young in Page Springs, Arizona, 2010. Photo by Robert Albrecht.

BECOMING A SCULPTOR

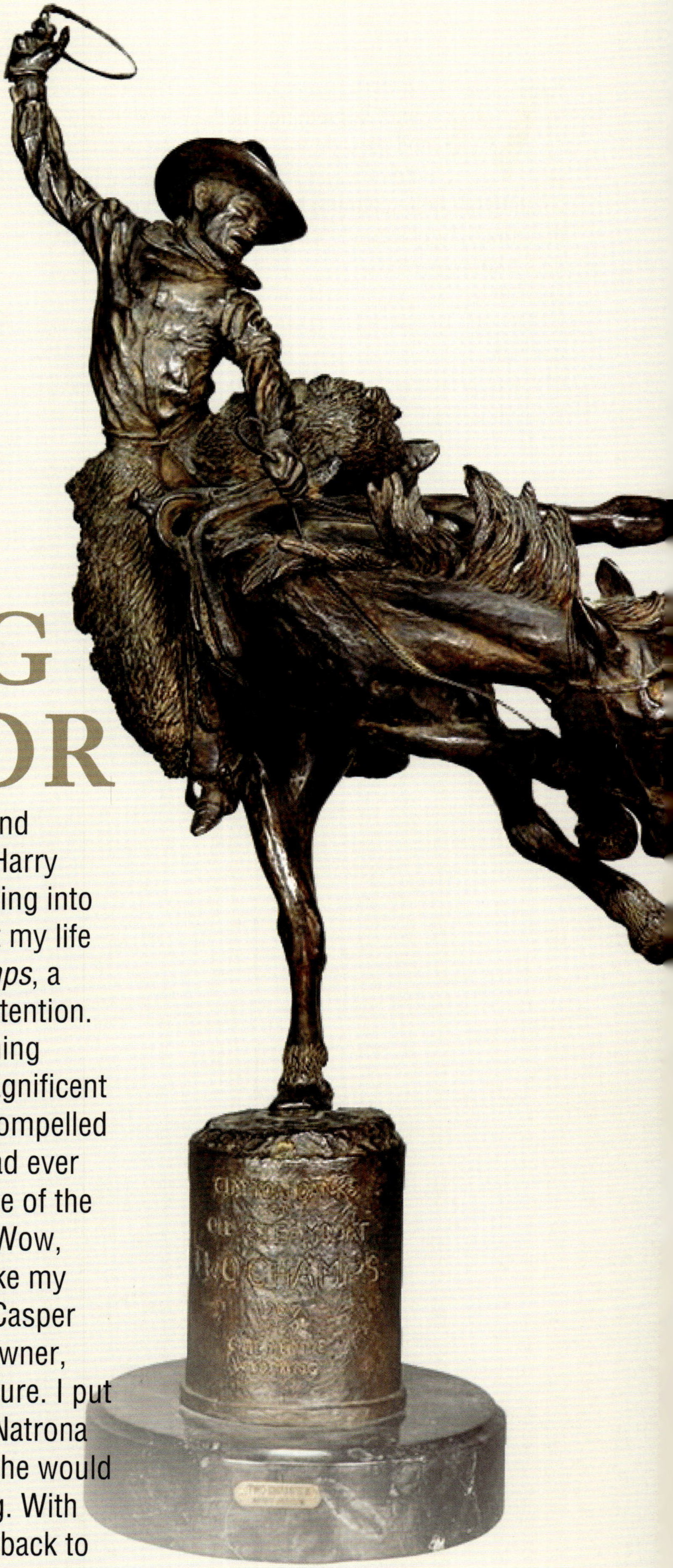

In 1979, Sy Gilland and I were out hunting and decided to visit his cousin, a caretaker at the Harry Jackson studio in Lost Cabin, Wyoming. Walking into Jackson's studio and home, I had no idea that my life was about to change. There it was, *Two Champs*, a bronze sculpture that instantly captured my attention. It depicted a cowboy riding the famous Wyoming bucking horse, Steamboat. Looking at this magnificent bronze, with its raw power and beauty, I felt compelled to touch it. It was the most beautiful thing I had ever seen. I wanted to have it, but was told the price of the sculpture was $35,000. I thought to myself, "Wow, I could never afford that! But maybe I can make my own." I visited Goedicke's art supply store in Casper the very next day and explained to John, the owner, that I needed supplies to build a bronze sculpture. I put all the materials in my truck and drove to the Natrona County Library, where I asked the librarian if she would show me all of the books she had on sculpting. With books and sculpting supplies in hand, I drove back to my trailer house and started creating my first sculpture.

Two Champs by Harry Jackson.

My first bronze sculpture was going to be about something I had a knowledge of and passion for, and that was bull riding. After studying the library books, I began creating my first sculpture in wax. It should be noted that most of my learning came from the school of "I didn't know any better, trial-and-error" method, an extremely slow process. I worked on weekends and nights, and it seemed to take forever. I had two weeks of paid vacation per year, so I took one week to devote all of my attention and time to getting it done. My buddies at work thought I was crazy to spend my vacation time alone, in my trailer house, working on a sculpture. But I had a burning desire to finish this piece. Somehow, I knew it would change my life. I finally completed the sculpture, which I titled *Spinning and Winning*, because bulls that spin usually score higher points than bulls that just jump and kick. The next step was to get it cast in bronze. I had heard about Caleco Foundry, a lost wax bronze-casting foundry in Cody, Wyoming. I drove to Cody and was informed that it would cost $1,000 to cast my first sculpture! I had no idea it was going to be that expensive, but I was committed and used my savings to get it done.

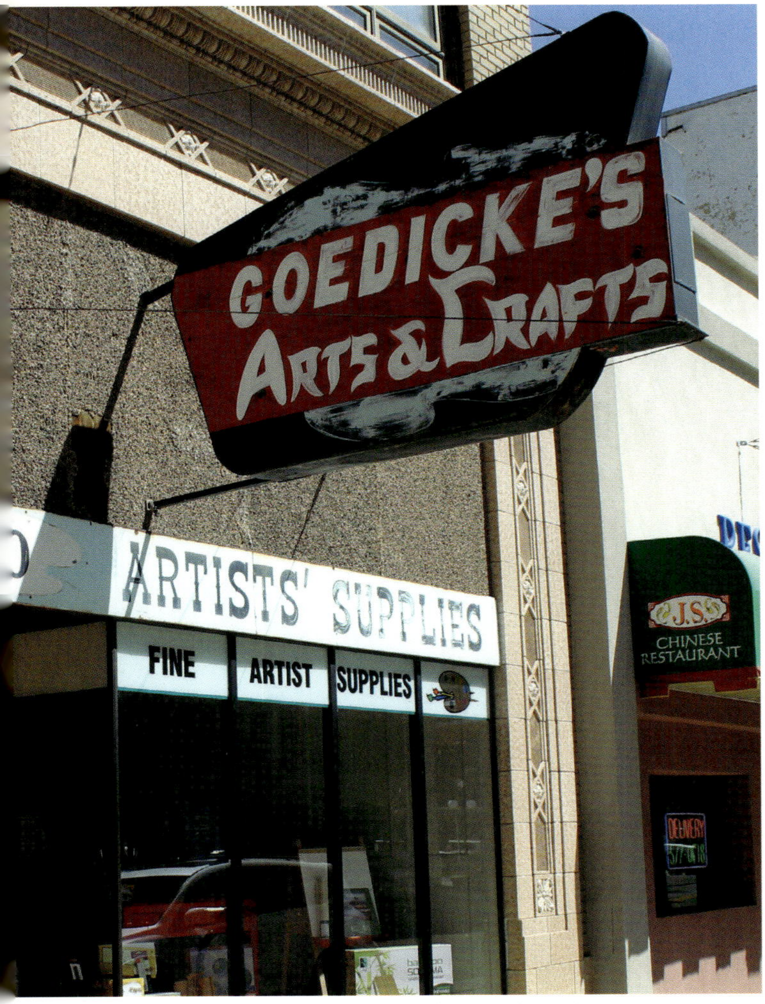

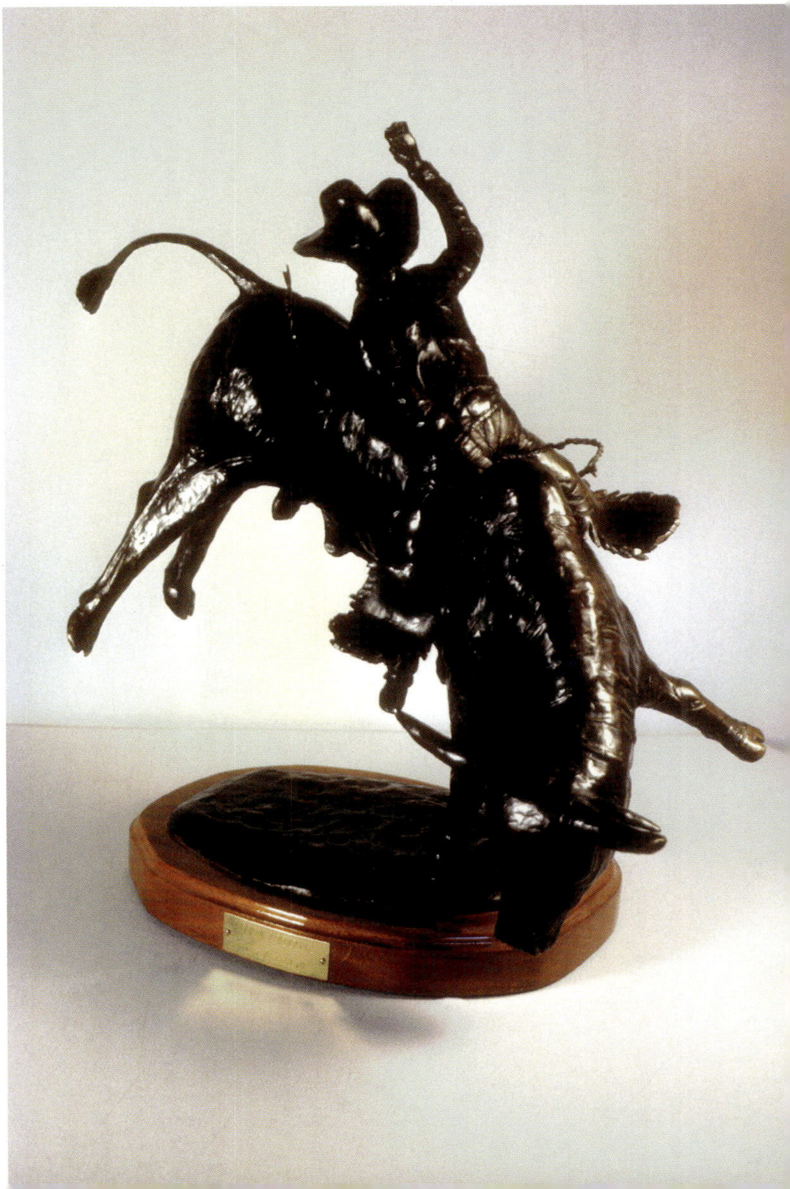

Above: Goedicke's Arts & Crafts, Casper, Wyoming.
Right: Chris' first bronze, *Spinning & Winning.*

THEY SAY A PERSON NEEDS JUST THREE THINGS TO BE TRULY HAPPY IN THIS WORLD: SOMEONE TO LOVE, SOMETHING TO DO, AND SOMETHING TO HOPE FOR.

–TOM BODETT

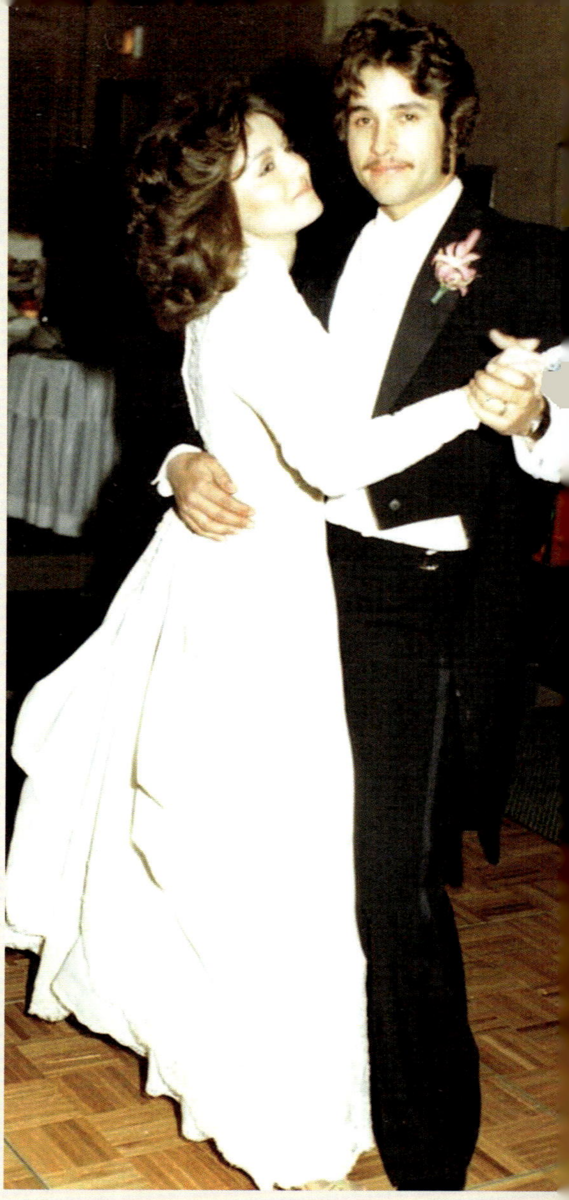

MONUMENTAL CHANGES

I met Lynne Chavez, the love of my life, on Valentine's Day in 1980. When people ask how we first met, I like to tell them one of two stories: I either bought her box lunch at the church social; or I met her dancing on ladies night at a bar. The truth is, I was sitting at a table with a couple of work buddies when the prettiest girl I had ever seen walked by. Next thing you know, I found myself asking her if she wanted to dance. She said, "Yes," and we both fell hard in love. We were married nine months later. Thirty-five years later, we are still dancing together. There are lots of great tips for a successful marriage. One secret I like to share is that, when married, a man can be happy or he can be right, but he can't be both!

We started dating when I told Lynne my dream of becoming a professional artist and that I'd traveled to Cody to pick up my first bronze sculpture. I was as excited as a young kid on Christmas morning when I held my first bronze sculpture in my hands. I wasn't sure what to do next, when Bucky Hall, the owner of Caleco Foundry, told me he thought the bronze was good for my first effort and that I should let him enter it in the Cody Chamber Art Show. I had never entered an art show before. Bucky told me he would take care of it and put it in the amateur sculpture division. Much to my surprise, I won first place and $15. That 15 bucks is long gone, but I still have the blue ribbon hanging in my studio. I remember how good it felt to win that first ribbon. It gave me a bit of validation, and I thought, "I'm on to something here; this is what I want to do with the rest of my life." I was going to do whatever it took to become a professional bronze sculptor.

When Lynne and I got married, we bought a little two-bedroom house with a barn, and I leased the adjacent 20 acres. Lynne had just graduated from cosmetology school and was working in a salon. I would sculpt at night and on weekends after work. Slowly, I began to finish more sculptures. I created pieces of all the rodeo rough stock events, as well as western and wildlife subjects. When I first started, I didn't realize how expensive it was to cast sculptures in bronze. I spent a lot more money at the foundry than I did selling art. After a couple of years, I sold my first bronze! I decided to take night classes at Casper College in drawing, painting, and photography. To make extra money to help pay for my foundry bills, I started two small businesses on the side: one was buying and fixing up cars, and the other was running a six-horse pack string that I leased to outfitters. I kept my full-time job at Tuboscope and continued to work nights on my art. I began selling more drawings and a few paintings, as well as a bronze now and then. My first one-man art show was held at First Interstate Bank in 1983. I wasn't going to give up on my dream, but I knew that as long as I was doing art part time, all I would ever be is a part-time artist.

I had been sculpting for a couple of years and was still working in the oilfield when I decided it was time to move my career along by getting into a big-time art gallery (or, for that matter, any gallery) that would

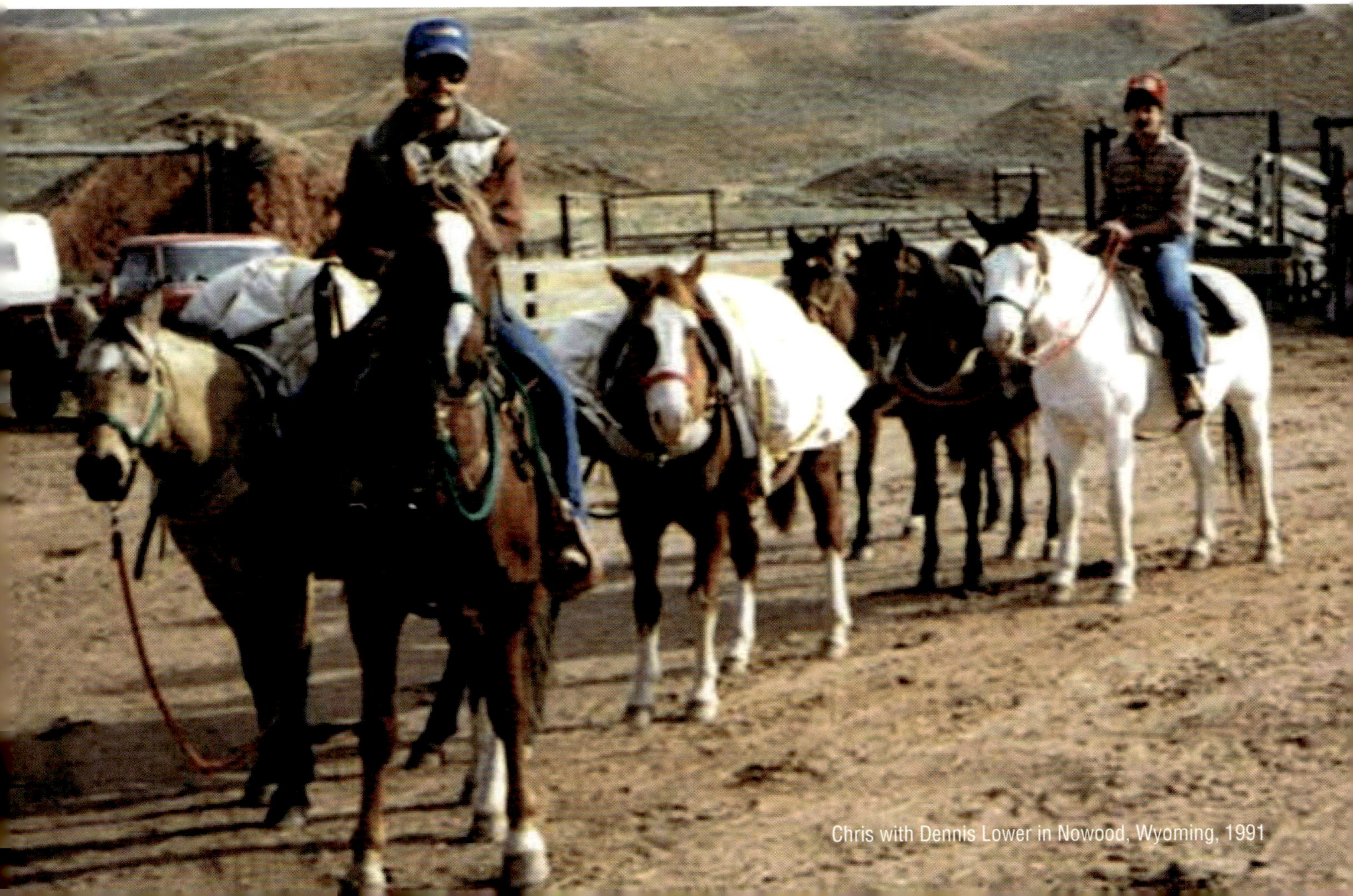

Chris with Dennis Lower in Nowood, Wyoming, 1991

handle my work. Lynne and I loaded up my bronze sculptures and drove to Jackson Hole, Wyoming. After scoping out all of the art galleries in town, I made a list of what I thought were the very best. Standing outside the first gallery, I tried hard not to be nervous, even though I was. "The worst thing they can do is tell me 'No,'" I said to myself. So, with my portfolio in hand, I went in and asked to speak to the director. After showing him images of my work, he politely told me they were not accepting new artists at that time. The next gallery owner said, "I'll be honest with you. I'm looking to represent artists who are already made." I thanked the owner for being upfront with me and went on to the next gallery on my list. They also said, "No." I started thinking that this was going to be a little tougher than I had expected. I was further declined at the fourth and fifth galleries. When one director wished me "good luck," I said, "Thanks, but if you want luck, sometimes you have to go out and make it." Feeling dejected, I returned to the car, where Lynne had been waiting. I told her that even though I was doing my best artwork, I realized that it wasn't quite good enough to show in these galleries. Being brutally honest is difficult, but I resolved then and there to go home, study, and work harder to become a better artist.

Lynne and I had been married for five years when we decided to start a family. She was seven and one-half months into her pregnancy when, on April 5, 1985, she told me something was terribly wrong. I rushed her to the emergency room, where the doctor determined she had Toxemia, a blood poisoning caused by toxins from a bacterial infection. We learned that they could not control Lynne's blood pressure, and she was at risk for having a stroke. I had planned to be with Lynne for the delivery, but instead, I found myself waiting outside of the operating room while she had an emergency cesarean delivery. After waiting and praying, the nurse came by with a little bundle. It was our tiny son, JC. I had never seen such a small baby. With no body fat, he only weighed three pounds, which meant he would spend the next 30 days in an incubator. He was a tough little fighter, and we took him home after one month in the hospital. Our daughter, Natalie, was born 19 months later on Nov. 21, 1986. Lynne again contracted Toxemia and had another emergency cesarean delivery. Natalie, only a few weeks premature, weighed five pounds, and we took her home after five days in the hospital.

March 13, 1986, was the day that I quit my corporate oilfield job. Walking away from a predictable income, I was finally pursuing my dream of being a professional sculptor. My son, JC, was ten months old, and Lynne was pregnant with Natalie. Everyone told me it was the wrong decision. After all, I had a mortgage and a family to support. But there are times in life when you have to make a stand and turn your dreams into reality. I just knew it. I knew deep inside that I was doing what was best for my family. I believed my instincts. So, listening to my heart and trusting my gut, I took a leap of faith and have not once regretted the decision. If you want something bad enough, you have to be willing to take a chance and put in the effort to make it happen. I wanted to make a living doing something I loved and was passionate about. If you have a dream that is the driving force in your life and you have to give it up, you'll feel lost and incomplete. I decided I was not going to spend my life just showing up for a steady pay stub at the end of the week.

I moved my studio out of the second bedroom when the kids started to arrive. I built a 12'x24' shop close to the house and went to work in that little studio every day. I put in the time and became more skilled with each piece that I created. I was learning by doing. The secret and challenge to being an artist is that you have to make art, and lots of it, because there are no shortcuts. It's about commitment, day by day, year after year. Your mastery of a craft is directly proportional to the sheer number of hours you spend in the effort.

Believe me, there are no overnight successes in the art world. The notion of the right gallery or art agent "discovering" you and paving the way to your artistic success is a myth. Building your art career is a lifelong struggle. If you want to be great at something, you need to put time in the studio with the materials in your hands. It is accomplished through dedication, hard work, and a love for what you are doing. Love is an emotion that you can't fake, and you cannot be great at anything without loving it. Caring about the work you do is the single best indicator that others will care about it, too. I know that what is in my heart is no different than what is in your heart. If you believe that other people are like you, then you hold the key to making art that matters.

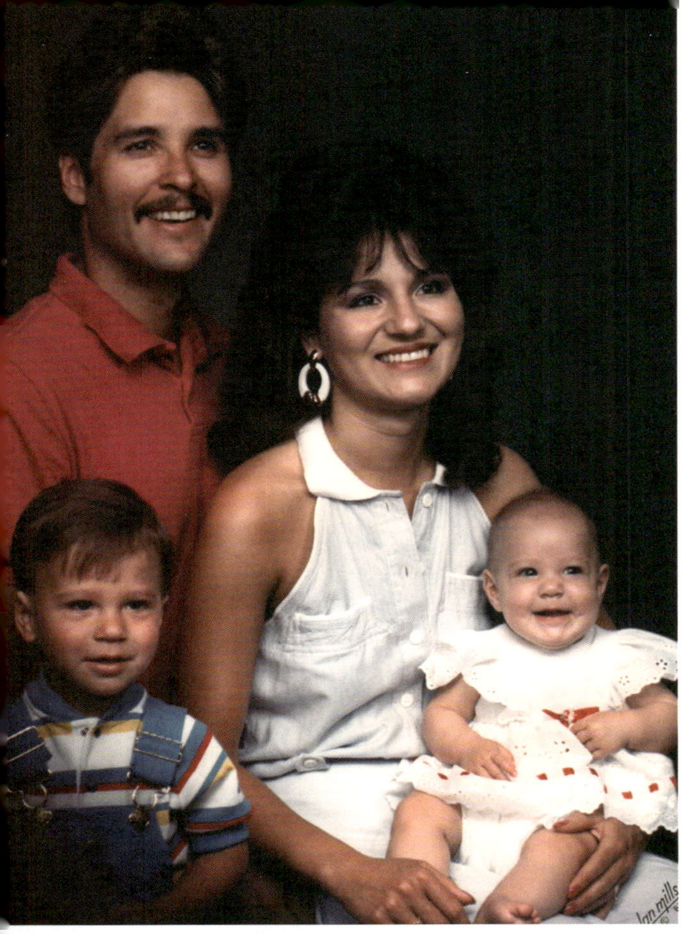

I KNOW WHAT IT IS LIKE TO HAVE A DREAM AND YOU ARE THE ONLY ONE WHO CAN SEE IT.

–CHRIS NAVARRO

Top to bottom: Chris, Lynne, JC, and Natalie, 1987. Natalie riding Kit for the Wyoming Junior Rodeo Association in 1999. Chris and JC, 1989. JC with *Mustang Pride*, 2003. Natalie and Chris dancing at the Buffalo Bill Art Show in Cody, WY, 2015.

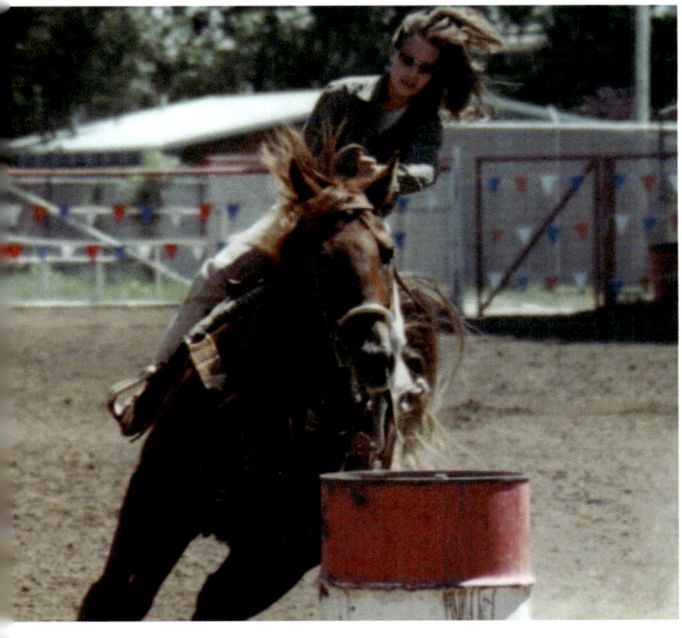

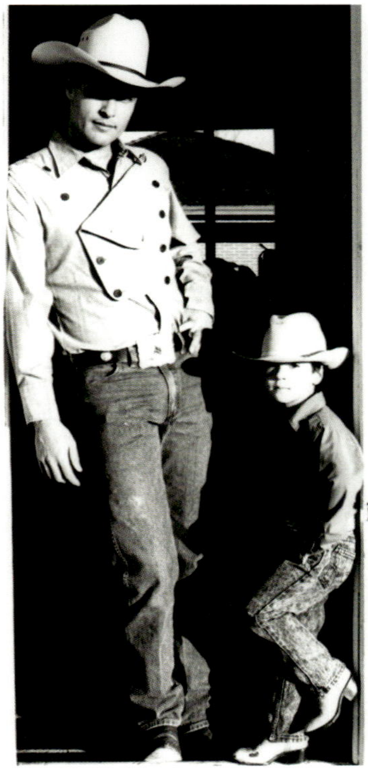

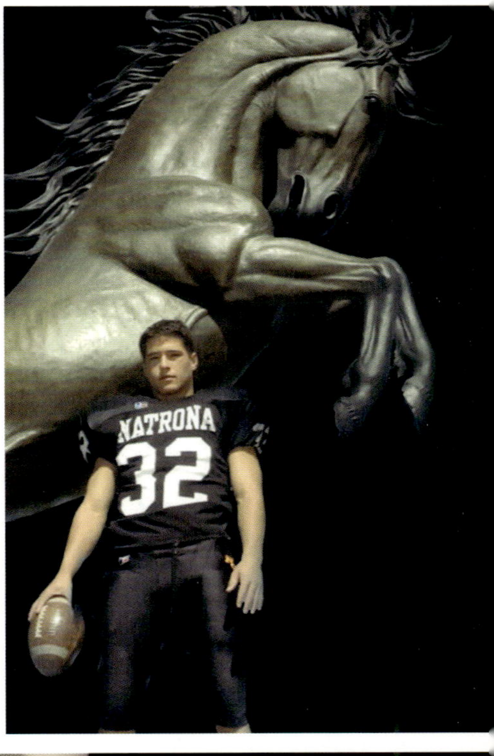

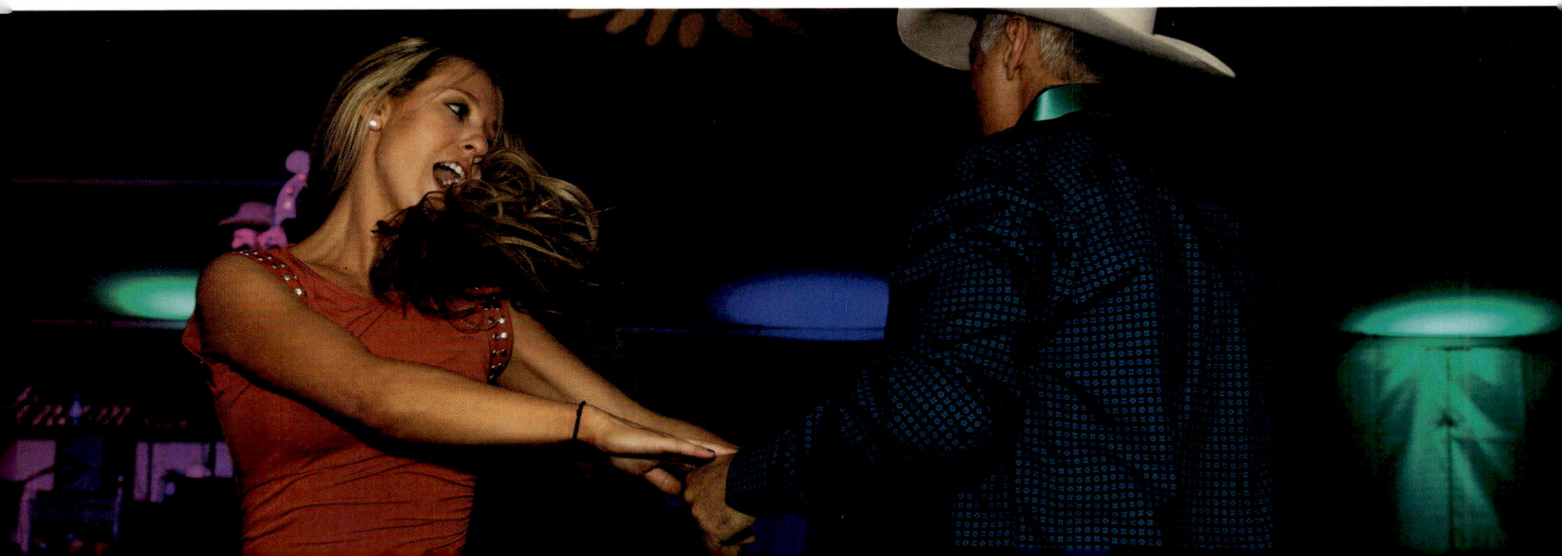

SCULPTURE IS
A SYMPHONY
OF MENTAL
AND PHYSICAL
CHALLENGES.
–CHRIS NAVARRO

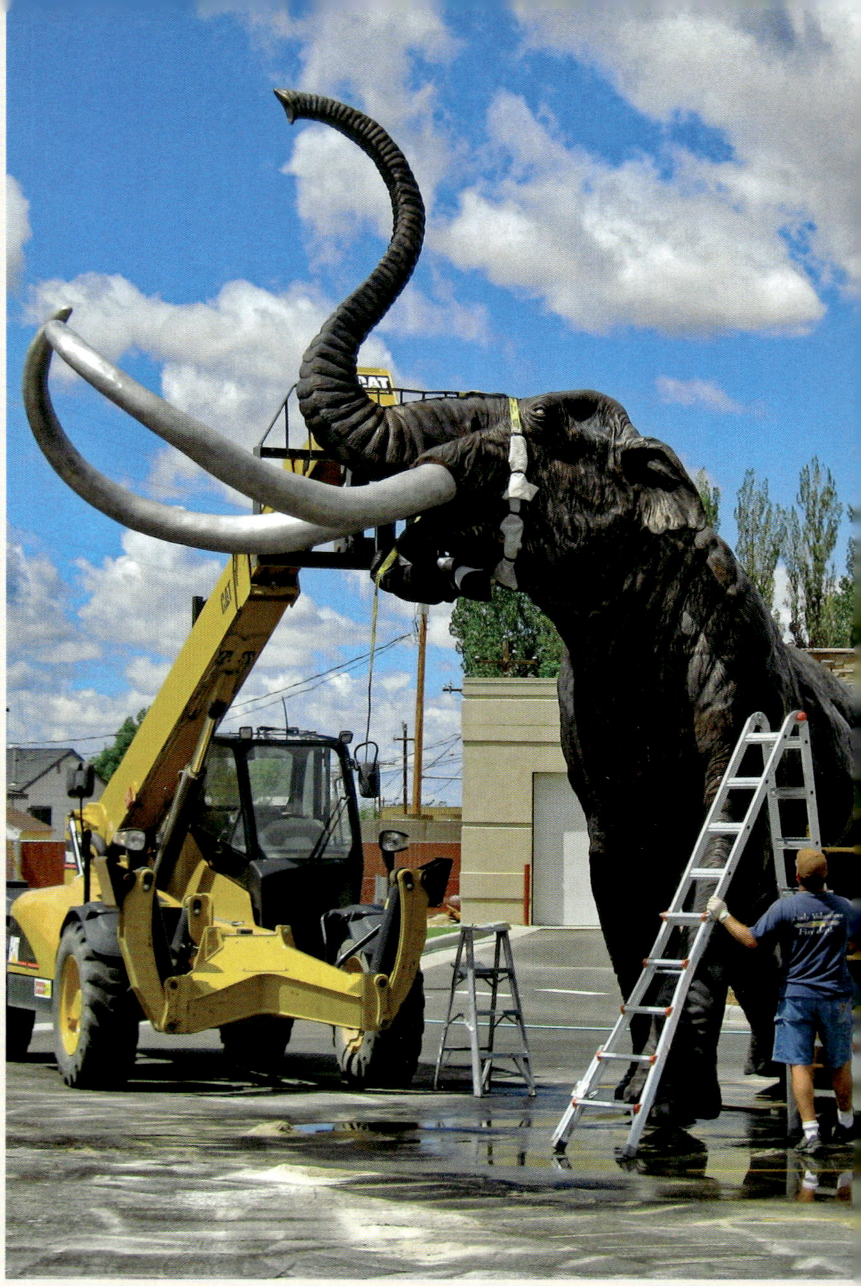

ART THAT SPEAKS

Having been a professional artist for more than 30 years, I would like to pass along those experiences which have helped me in my pursuit of making a living from doing what I love. I do not claim to know all the answers, but I will gladly share what I've learned with those who wish to make a similar journey.

We begin life with unlimited potential. Every child is an artist. If you want to see a group of artists, get a bunch of 4-year-old kids together, spread out some crayons and paper, and then sit back and watch them create. Children have no fears or preconceived concepts about art. They understand "fun," so they enjoy art for the pure and simple pleasure of experiencing it. Unfortunately, many people lose their sense of play as they grow older. They worry too much about what others think and seek the approval of their peers to validate what they're doing. As I have grown older, I realize the most important approval is my own.

From the very beginning, I had to find the path on my own, but I have never considered myself a self-taught artist; I am a self-educated artist. I have learned from the books I have read and the experiences and mistakes that I've made. I do not believe that we're born with a limited amount of talent, knowledge, or ability. Talent and knowledge can expand and grow. I have never allowed my lack of talent or knowledge to stop me from doing what I believe to be meaningful. Art is more the product of a commitment made by ordinary people than it is the product of unique talent possessed by only a chosen few.

My sculptures tell a story by using composition, design, movement, and line. These stories include relationships and interactions with people, animals, and landscapes. Irony, humor, conflict, and resolution are all crucial elements woven into a sculpture's narrative. People will identify more with art if the story is a powerful one. Creating a strong title is important, as it helps to enhance the story of the sculpture. I sometimes think of the title first, because it provides me with a concrete image. The sculpture, then, becomes a representation of that title. When looking for ideas to create new sculptures, I use all the tools that are available. The enjoyment one gets from looking at sculptures depends on the specific challenges that the works of art contain.

Creating art has always made me feel part of something larger than myself. I have created much of what is known as "western art." I've been a horseman and cowboy all of my life, and western art is a natural extension of my passion for that way of life. However, I have created many inspirational and spiritual works that do not fall into the western art genre. In creating sculpture, I do not put limits on myself or the subject matter. I do what excites and challenges me, and that is one of the reasons I love doing public monumental sculptures.

The creation of monuments is extremely time-consuming and labor intensive. Spending hours on ladders and scaffolding is physically demanding, but the labor gives me great personal satisfaction. It's also mentally challenging, requiring an initial design and the creation of a clay model. To cast my clay models in bronze, I prefer the lost wax method, the process by which a duplicate metal sculpture is cast from an original sculpture. I know that if I have a tool in my hand and I invest enough time and effort, no project or idea will be too big, and I will get it done. The best feeling as an artist comes when you put everything you have into something difficult and you finish it, completely spent.

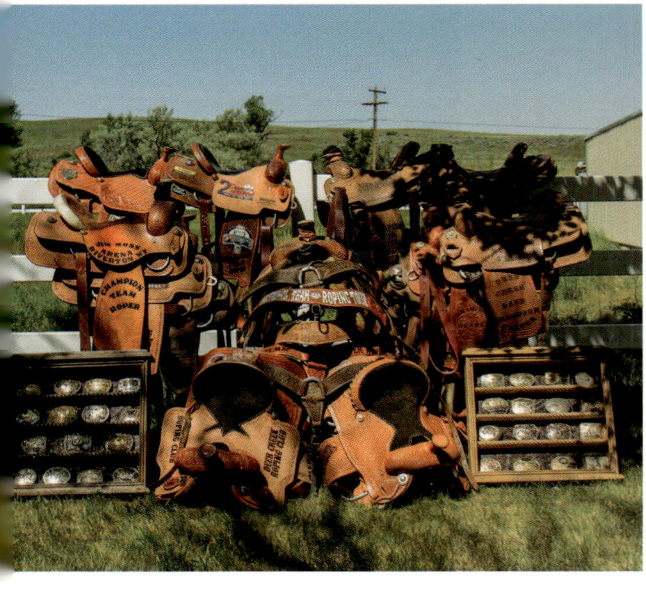

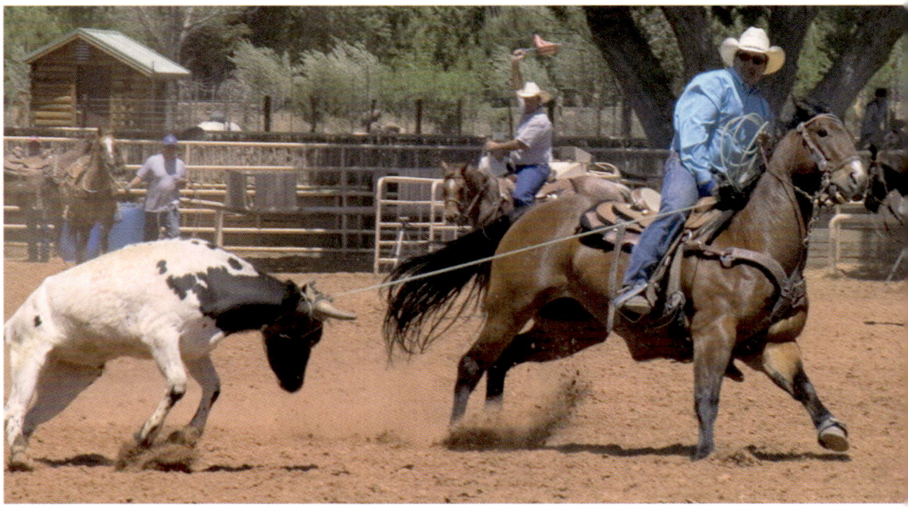

Left: Collection of rodeo winnings over the years, 2015
Above: Chris roping with Man in Page Springs, Arizona, 2008.

THERE IS NOTHING WORTHWHILE IN LIFE THAT IS NOT HARD TO GET. THERE IS LITTLE OR NO VALUE IN EASY PERFECTION REACHED BY MANY.
–CHRIS NAVARRO

DEALING WITH CRITICISM

Just as early man created images on cave walls, we all have an inherent need to express our individuality. One of the reasons that I became an artist was to express who I am and what I believe. But when you open the window of your soul and share your art with others, you expose yourself to criticism, judgment, and rejection. It is difficult not to take criticism personally when you've invested so much of yourself in the creation. We all suffer setbacks from time to time; it is the way we react to those setbacks that matters. That is why I like to take rejection and make it work for me. When someone tells me that I'm not good enough or that I can't do something, it puts a fire in me and fuels my desire to not only disprove the naysayers, but also to prove that I am capable. Believe me, I don't like rejection, failure, or looking foolish, but I'm not afraid to take risks. Life is full of challenges, and that is what gives meaning to life. There is little value in easy perfection. Don't do it because it's easy; do it because it's hard.

There will always be negative people and haters out there. Your happiness should not depend on what's going on in someone else's head. You have no control over that. What matters is how you view yourself and what is going on inside of your own head.

It is important to keep your sense of humor in all things. Humor is the armor that protects you in life; it is the great lubricant that makes the difficult things easier to bear. So, laugh at yourself and roll with the punches.

For the artist who thrives on challenges, rejection is not a problem. The true responsibility of an artist is to put forth their best effort and strive for continual improvement. In the end, that is all one can do.

Elements of Success

To me, Michelangelo is the greatest artist who has ever lived. He passed away in 1564 at age 89. At that time, the average Italian man had a life expectancy of 43 years. I believe the reason for Michelangelo's long and productive life is that he awoke every day with a passion and a purpose, and this is the way that I choose to live my own life.

I see no downside to that philosophy.

I have been extremely fortunate to make a living with my art for the last 30 years. I was 23 and did not have much going for me when I started sculpting. I had no money or formal training in art. What I did have was a lot of confidence and ignorance. Yes, it has been a crazy roller coaster ride, but hell, who wants to ride on a merry-go-round all of the time?!

The great thing about working with bronze is that it's such a strong, durable, and permanent medium. All artists want to live on in their work. To know that my monuments will stand in the sun long after I'm gone is extremely rewarding. Sculpting is what I do for a living, and I don't plan on retiring. It's what I truly love, and I hope others can see this through the works I have created, because the most worthwhile aspect about art is seeing what's in someone else's heart. When it's all said and done, I don't think it's about how many years you have lived in this world, but rather what you leave behind that truly matters.

Seeing Harry Jackson's *Two Champs* sculpture all those years ago made me want to become a sculptor. It lit a spark in me that still burns today. When others look at my life's work, I hope it will light a spark in them to be inspired with hope and to live life with determination. My advice is to never give up, and do not take "No" for an answer. Believe in yourself when no one else does. Do not be afraid of failure or of being knocked down. Just keep getting up and do the best that you can with what's in front of you. Never feel as though you have lost when you have given it your all. It is a waste of time to worry about the amount of talent that you have or do not have. With sincere effort, you can always expand your knowledge and talent, which helps you create your own reality. Desire, determination, and dedication are the ingredients of success in any field. To be successful at something that you care about is a matter of being someone who does not quit, and this ability is available to everyone. You never really know what you can do until you try. Remember, every "expert" was a beginner at some point in their life. You can't let fear of the unknown keep you from following your dreams, so do not be afraid to embrace the struggle. Go out there and make a living doing something you're passionate about. Life is too short not to!

KEEP AWAY FROM PEOPLE WHO TRY TO BELITTLE YOUR AMBITIONS. SMALL PEOPLE ALWAYS DO THAT, BUT THE REALLY GREAT MAKE YOU FEEL THAT YOU, TOO, CAN BECOME GREAT.

—MARK TWAIN

RODEO

RODEO CAREERS CAN END WITHOUT WARNING, AS QUICK AS THE NEXT TRY AT AN 8-SECOND RIDE.
–JOHN BRANCH

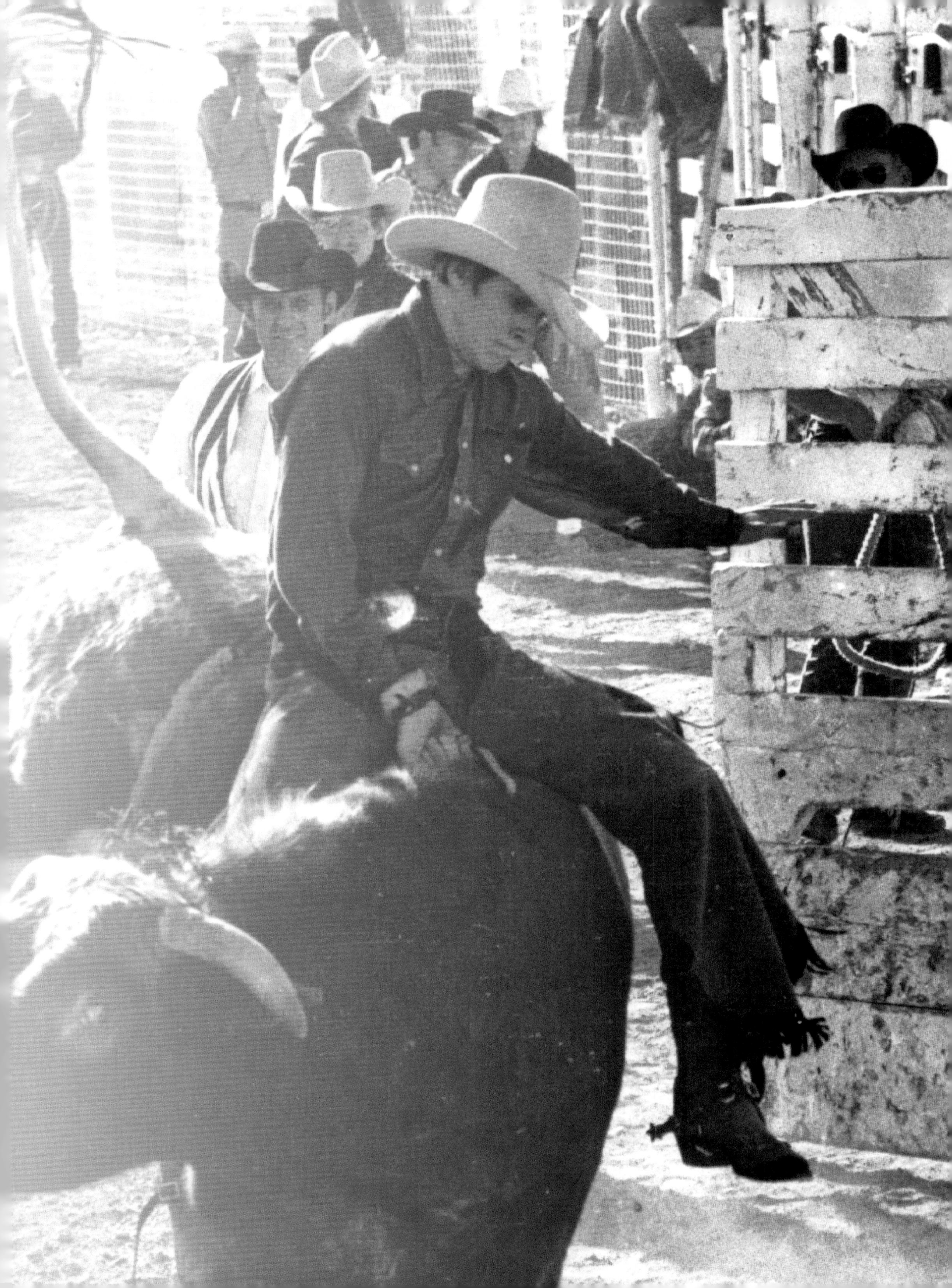

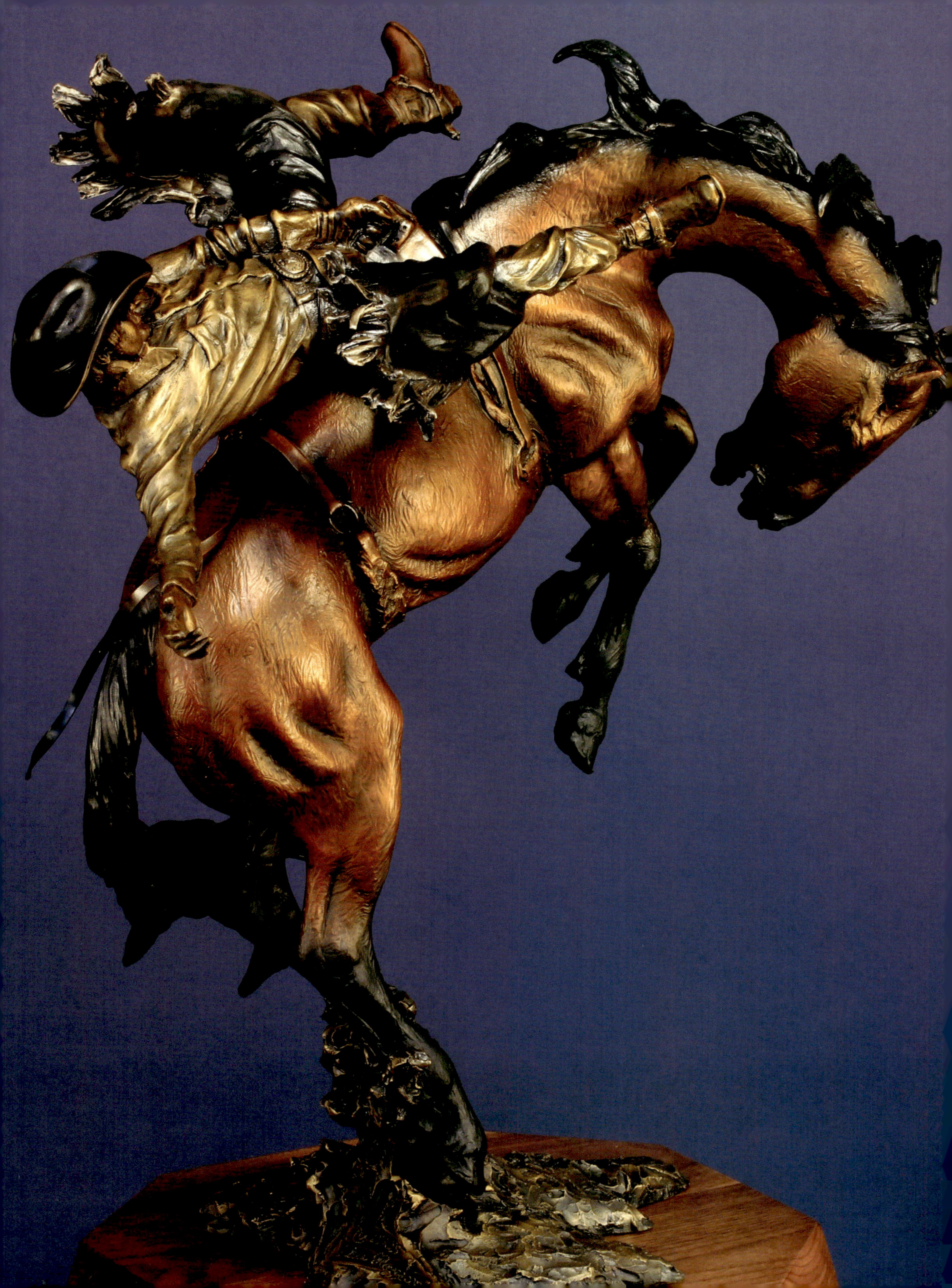

DON'T COMPLAIN OR ASK WHY. JUST LIVE EACH DAY AND PUT OUT THE TRY.
–CHRIS NAVARRO

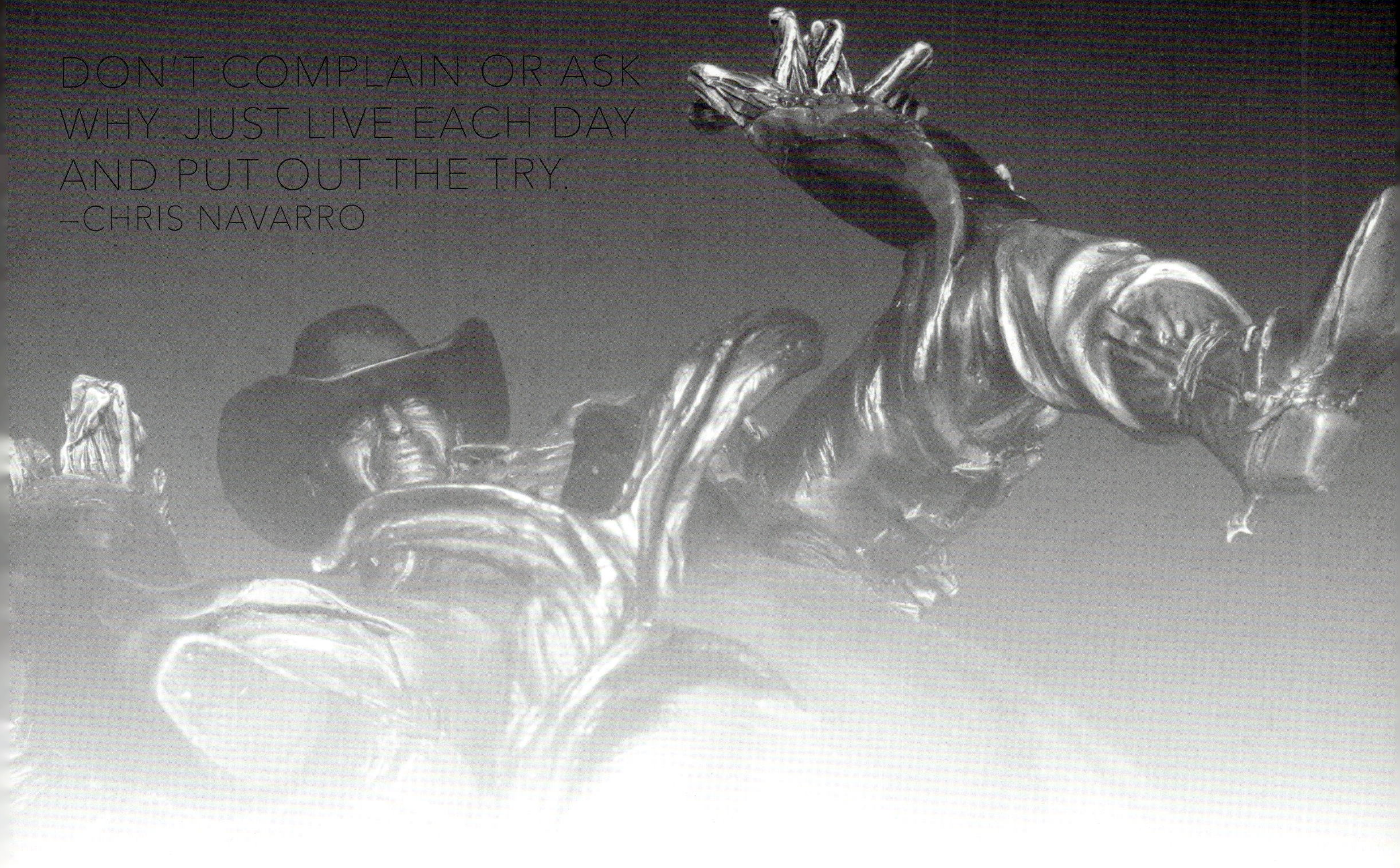

A WILD RIDE (2012)

Bronze, 21" x 15" x 11"

I started competing on bareback broncs and bulls when I was 16. Bull riding may be the most dangerous event, but bareback is the most physically demanding. I wanted to capture the power, excitement, and raw beauty of this rodeo event. Competing in rodeo and sculpting the events has been a passion in my art and life for as long as I can remember.

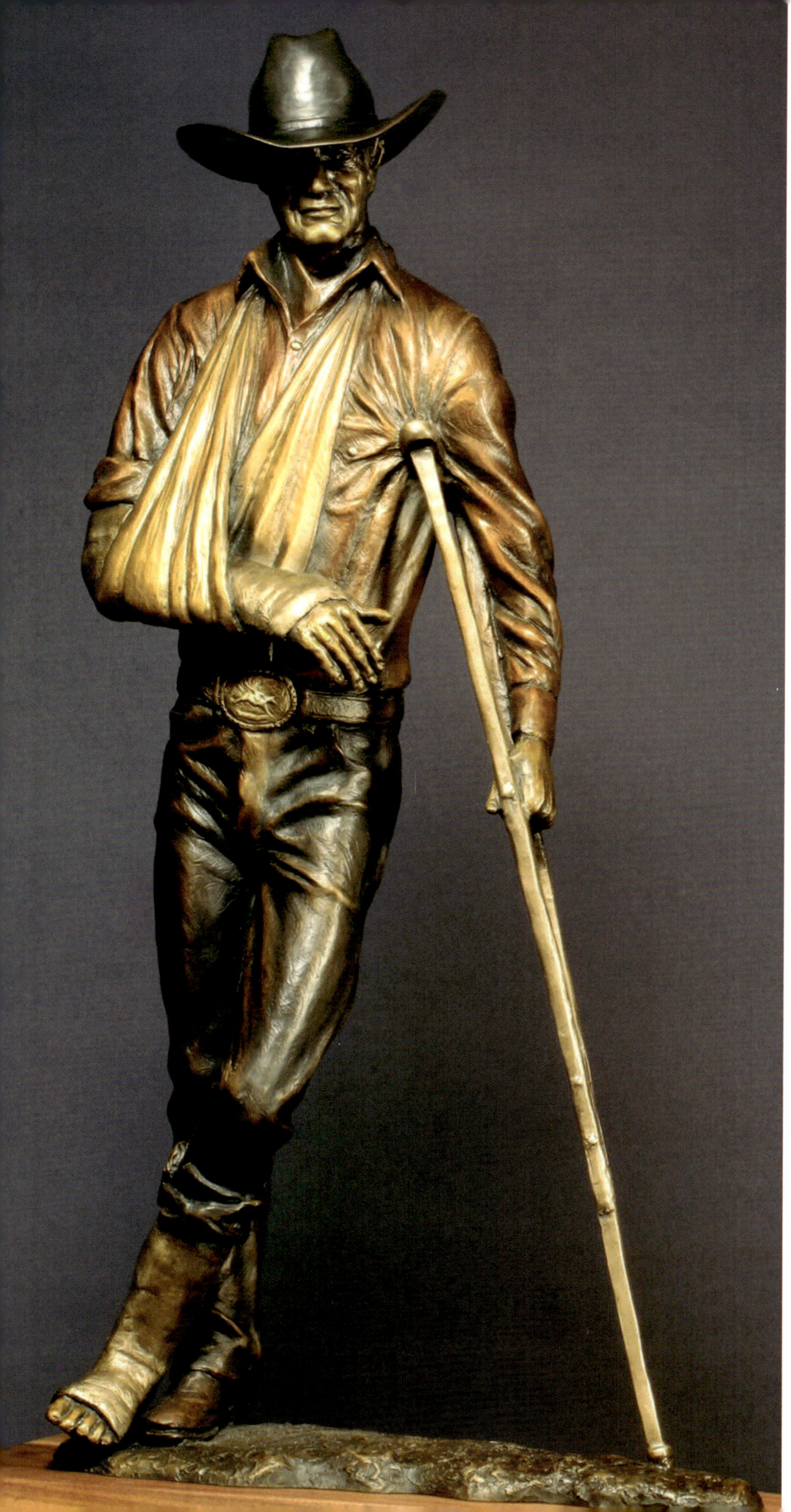

TOUGH
TIMES DON'T
LAST; TOUGH
PEOPLE DO.
–ROBERT H.
SCHULLER

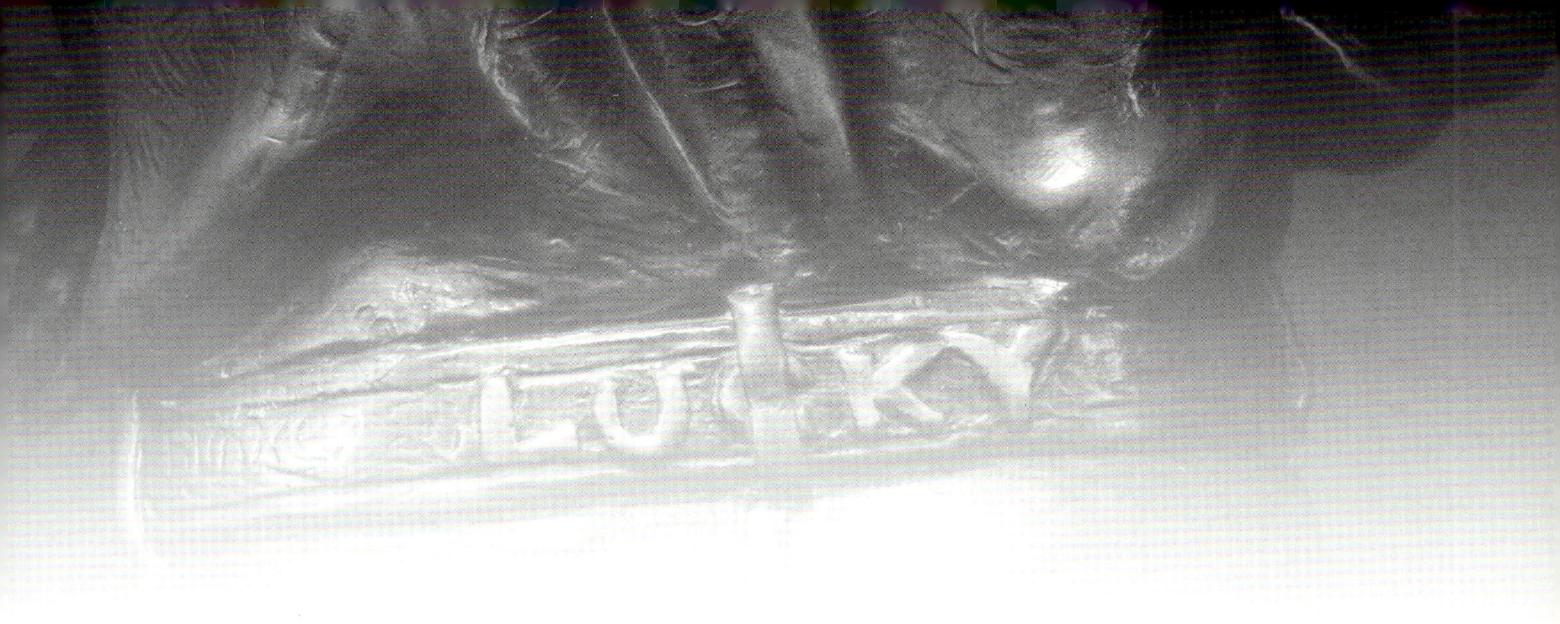

BROKEN JUST ABOUT EVERYTHING BUT MY WORD (2012)

Bronze, 27'' x 15'' x 9 ''

You will notice a broken nose, a black eye, and a big scar running down the left side of this cowboy's face. And stamped on the back of his belt is his name, "Lucky!" Lucky might be all broken up, but the one thing he will never break is his word. "A man's word is his bond" is the cowboy code by which I live.

I have been asked if this sculpture is a self-portrait. It sure could be with all the injuries I have sustained in my rodeo career and while working horses. I believe being a rodeo cowboy was good training in becoming a professional artist. You have to be physically and mentally tough and learn to compete when you are hurt. You don't get paid unless you come through and deliver. When you get knocked down or bucked off, you just keep getting up and getting back on. You never know what you can do unless you try.

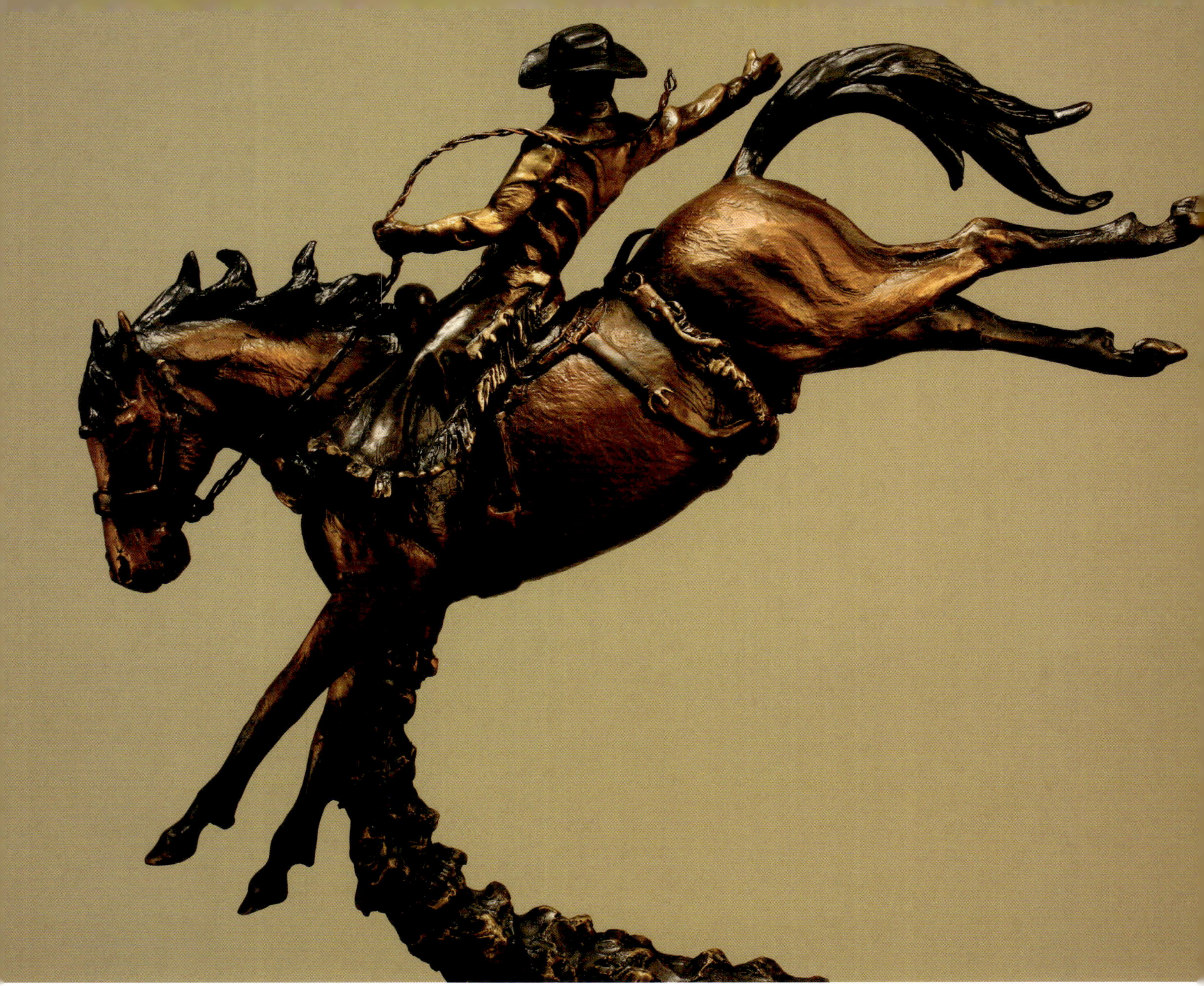

FIRE IN THE REIN (2012)

Bronze, 10'' x 9.5'' x 4.5''

Fire in the Rein is a sculpture of saddle bronc riding in which I use the title to help tell a more interesting story. Rodeo cowboys will say that when a horse or a bull really bucks hard, he has a lot of fire. So I like to use the double play and meaning of the word "rain" as a buck rein, i.e., the cowboy feels the power and buck of the horse through the buck rein.

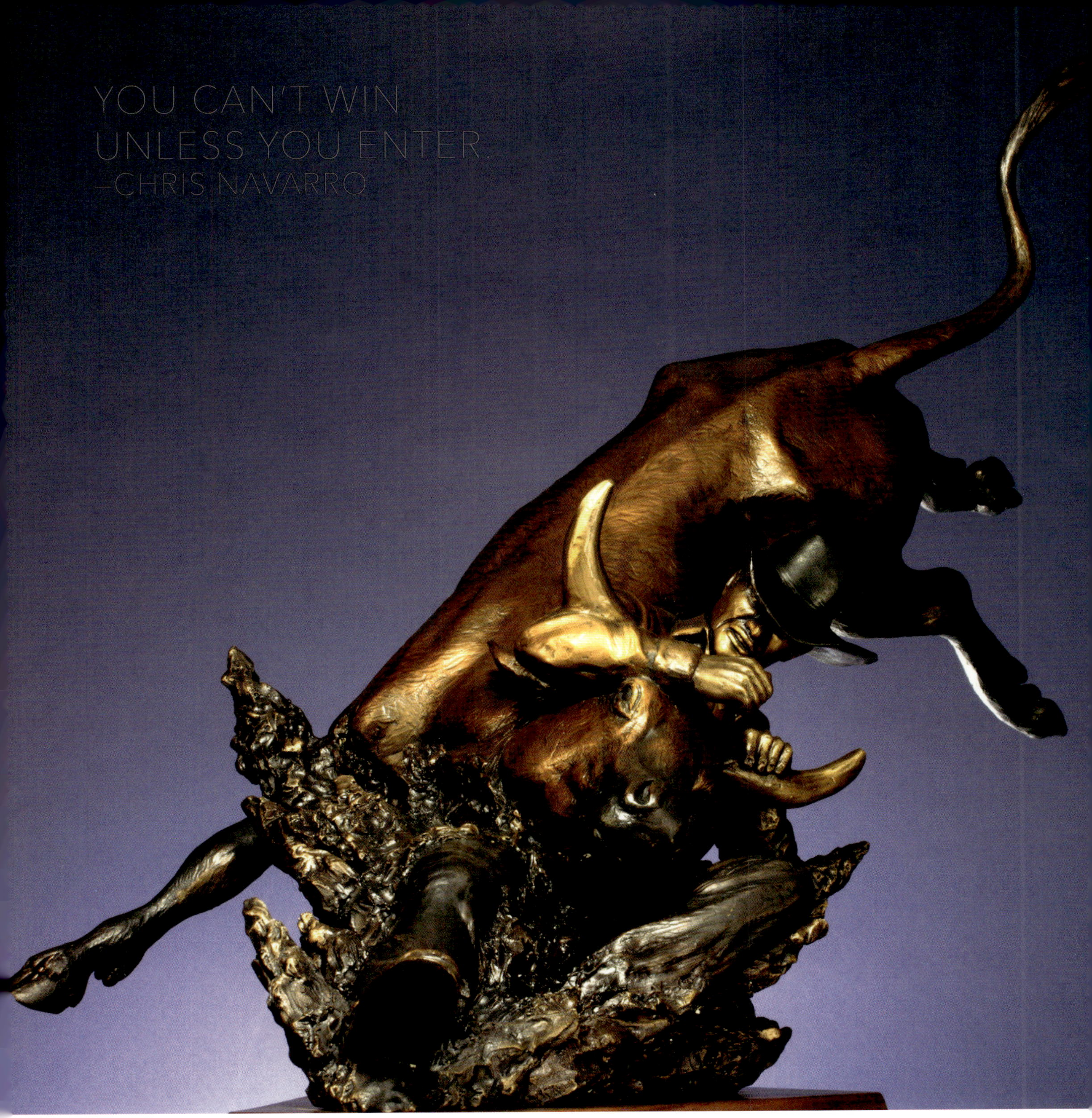

ALL OUT (2013)

Bronze, 20" x 31" x 14"

This bronze sculpture won the Calgary Stampede Trophy Bronze Competition for steer wrestling. *All Out* is commissioned to be presented to the champion steer wrestler at the Calgary Stampede, 2013 through 2017, along with $100,000 in prize money.

GET BACK ON (2007)

Bronze, 11" x 18" x 10"

When life (or a horse) brings you down, you have to get up and get back on! This sculpture is about facing adversity. As we go through life, we are going to hit setbacks and be knocked down. We have to remember that we are never a failure if we always get up and get back on.

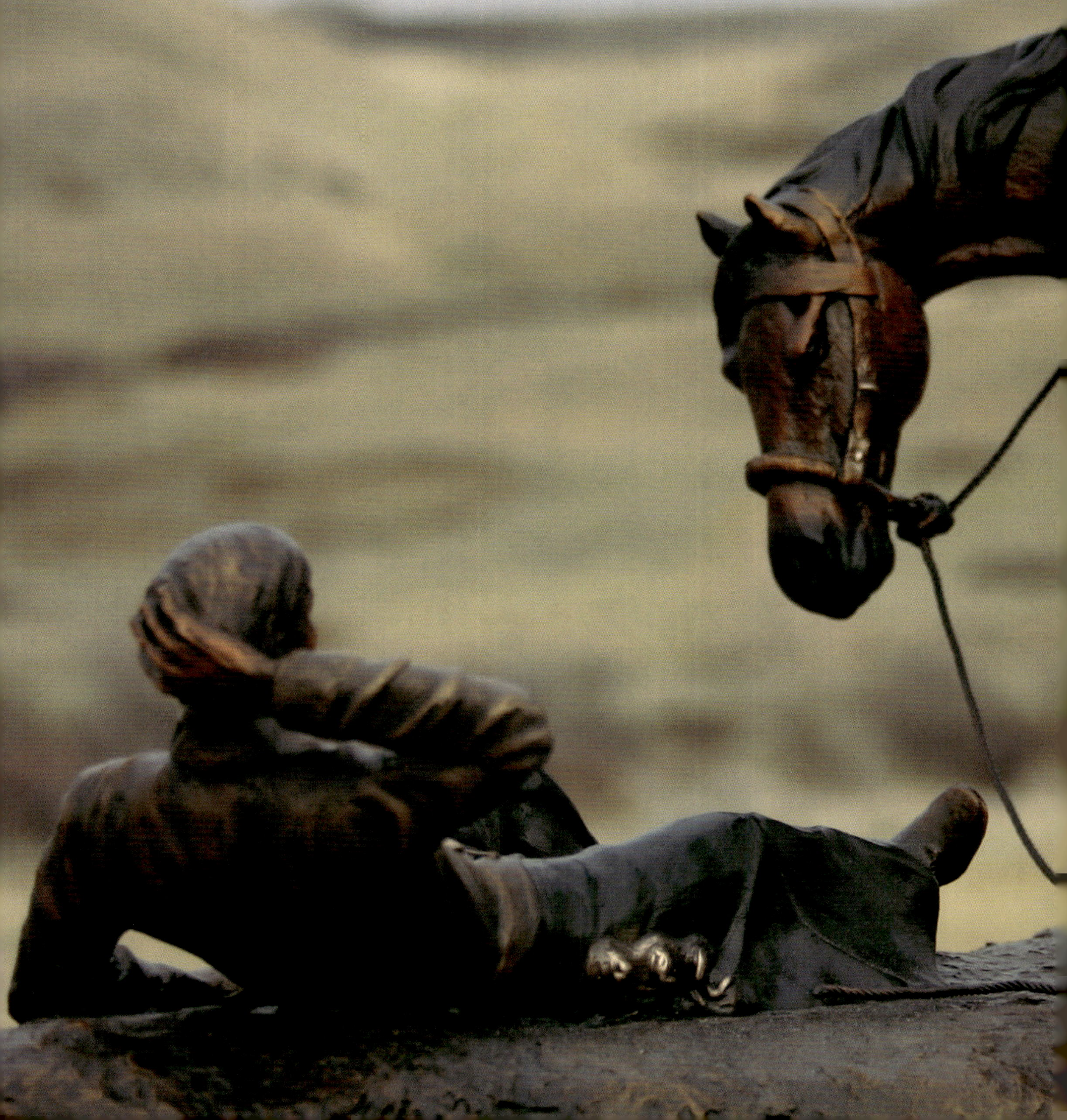

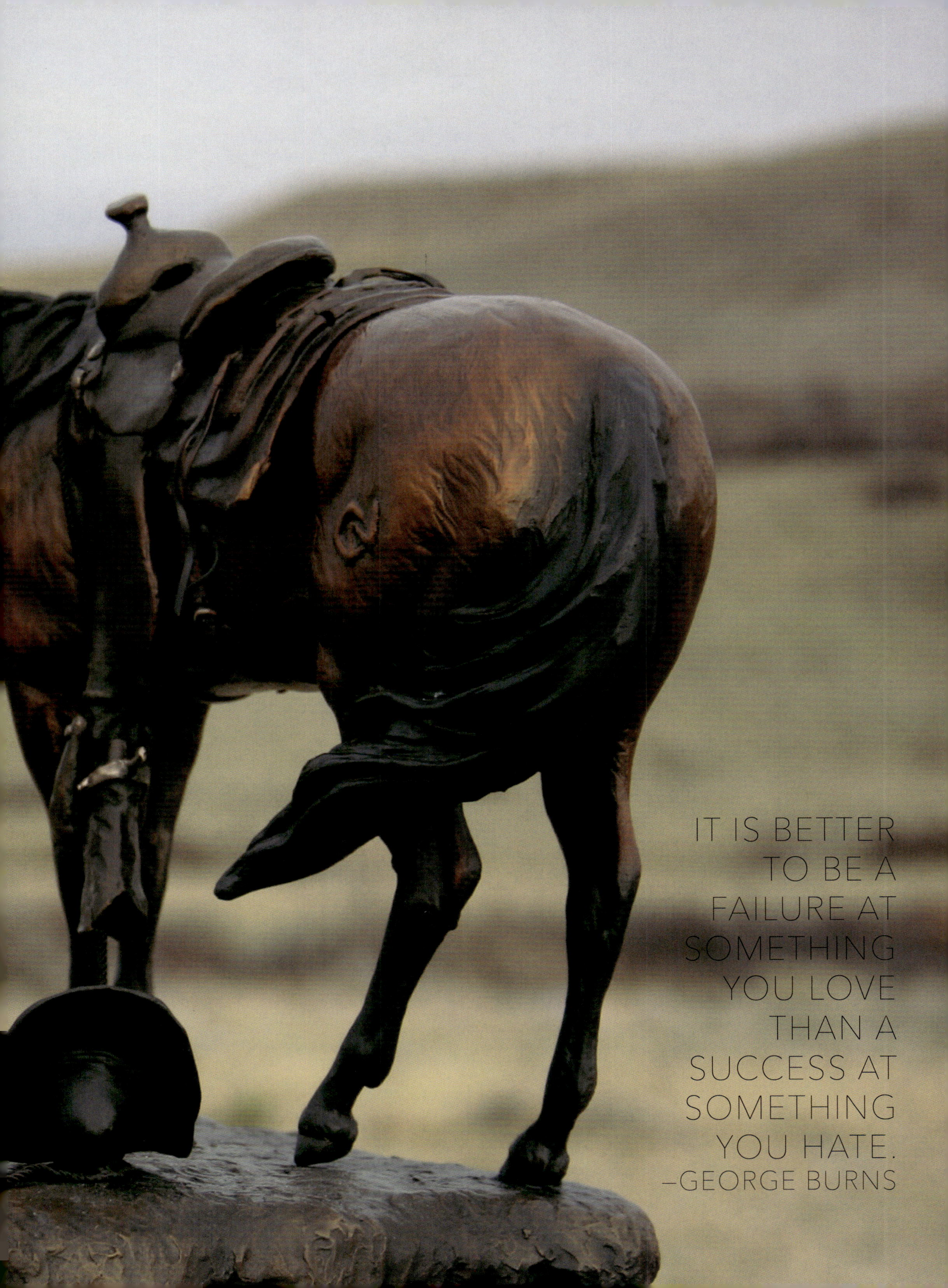

IT IS BETTER
TO BE A
FAILURE AT
SOMETHING
YOU LOVE
THAN A
SUCCESS AT
SOMETHING
YOU HATE.
–GEORGE BURNS

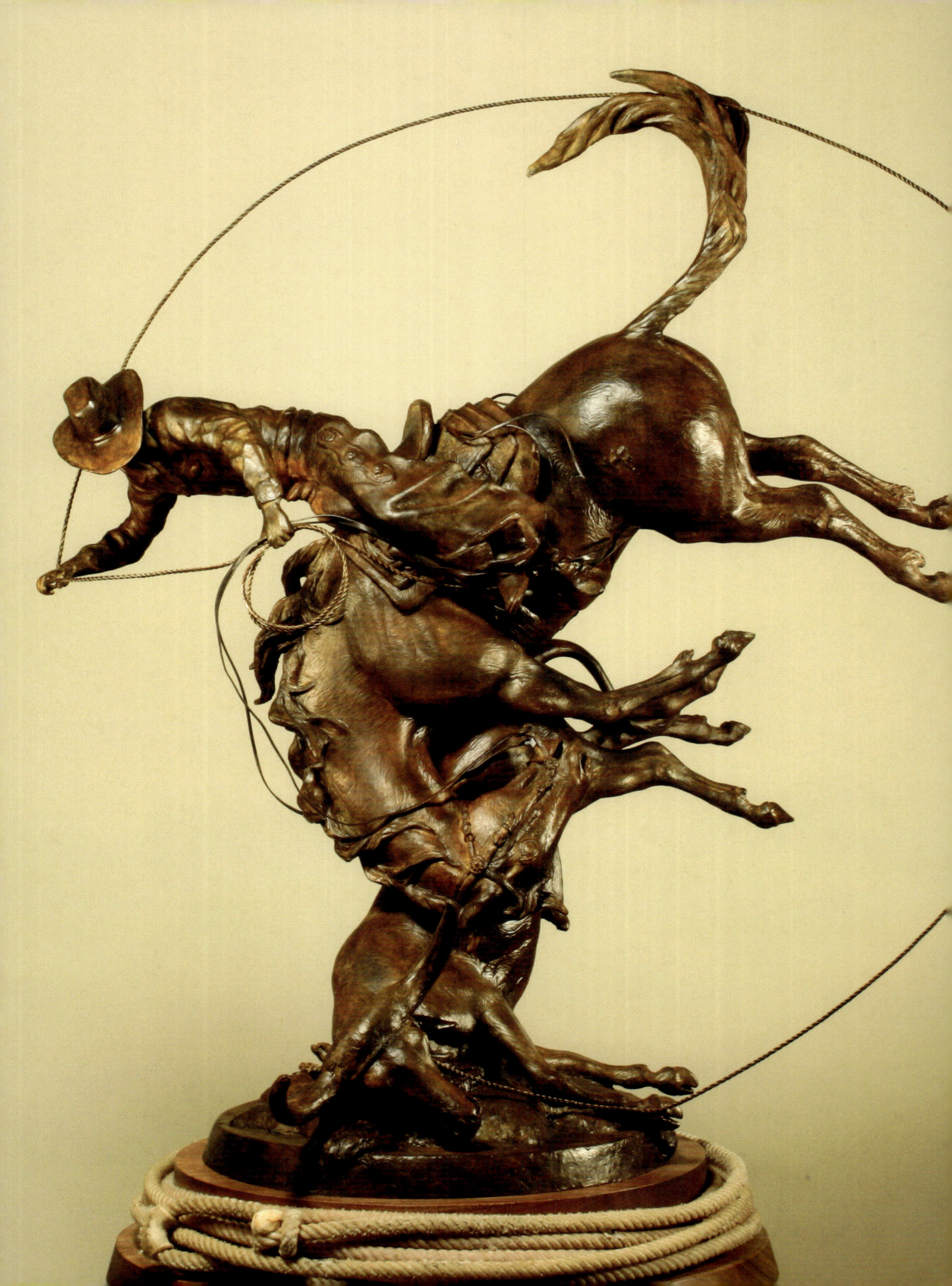

HECK OF A WRECK (2011)

Bronze, 29" x 26" x 16"

When I look at this sculpture, it brings back memories of my own heck of a wreck at the Indian Head Ranch on Sept. 26, 2014. I was in a full-speed matched horse race when I collided with a loose, riderless horse, which caused my horse to go down, flip over, and land on me. The cantle of the saddle landed on my left shoulder, and I broke my collarbone, shoulder blade, seven ribs, suffered a collapsed lung, and a concussion. I also received an expensive helicopter ride to the hospital, 12 new screws, and a stainless steel plate. Surprisingly, my horse came out unscathed with only some cuts and bruises, whereas I was laid up for three months. As soon as I was able, I got back on my horse and started roping again. You have three choices when something bad happens: you can have it define you; allow it to destroy you; or let it strengthen you.

PAIN IS JUST WEAKNESS LEAVING THE BODY.
–U.S. MARINE QUOTE

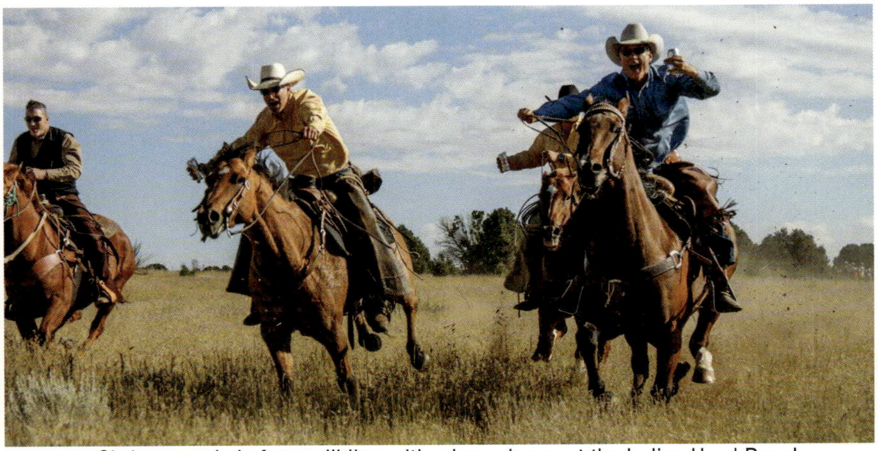

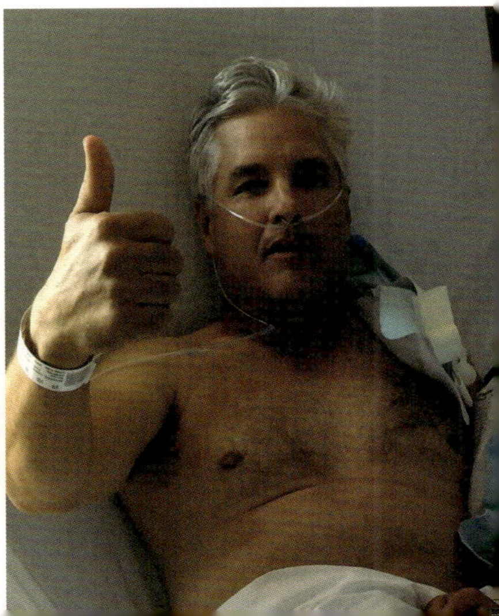

From left: Chris seconds before colliding with a loose horse at the Indian Head Ranch. Recovering in the hospital after his "heck of a wreck" in 2014.

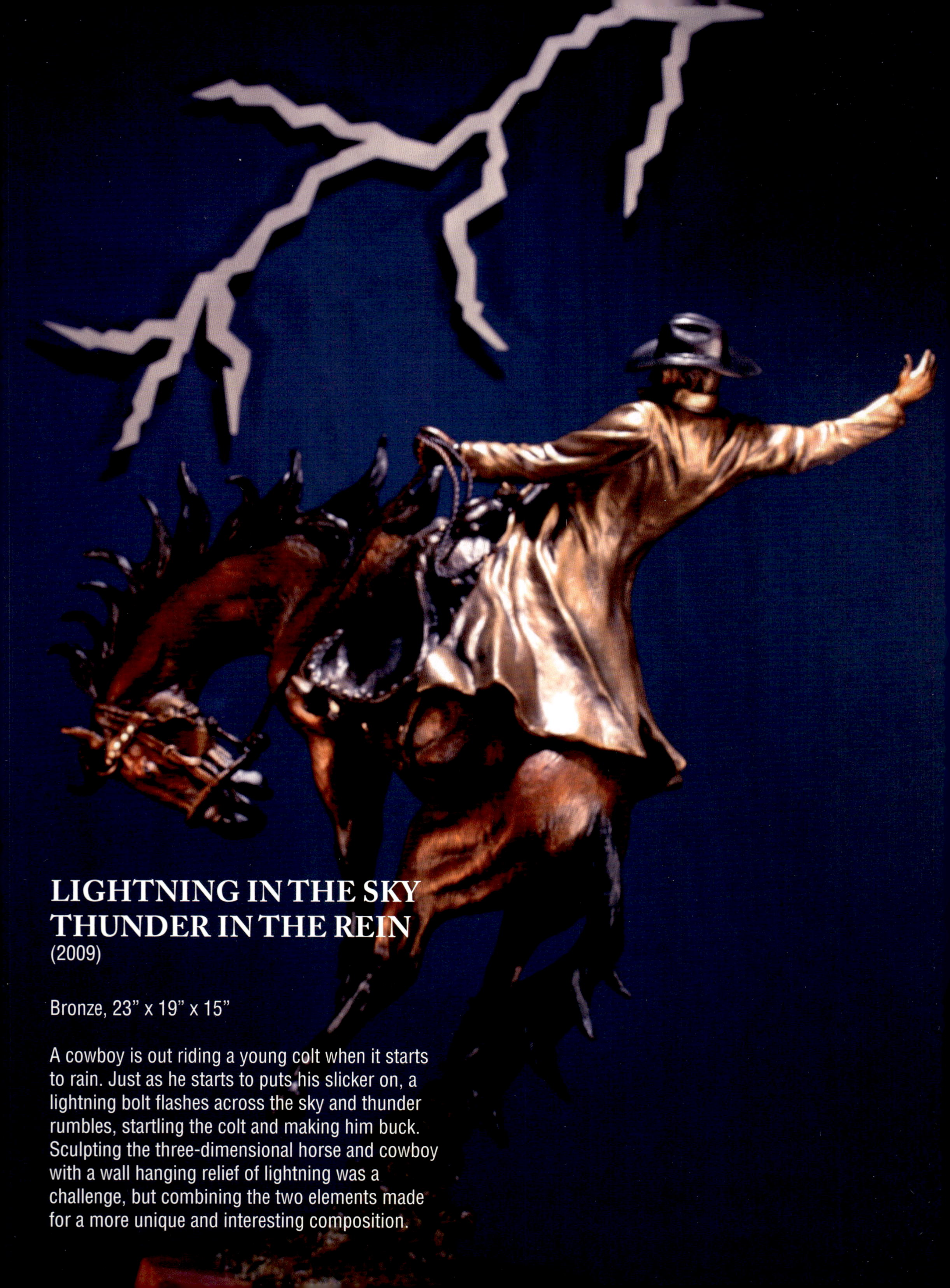

LIGHTNING IN THE SKY THUNDER IN THE REIN

(2009)

Bronze, 23" x 19" x 15"

A cowboy is out riding a young colt when it starts to rain. Just as he starts to puts his slicker on, a lightning bolt flashes across the sky and thunder rumbles, startling the colt and making him buck. Sculpting the three-dimensional horse and cowboy with a wall hanging relief of lightning was a challenge, but combining the two elements made for a more unique and interesting composition.

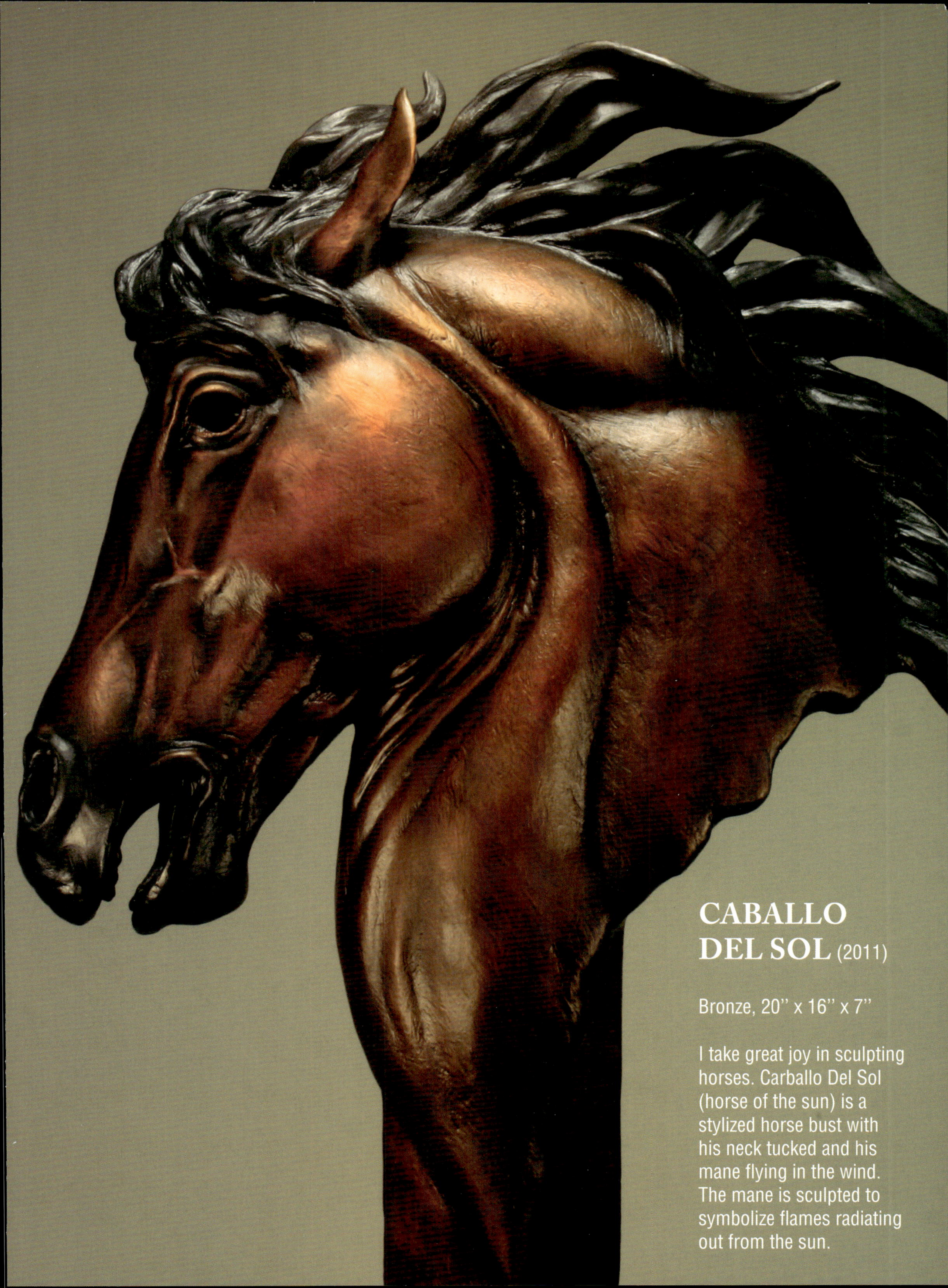

CABALLO DEL SOL (2011)

Bronze, 20'' x 16'' x 7''

I take great joy in sculpting horses. Carballo Del Sol (horse of the sun) is a stylized horse bust with his neck tucked and his mane flying in the wind. The mane is sculpted to symbolize flames radiating out from the sun.

WILDLIFE

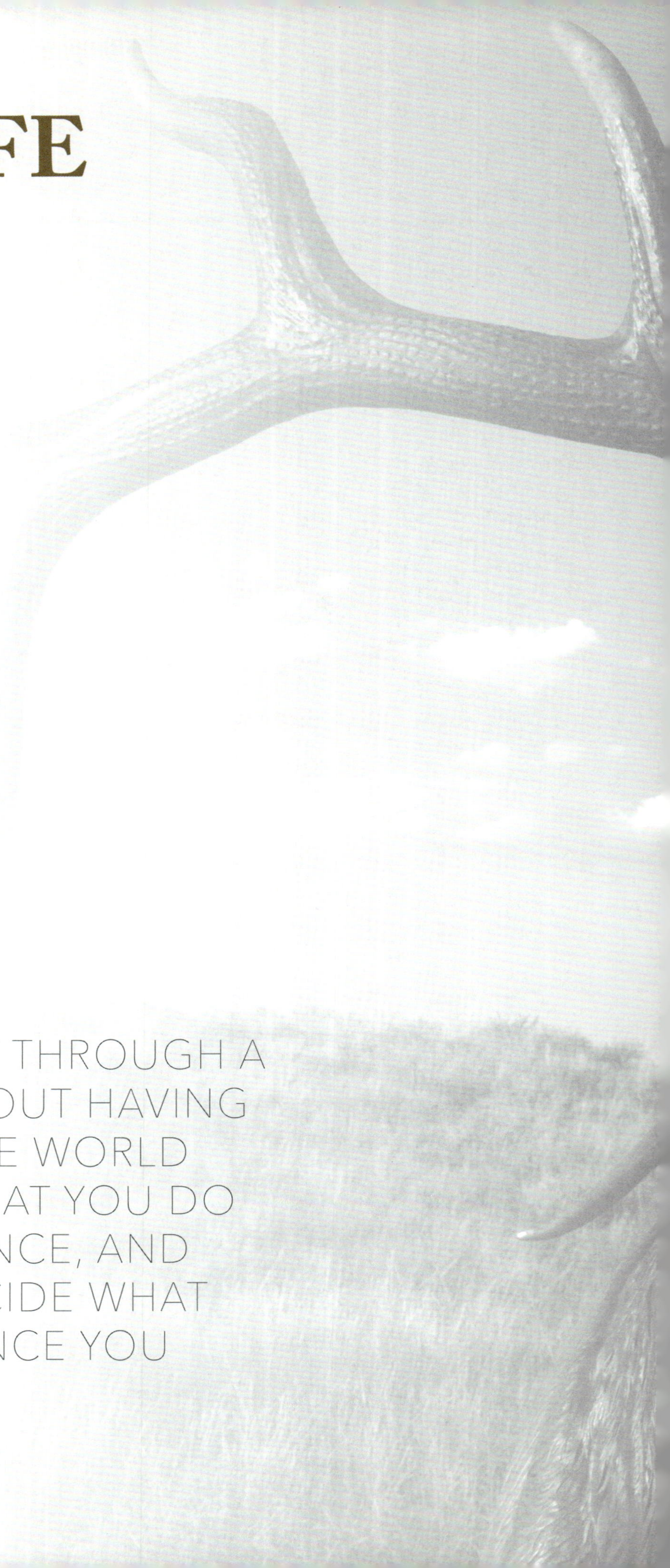

YOU CANNOT GET THROUGH A SINGLE DAY WITHOUT HAVING AN IMPACT ON THE WORLD AROUND YOU. WHAT YOU DO MAKES A DIFFERENCE, AND YOU HAVE TO DECIDE WHAT KIND OF DIFFERENCE YOU WANT TO MAKE.
–JANE GOODALL

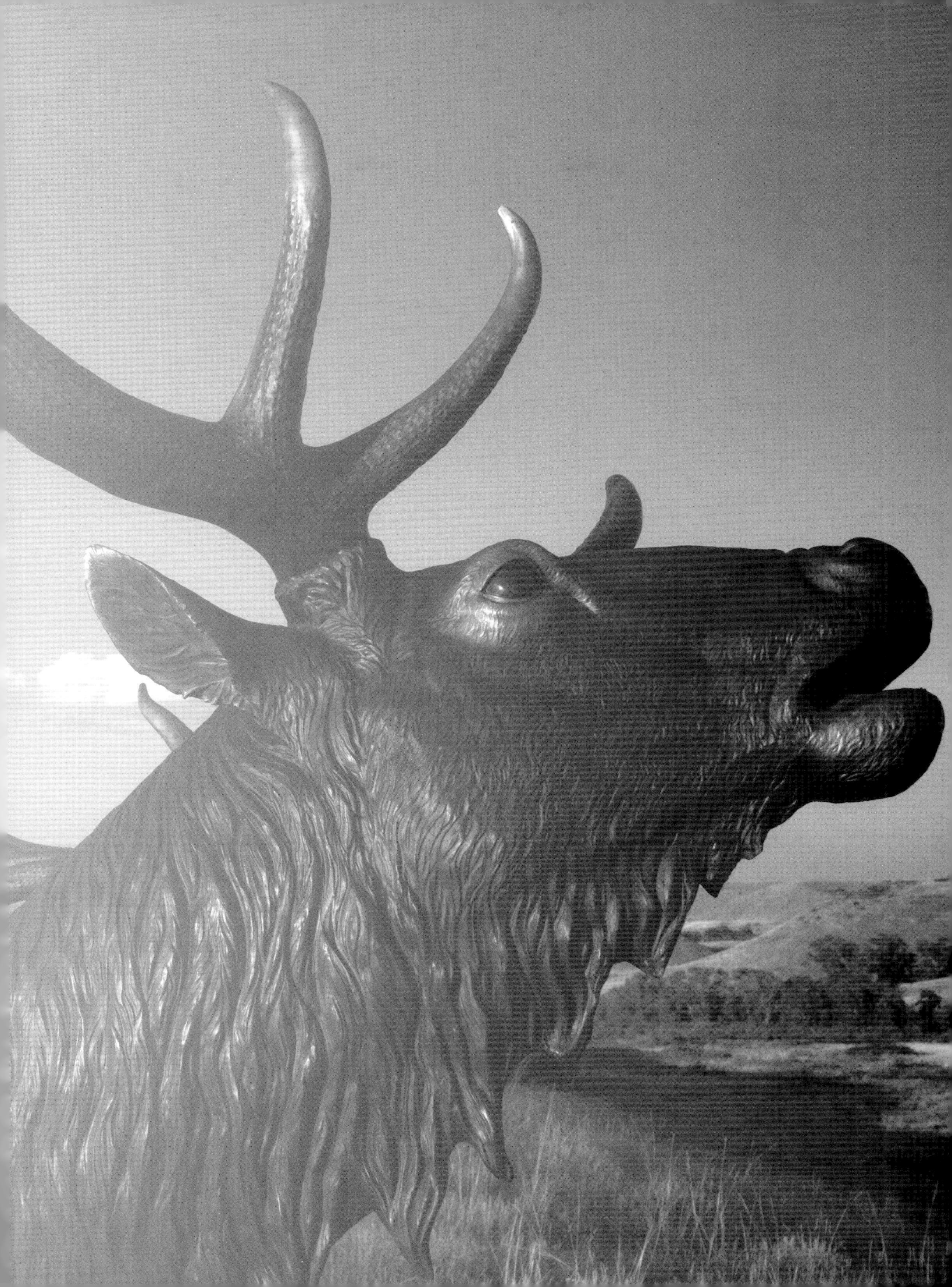

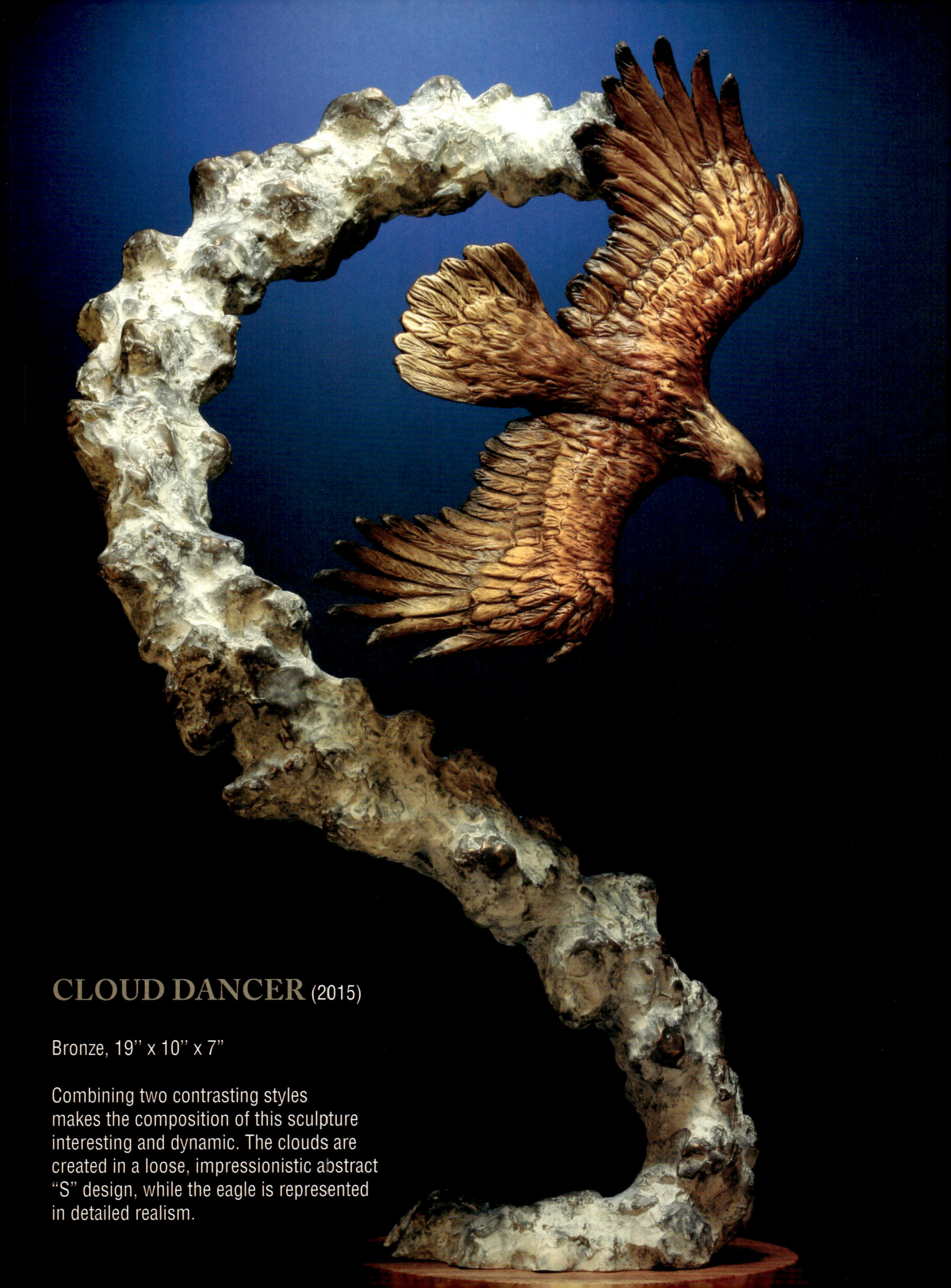

CLOUD DANCER (2015)

Bronze, 19'' x 10'' x 7"

Combining two contrasting styles makes the composition of this sculpture interesting and dynamic. The clouds are created in a loose, impressionistic abstract "S" design, while the eagle is represented in detailed realism.

HOME WRECKER (2009)

Bronze, 25" x 18"x 9"

Here is another title that adds to the story of the piece. A bull elk scrapes his antlers on an aspen tree that is home to a couple of magpies.

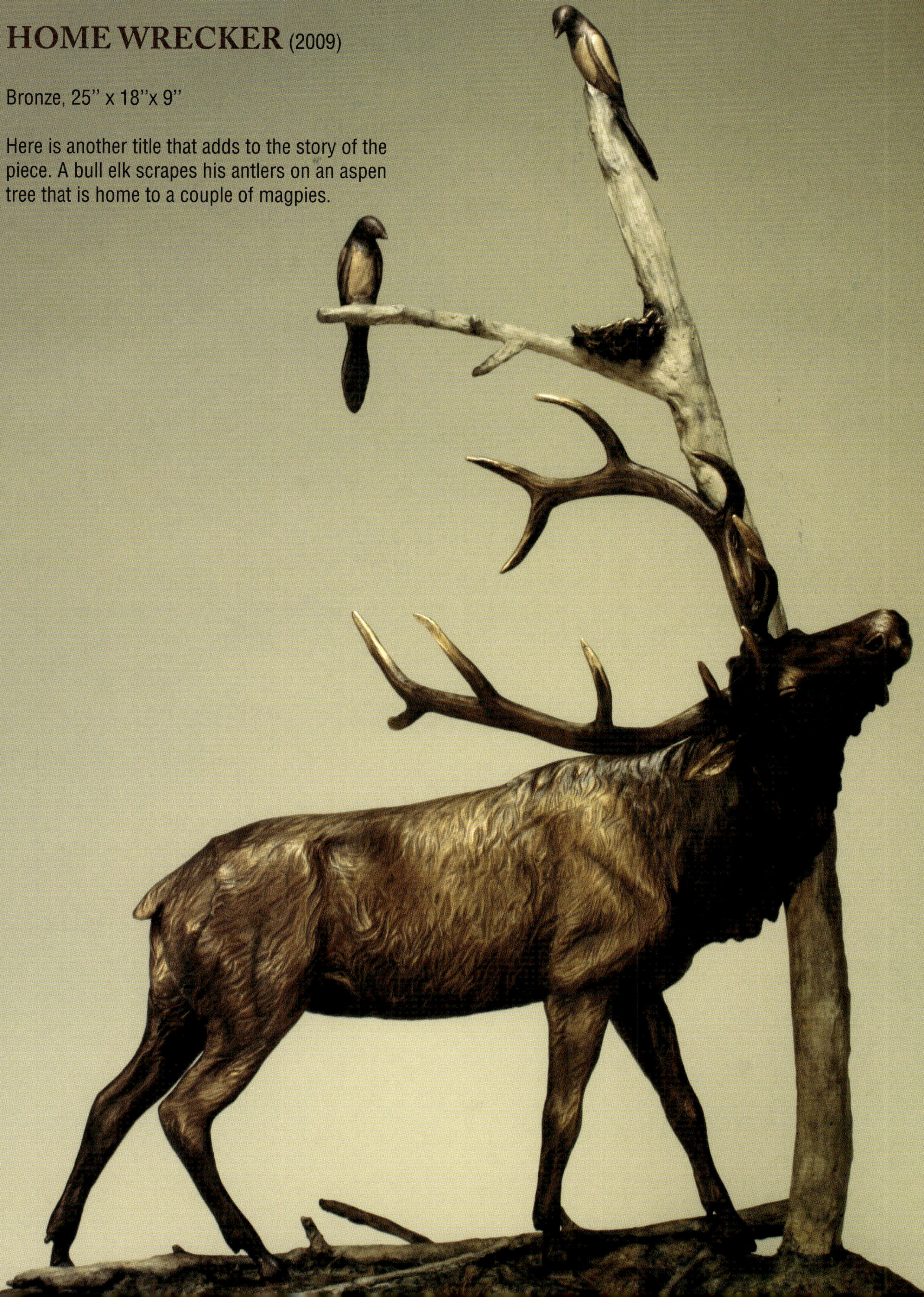

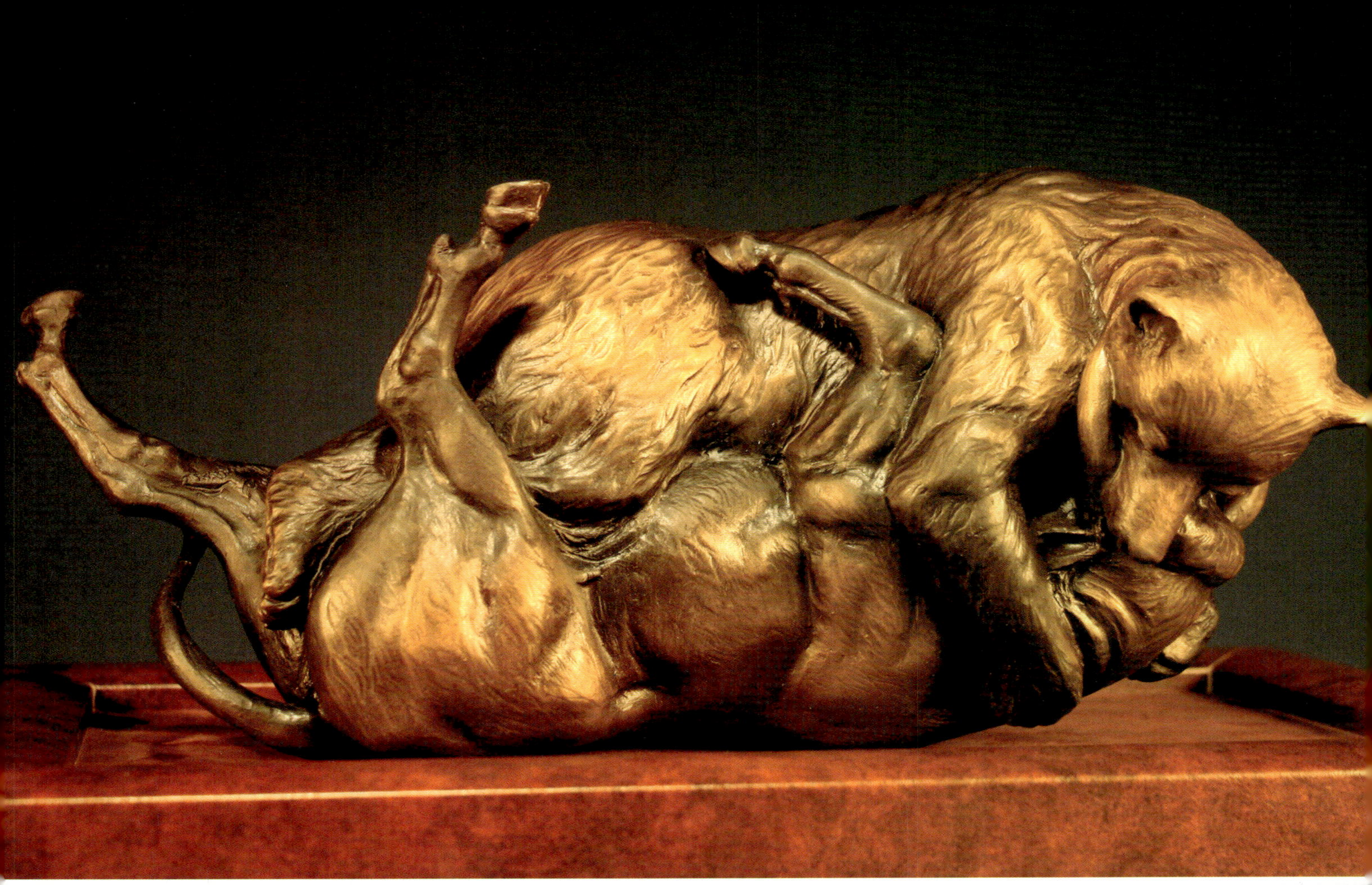

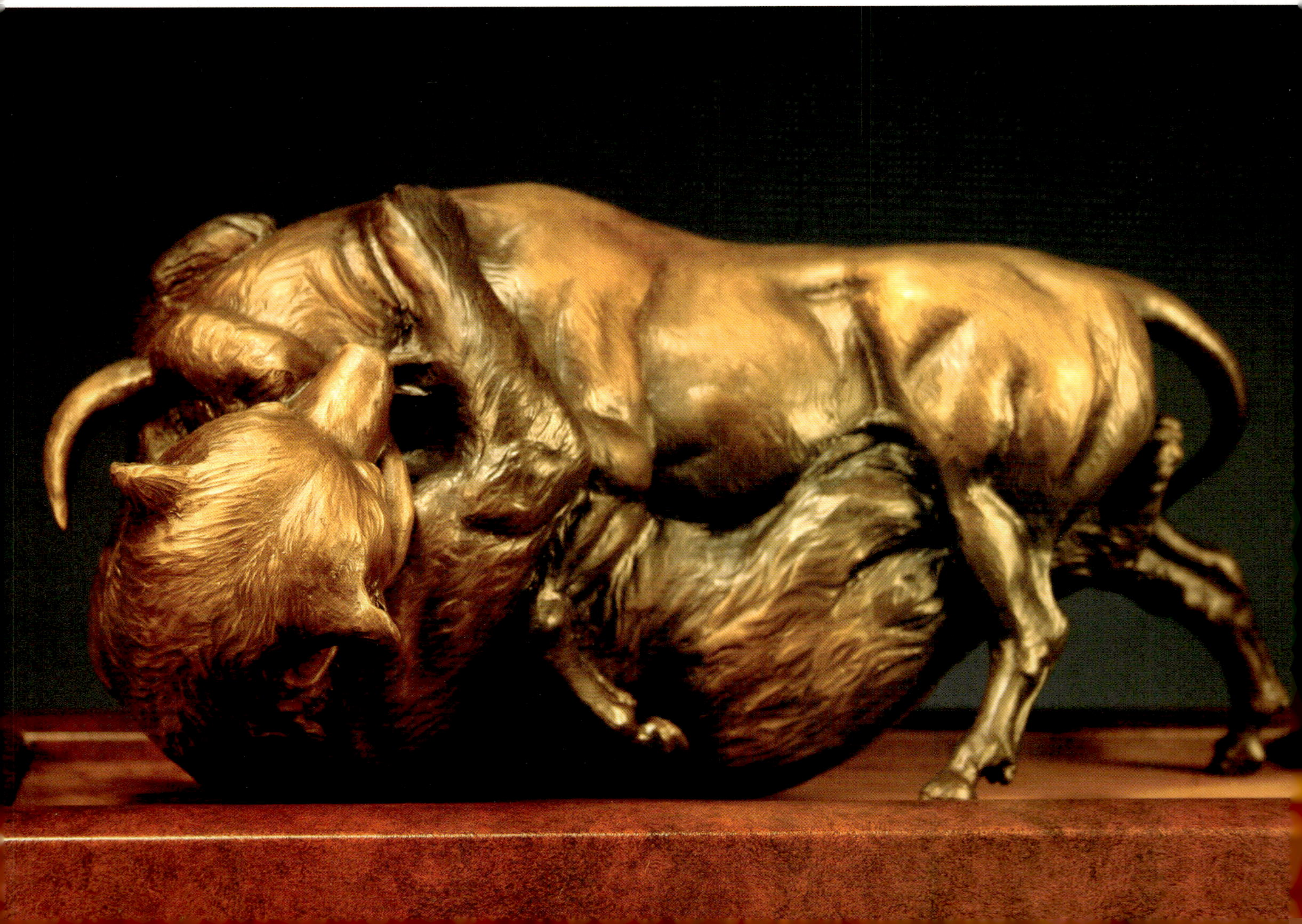

AN INVESTMENT IN KNOWLEDGE PAYS THE BEST INTEREST.
—BENJAMIN FRANKLIN

DUALITY OF THE BULL AND BEAR (2007)

Bronze, 6" x 15" x 8"

This bronze represents the changes and cycles of the stock market. In a bull market, rising share prices encourage buying, while in a bear market, declining prices prompt selling. This is the first "reversible" sculpture that I have designed. By picking up and flipping the sculpture over, you are able to change the meaning of the design. From one direction, the bull dominates the bear. Flip it over, and the bear dominates the bull. The ability to switch the sculpture shows the duality and change of the bull vs. bear markets.

RUNNING FREE (2002)

Bronze, 12" x 26"

Wild horses are herd animals and, when possible, live in groups. Each herd has a lead mare that is in charge of the day-to-day running of the family group, thereby keeping the herd safe. She also determines the routes to be taken when they move. The head stallion, meanwhile, will push from the rear, keep the band together, and provide protection from predators and other stallions.

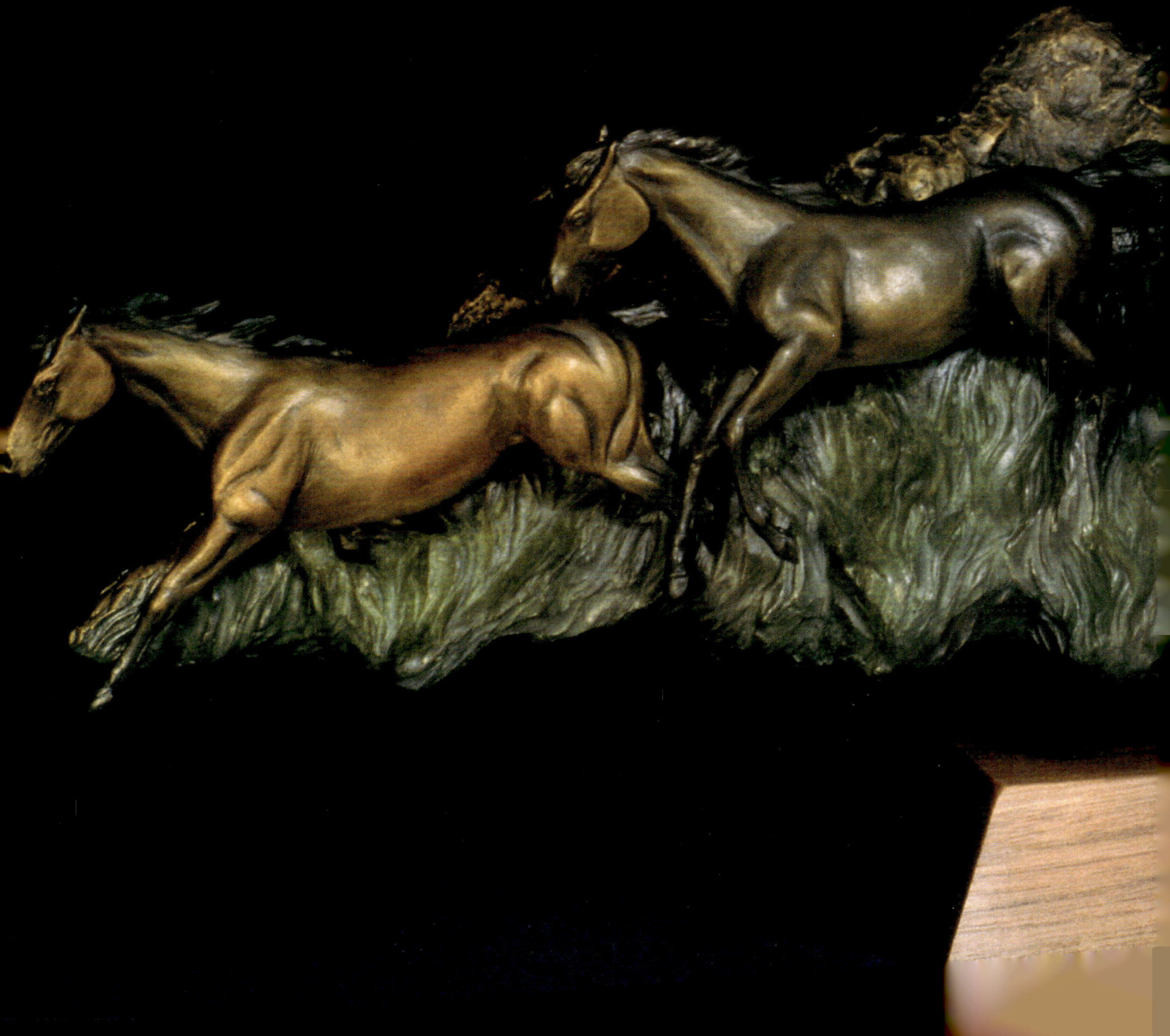

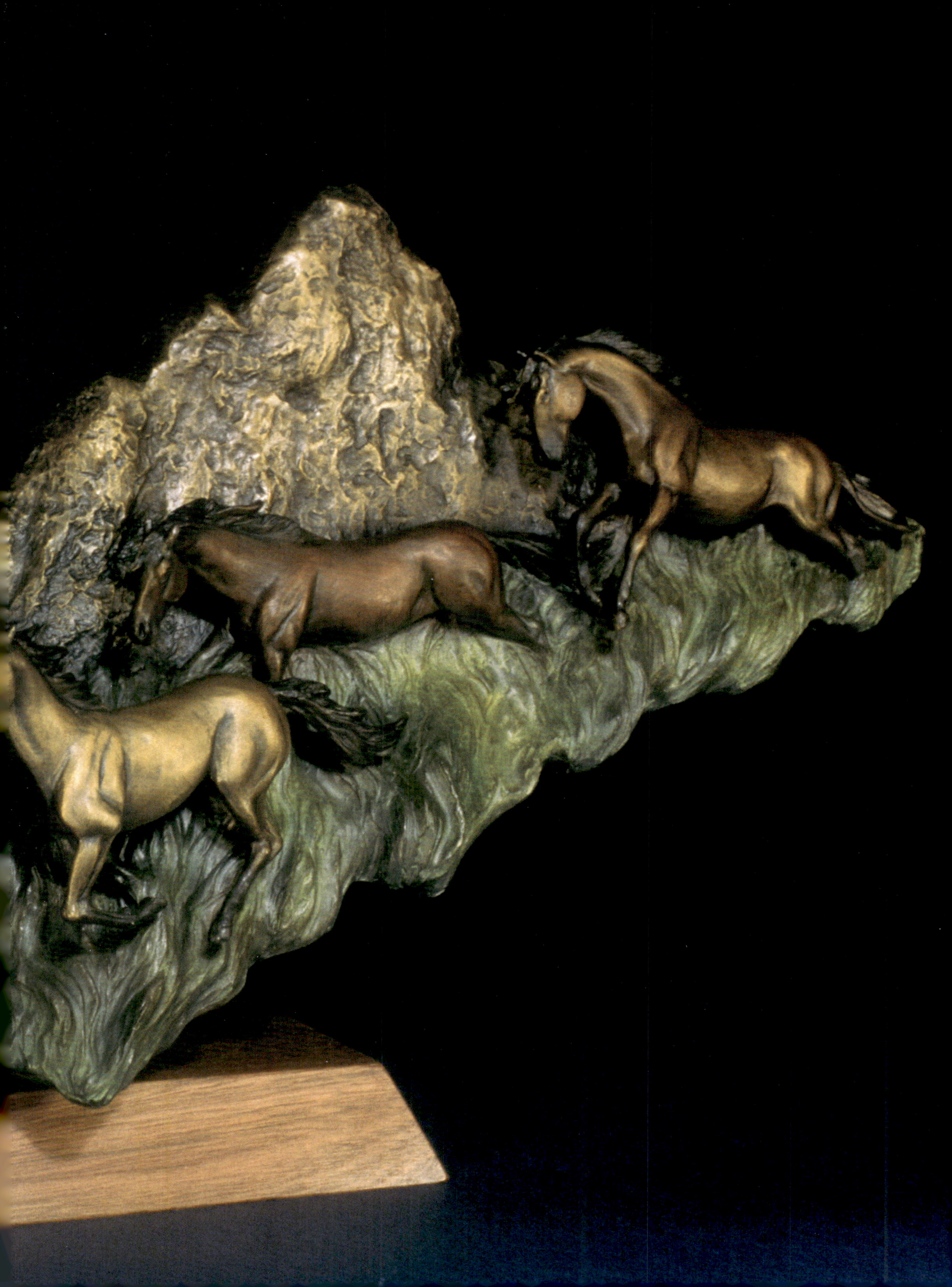

TASTES LIKE CHICKEN (2015)

Bronze, 16.5" x 12" x 6.5"

I decided to do a little artistic research and visited Maria's Restaurant & Cantina in Sedona, Arizona, where they have rattlesnake on the menu. After ordering a plate of rattlesnake, my wife said she didn't want any. That meant I got to eat the whole thing by myself, and you know something? It tastes like chicken! It tasted pretty good, but of course, most things do if you bread it and deep fry it.

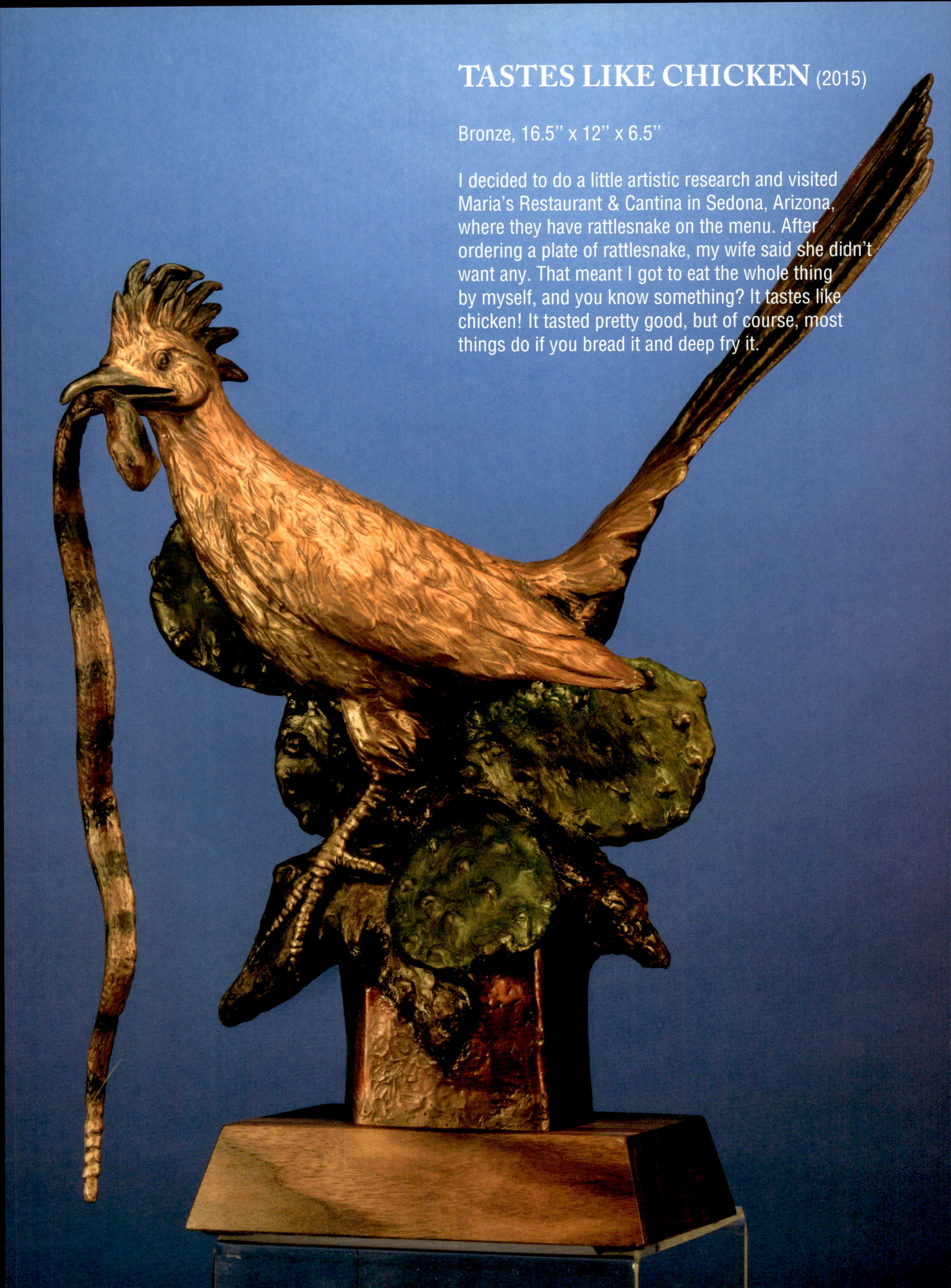

MOUNTAIN GRACE (2013)

Bronze, 30'' x 7'' x 6''

This sculpture has a strong vertical design, and the contrasting surface textures of the smooth cat against the rough rocks help give it more visual depth.

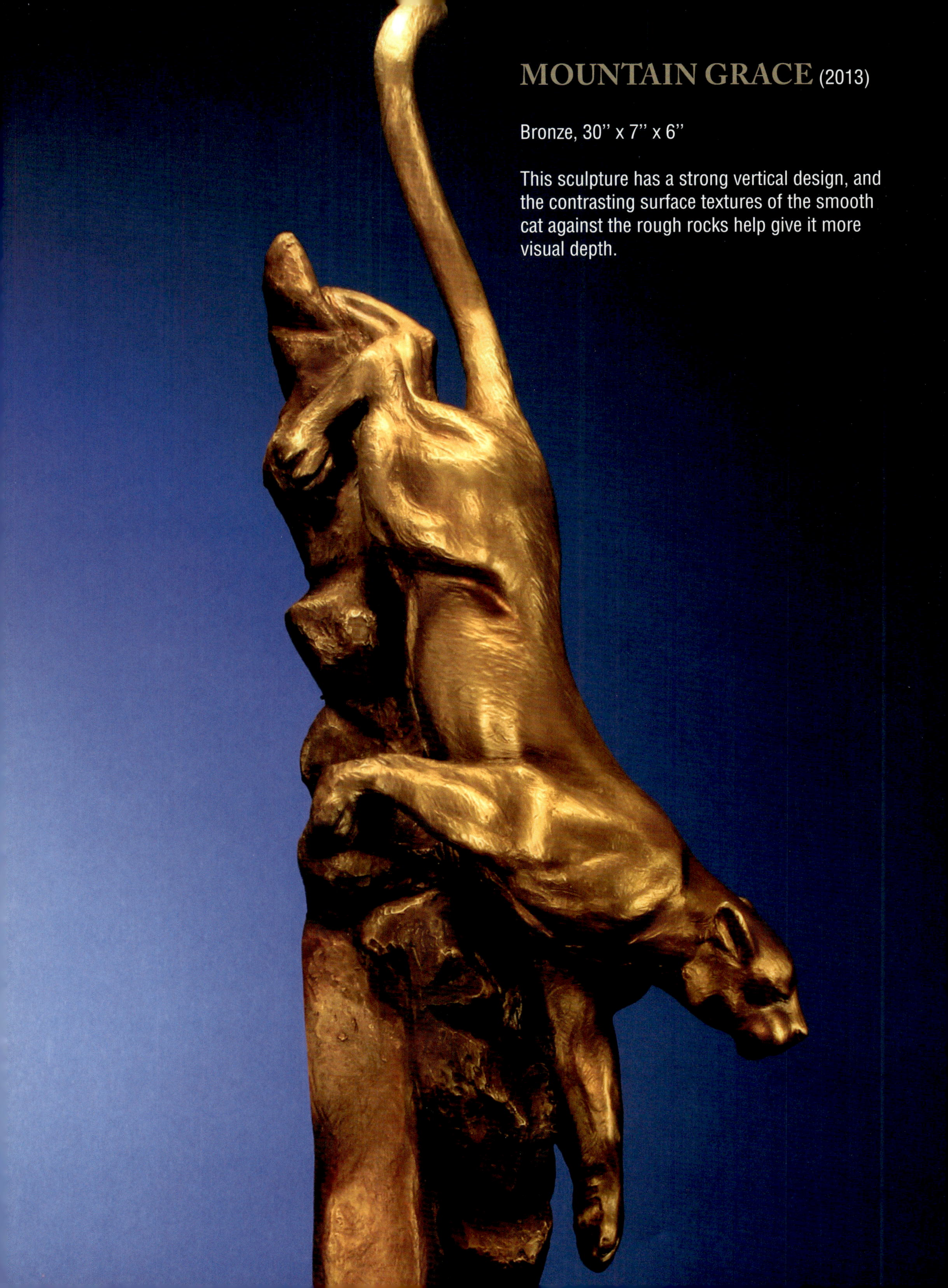

BALANCE, PROPORTION, RHYTHM, AND HARMONY ARE THE QUALITIES THAT ENCOMPASS BEAUTY.
–TED ORLAND

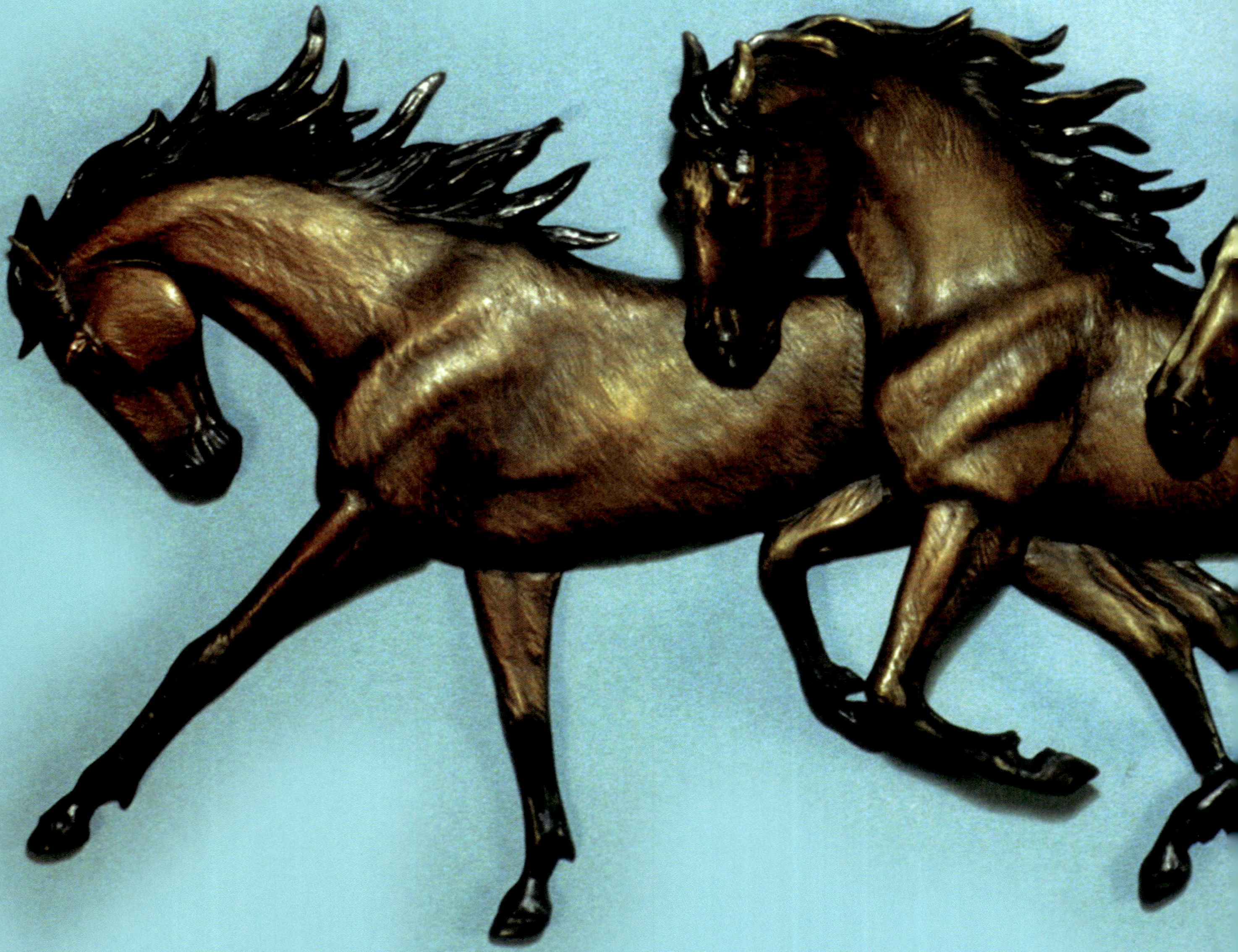

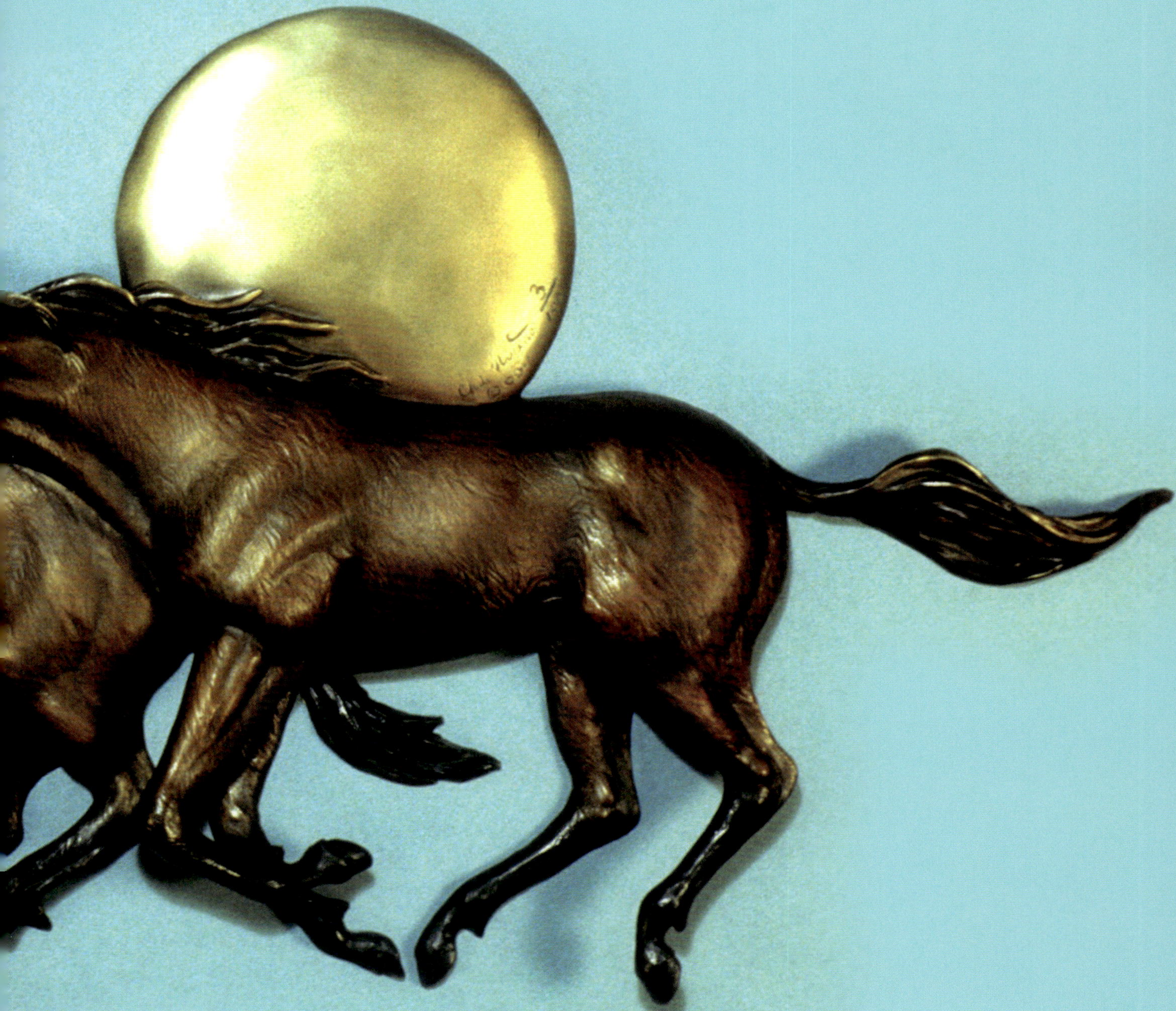

RACING THE MOON (2004)

Bronze (Wall Hanging relief), 13" x 31" x 2"

Three horses running under a full moon are shown in this wall hanging sculpture. All three are in full gallop, manes flying, under the moon's golden glow. The sculpture combines both low and high relief techniques that detail and emphasize the animals' swift movements.

NATIVE AMERICAN

I DO NOT FEAR DEATH.
–FOUR BEARS

ONE DOES NOT SELL THE LAND PEOPLE WALK ON.
–CRAZY HORSE

IT DOES NOT REQUIRE MANY WORDS TO SPEAK THE TRUTH.
–CHIEF JOSEPH

INSIDE OF ME THERE ARE TWO DOGS. ONE IS MEAN AND EVIL AND THE OTHER IS GOOD AND THEY FIGHT EACH OTHER ALL THE TIME. WHEN ASKED WHICH ONE WINS I ANSWER, THE ONE I FEED THE MOST.
–SITTING BULL

I CANNOT THINK THAT WE ARE USELESS OR GOD WOULD NOT HAVE CREATED US.
–GERONIMO

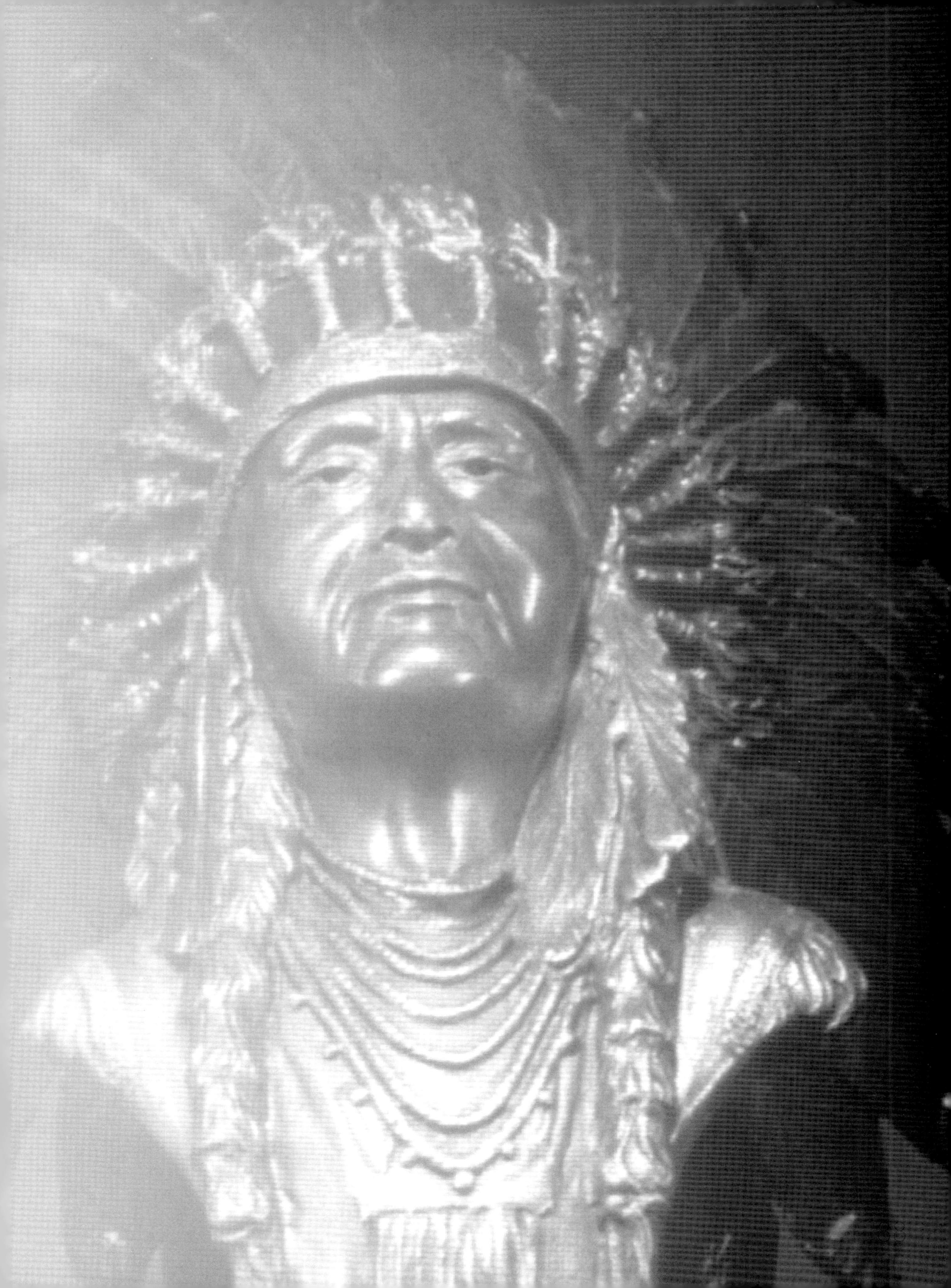

THE GREAT CHIEFS (1999)

Bronze, 17'' x 36'' x 7''

This is a collection of five Native American busts, including: Crazy Horse, the great war chief of the Oglala Sioux; Geronimo, the fierce warrior and Apache chief; Chief Joseph, the leader of the Nez Perce Nation who was known as a warrior for peace; Four Bears, the great fighter and leader of the Mandan Tribe (artists Charles Bodner and George Catlin painted a portrait of Four Bears in the 1830s); and Sitting Bull, the Sioux Lakota chief who was known as a great warrior and holy man.

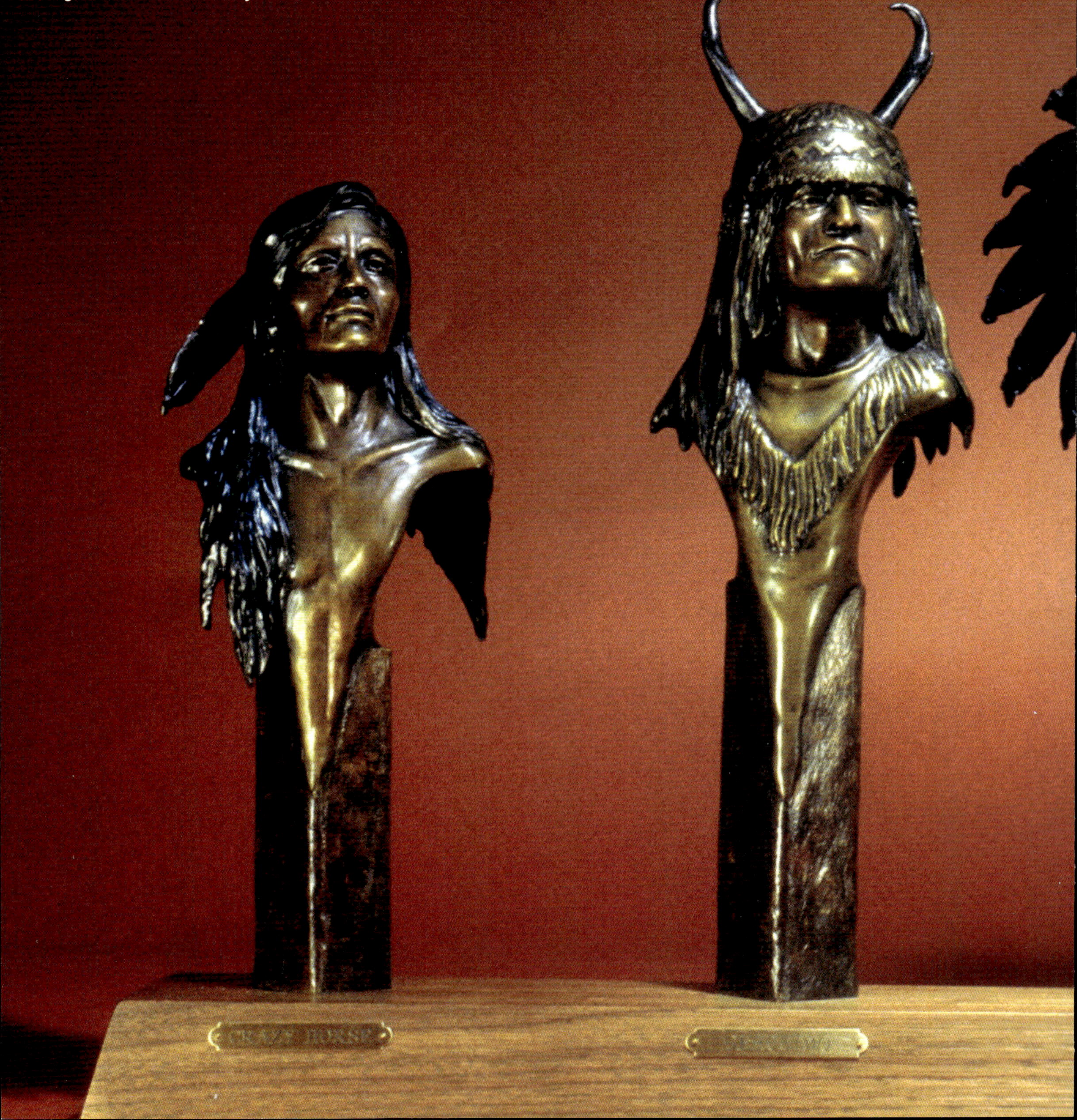

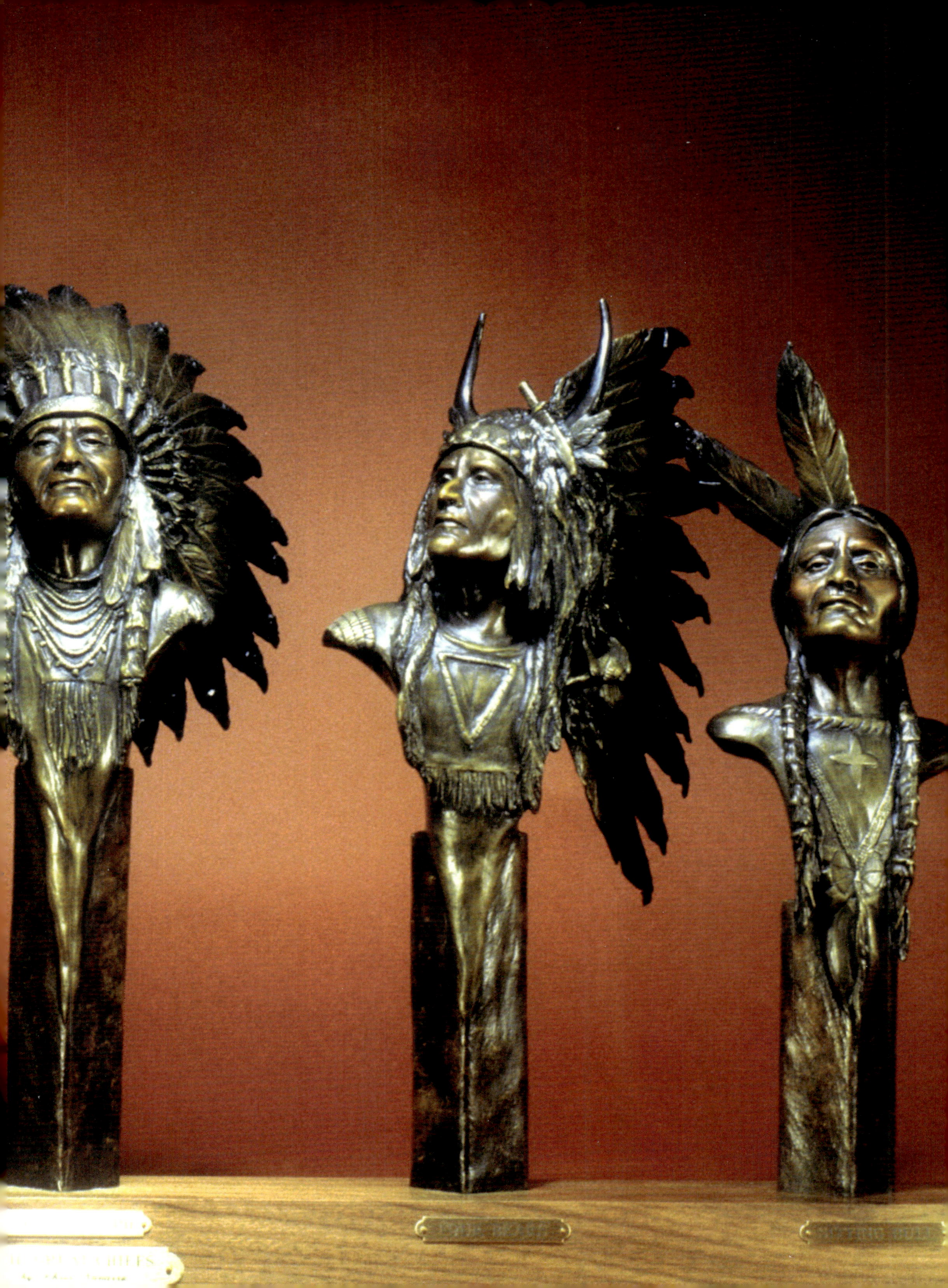

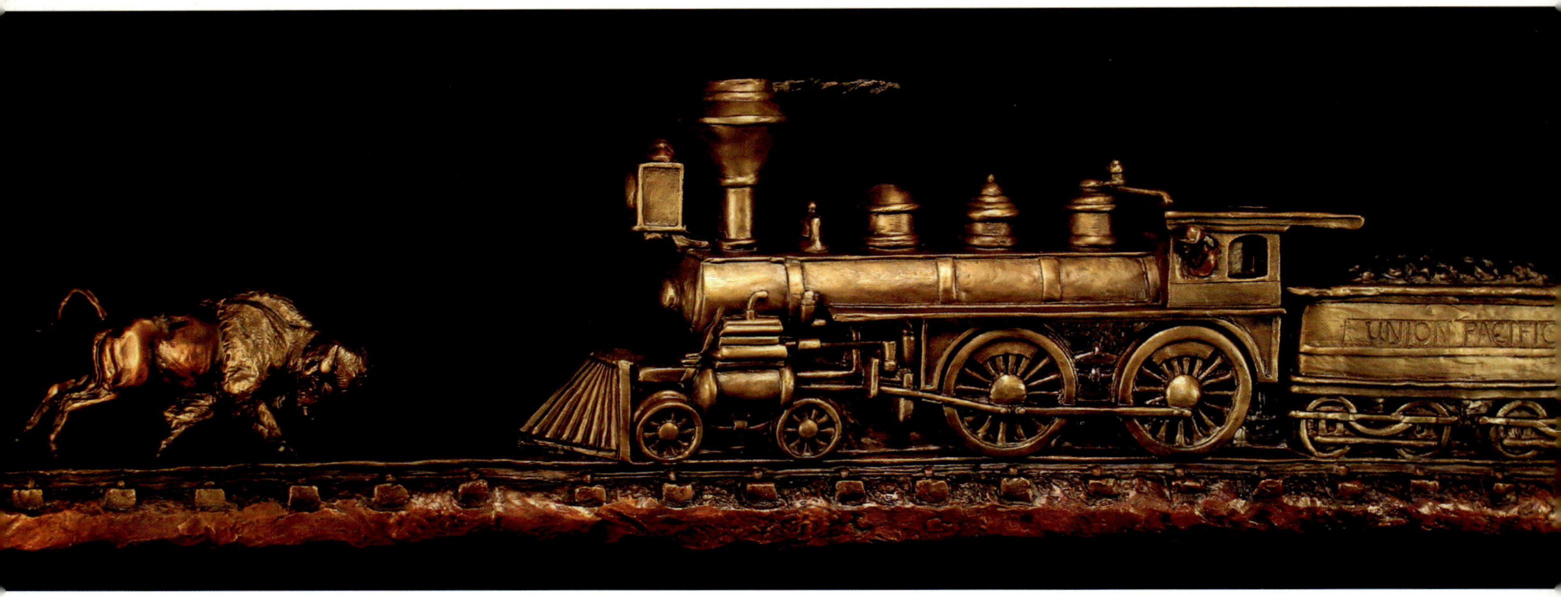

THE BUFFALO AND THE IRON HORSE (2013)

Bronze, 9.5"x 34" x 11.5"

Two competing symbols of white and American Indian cultures, the buffalo and the "iron horse," help explain the conflict and change on the Great Plains. By the 1880s, powerful, steam-belching railroad locomotives (or iron horses, as the Indians called them) replaced the near-extinct buffalo. The advance of iron horses not only hastened the demise of the buffalo, but also forever transformed the environment and the lives of human and animal cultures of the Great Plains.

In 1883, Sitting Bull was a guest of honor at the opening ceremonies for the Northern Pacific Railroad. When it was his turn to speak, he said in the Lakota language, "I hate all white people. You are thieves and liars. You have taken away our land and made us outcasts." A quick-thinking interpreter told the crowd the chief was happy to be there and that he looked forward to peace and prosperity with the white people. Sitting Bull received a standing ovation.

A cultural and historical era that had defined life for Plains Indians for thousands of years came to an end as iron horses crossed the prairies where millions of buffalo had once grazed.

BUFFALO RUNNER (2015)

Bronze, 16.5" x 26" x 10"

One tactic of the warrior hunters of the Great Plains would involve herding buffalo and driving them over cliffs, known as "buffalo jumps." This technique allowed hunters to harvest the massive animals for food, clothing, and shelter.

The *Buffalo Runner* sculpture depicts a warrior on horseback, using a buffalo robe to stampede a herd. The backside of the robe portrays the image of a running buffalo, which symbolizes the great power, spirit, and respect that Native Americans held for the buffalo.

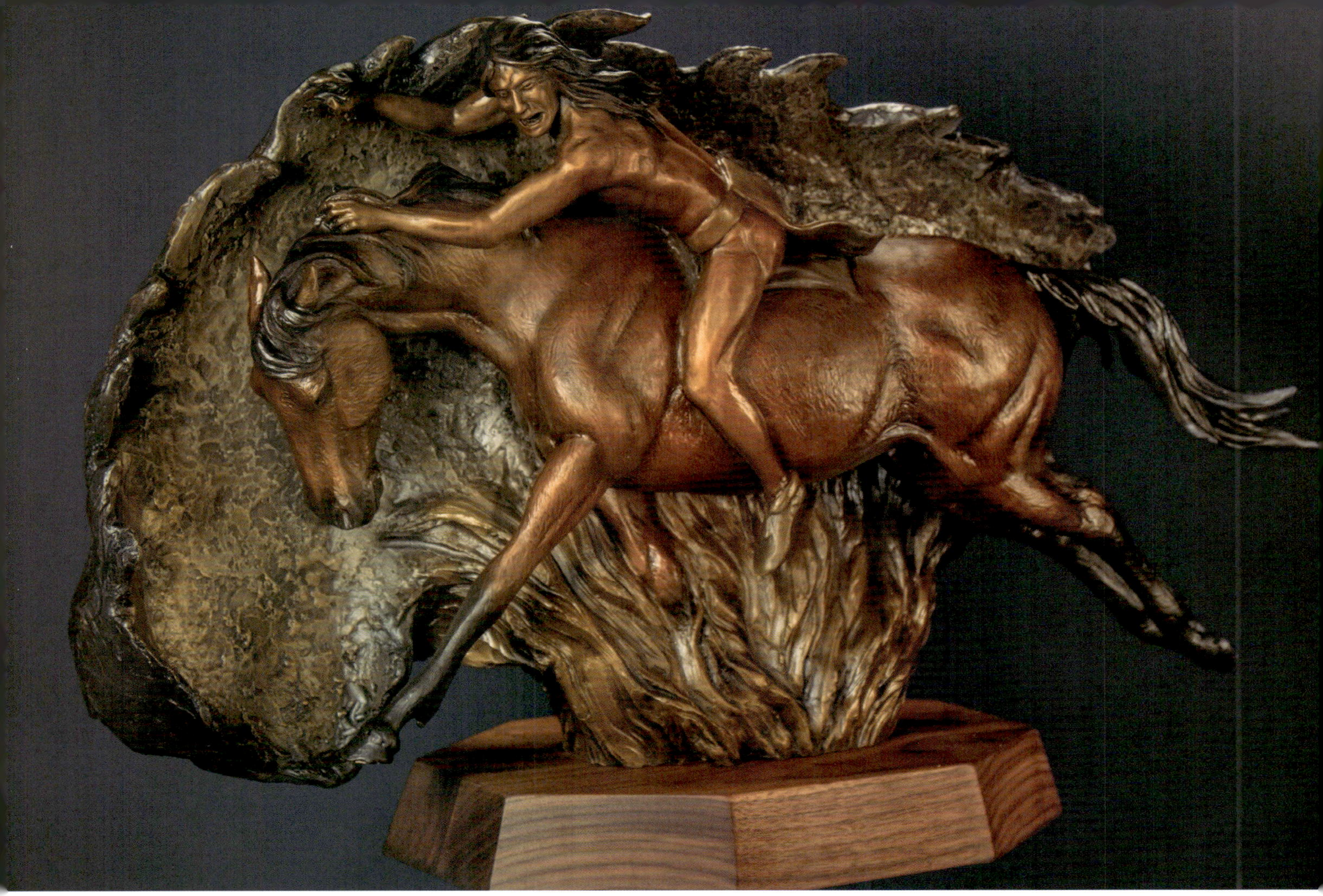

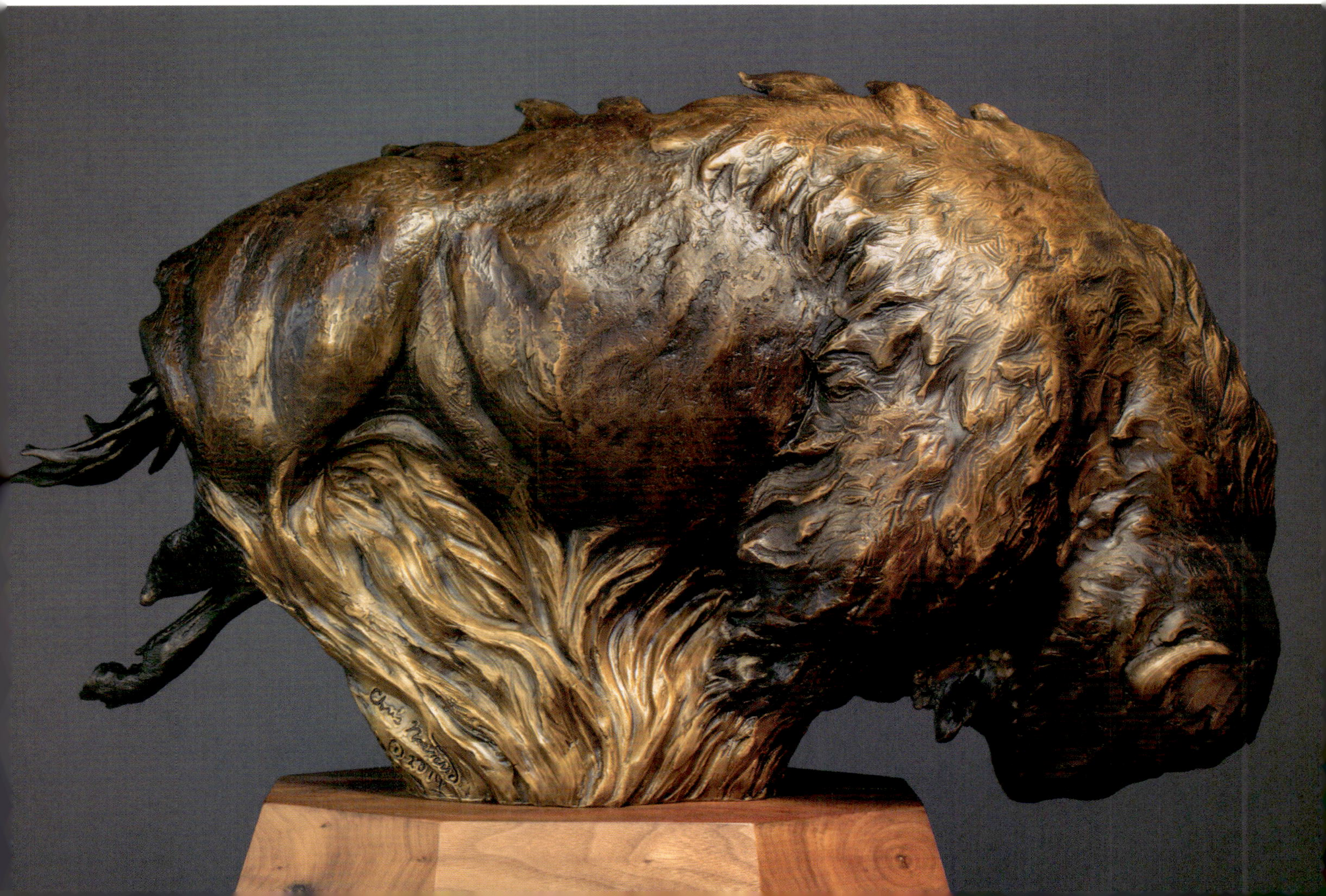

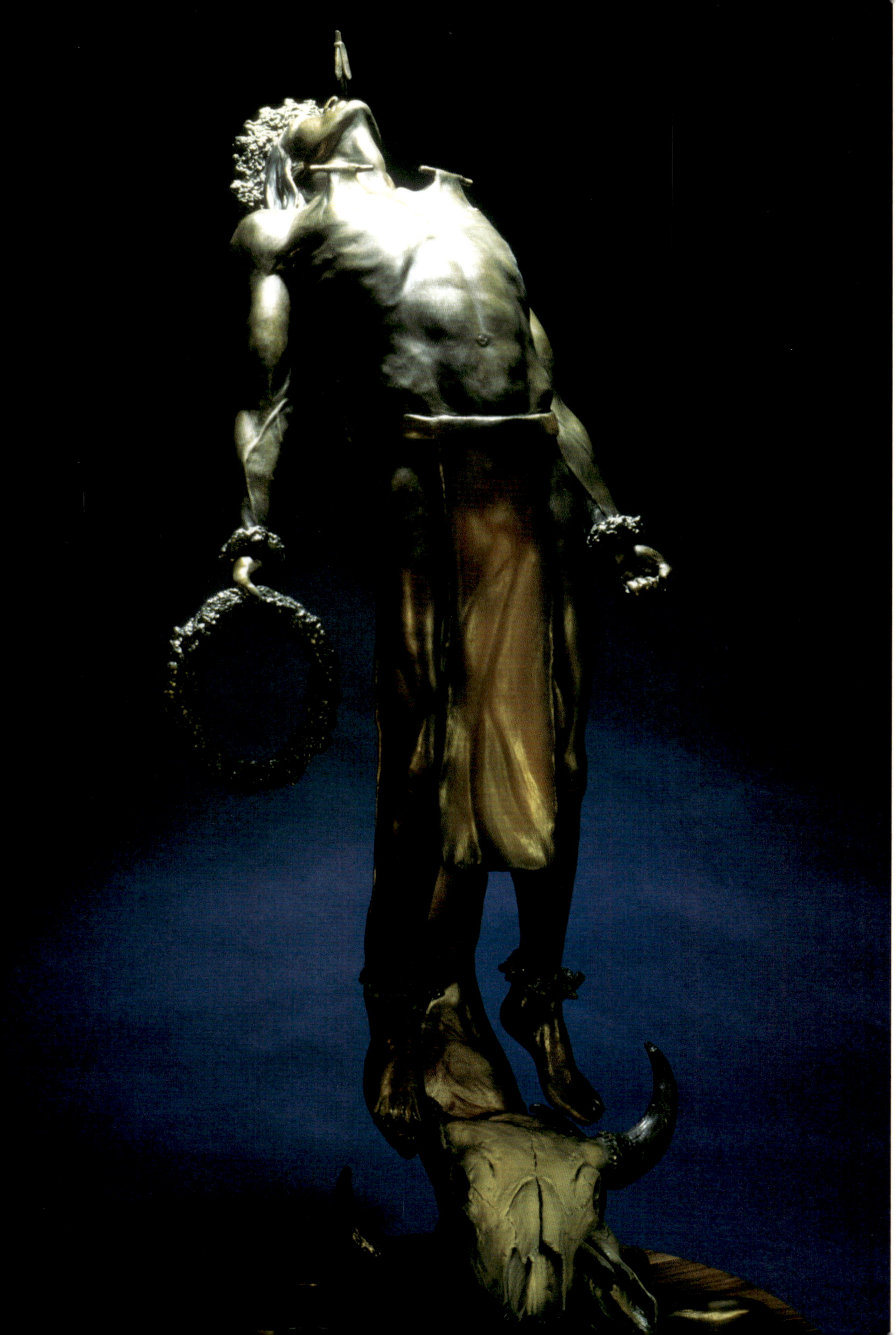

VISION QUEST OF THE SUN DANCE (2000)

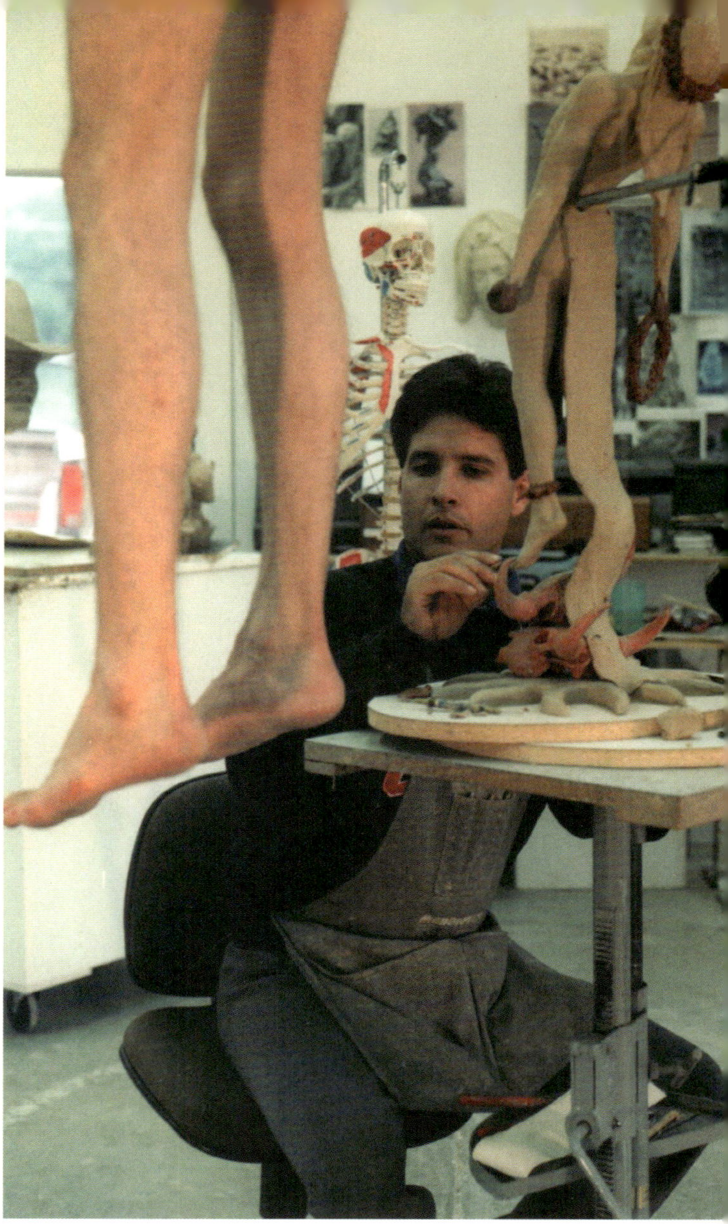

Bronze, 32" x 15" x 15"

Because hardship and the unexpected were so much a part of their lives, Plains Indians believed that through personal suffering, they would receive supernatural power in their favor. Suffering and testing were also forms of thanksgiving, because they proved, without doubt, their sincerity and gratitude to the Great Spirit for responding to their pleas. Sioux warriors believed that by suffering at the pole in the center of their sun lodge, they took upon themselves much of the agony of their people. As a sacred Native American ceremonial dance, the sun dance required exhaustive preparation, fasting, and self-mutilation. The sculpture portrays a sun dance warrior at the culmination of the ritual. Having completed his fasting and chanting, he is suspended by sticks that pierce his chest. He wears the sacred sage wreaths, and with his head thrust back, blows the eagle bone whistle. The sound of the whistle replicates an eagle's cry, which delivers the warrior's plea to the Great Spirit above. Beneath him, the buffalo skulls are bound to his legs in order to hasten the tearing free of his flesh. The sun and the skulls further symbolize the mystery of the Great Spirit.

I work with live models whenever possible, which allows me to respond and interact with my subject. For example, while sculpting *Vision Quest of the Sun dance*, I constructed a hoist and harness to suspend a live model from the ceiling of my studio. This allowed me to authentically represent the tension that the fatigued warrior felt in his muscles from being suspended.

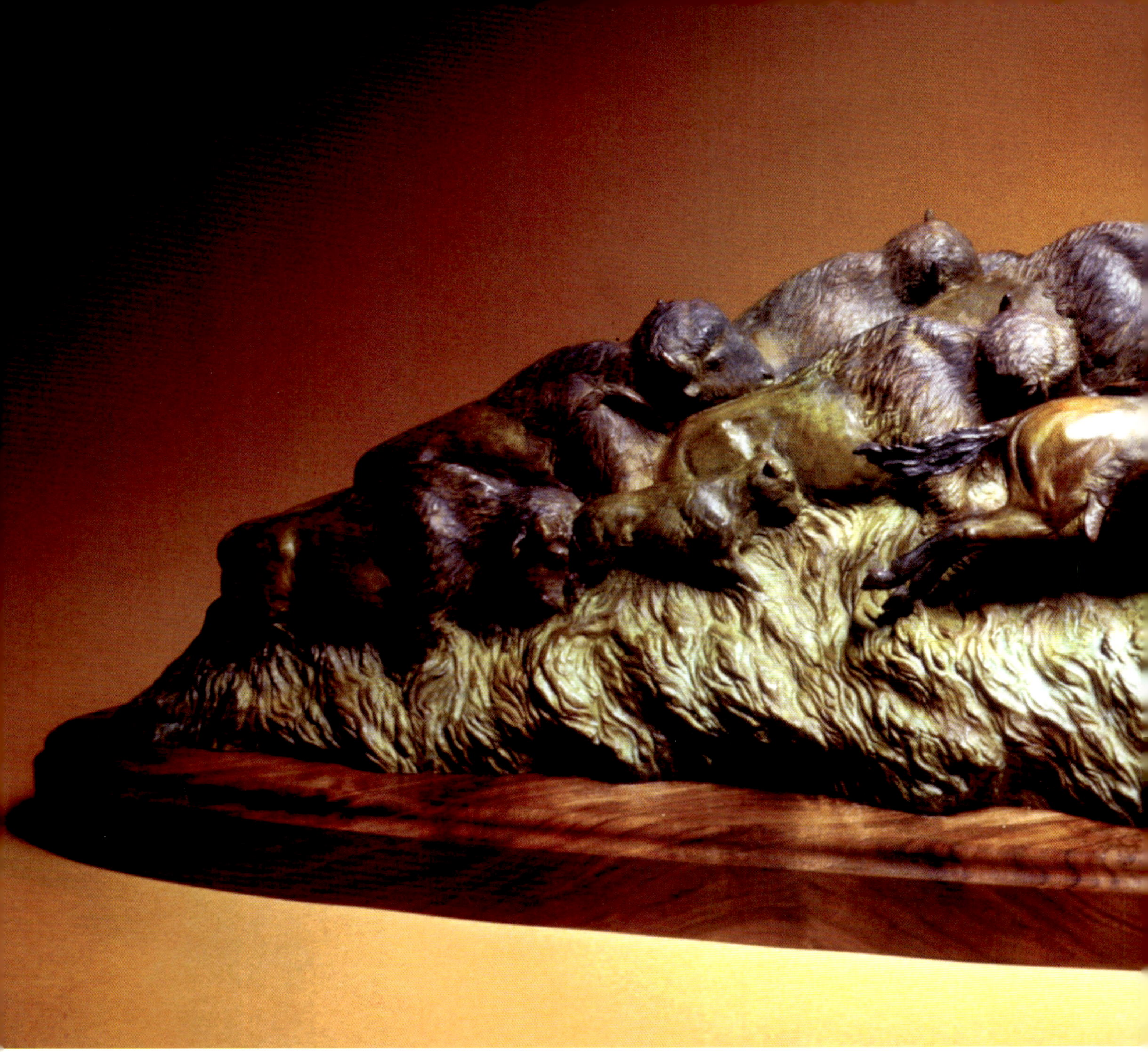

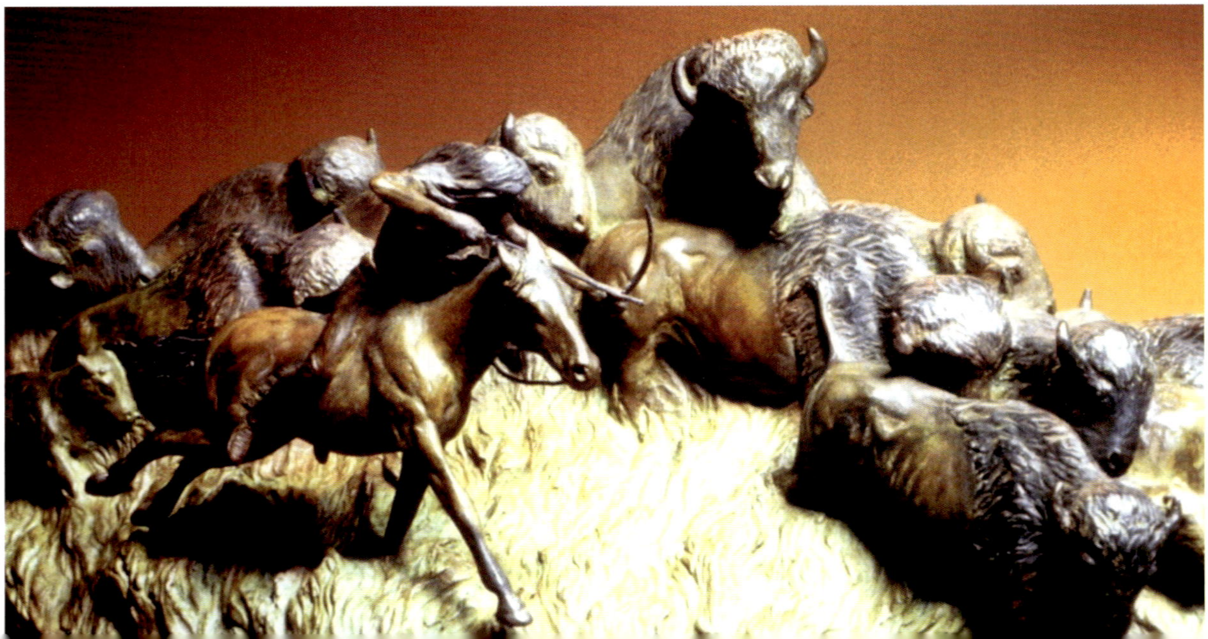

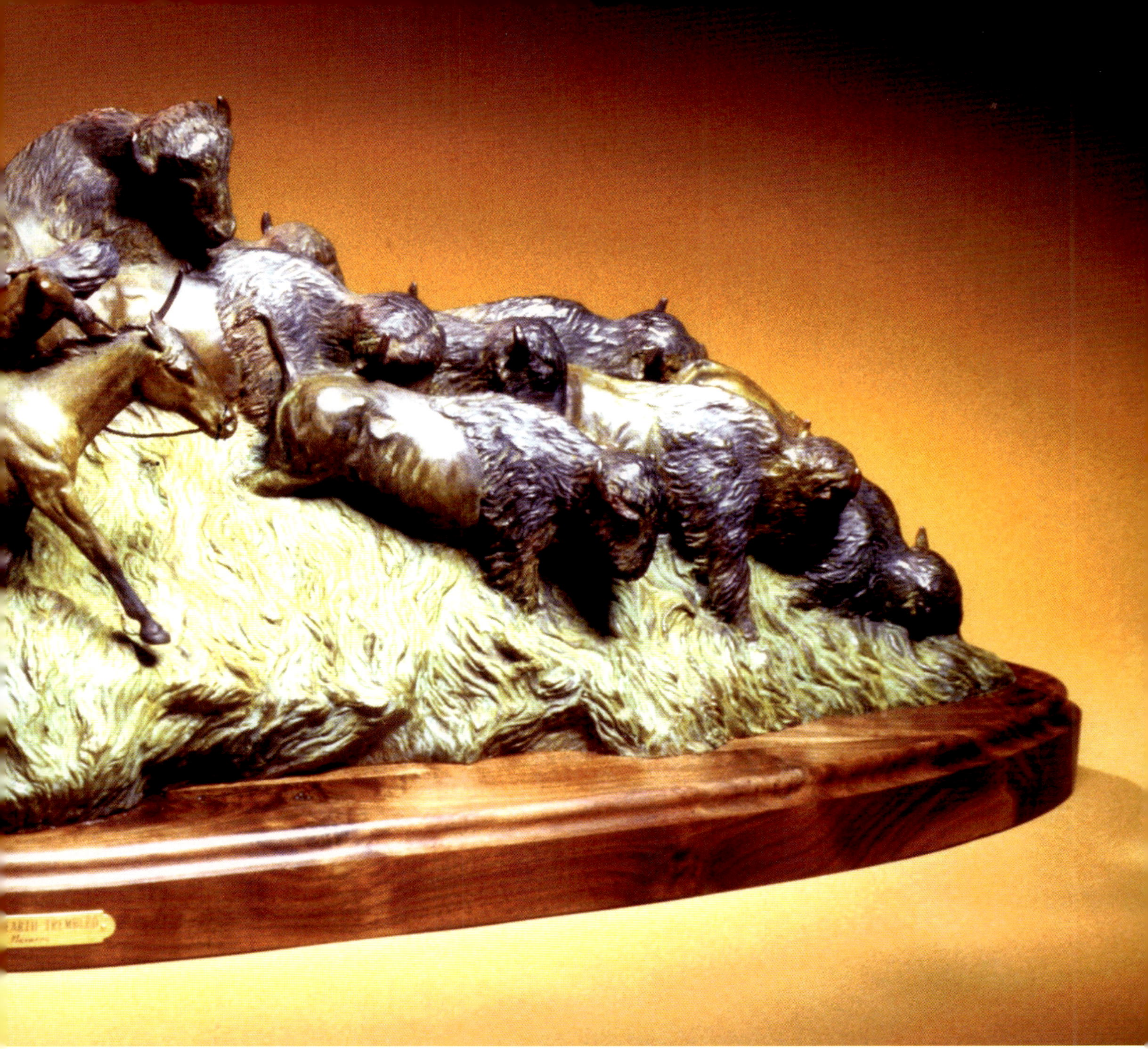

WHEN THE EARTH TREMBLED (1995)

Bronze, 13" x 40" x 12"

The coming of the horse changed many of the old ways for buffalo hunters. The buffalo chase on horseback combined the excitement of the horse race with the challenge of the hunt. The thrill and exhilaration were so fulfilling that it became addictive to the hunter. The buffalo hunter would put his horse into a full gallop the moment the herd broke – a test of horse speed against buffalo speed. Each hunter selected a single buffalo and attempted to ride within a bow's length away. The preferred target on the buffalo was the intestinal cavity just behind the last rib and edge of the shoulder, which allowed the arrow to penetrate the heart. This method of hunting buffalo became a real test between man and animal, as opposed to the later mass killings of buffalo by white men, which decimated the herds. Buffalo are no longer hunted in this manner, but there was a time not long ago when man, horse, and buffalo raced over the prairie and the earth trembled!

WESTERN LIFE

IT WAS A HARD LAND, AND
IT BRED HARD MEN TO
HARD WAYS.
—LOUIS L'AMOUR

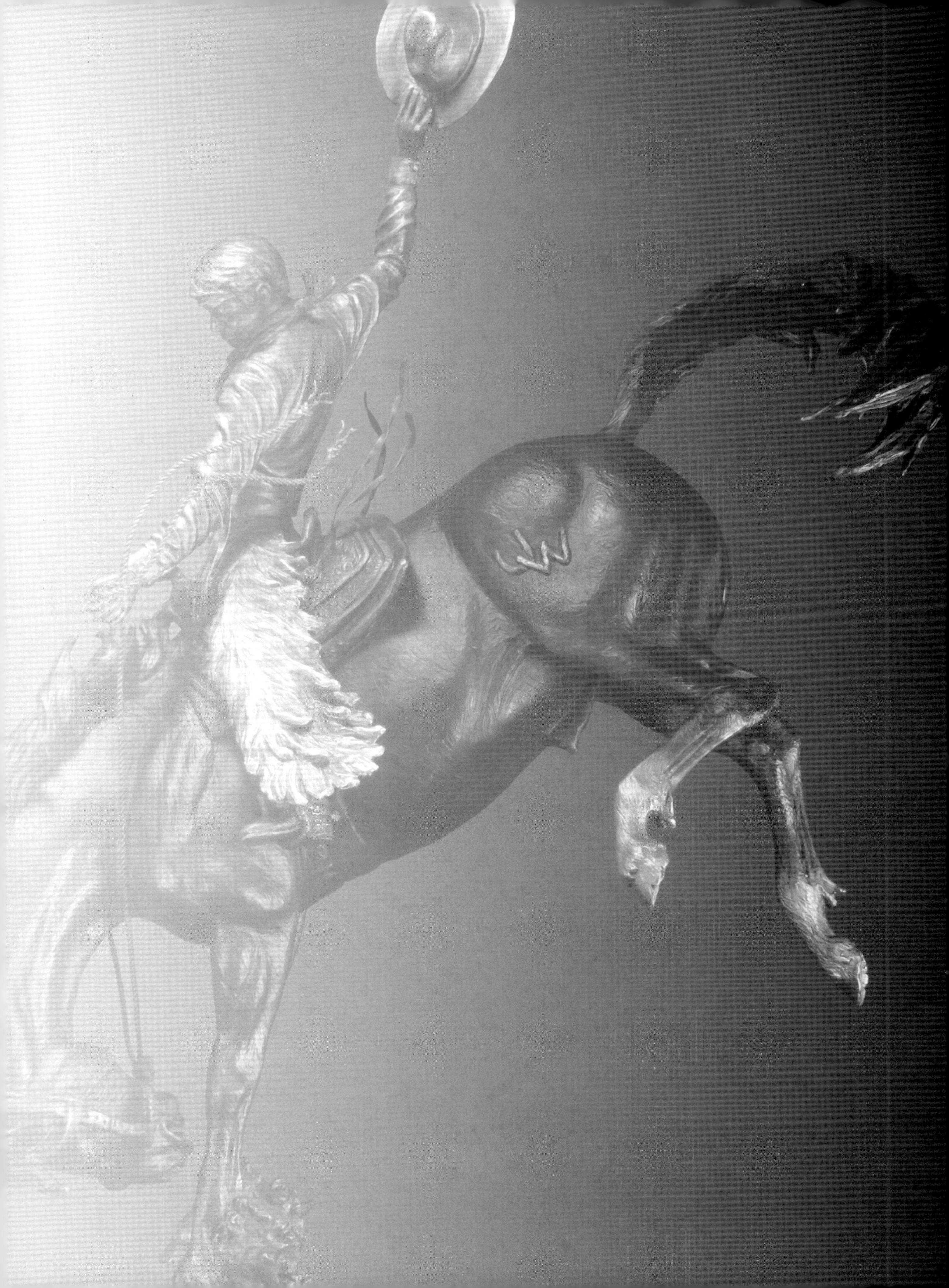

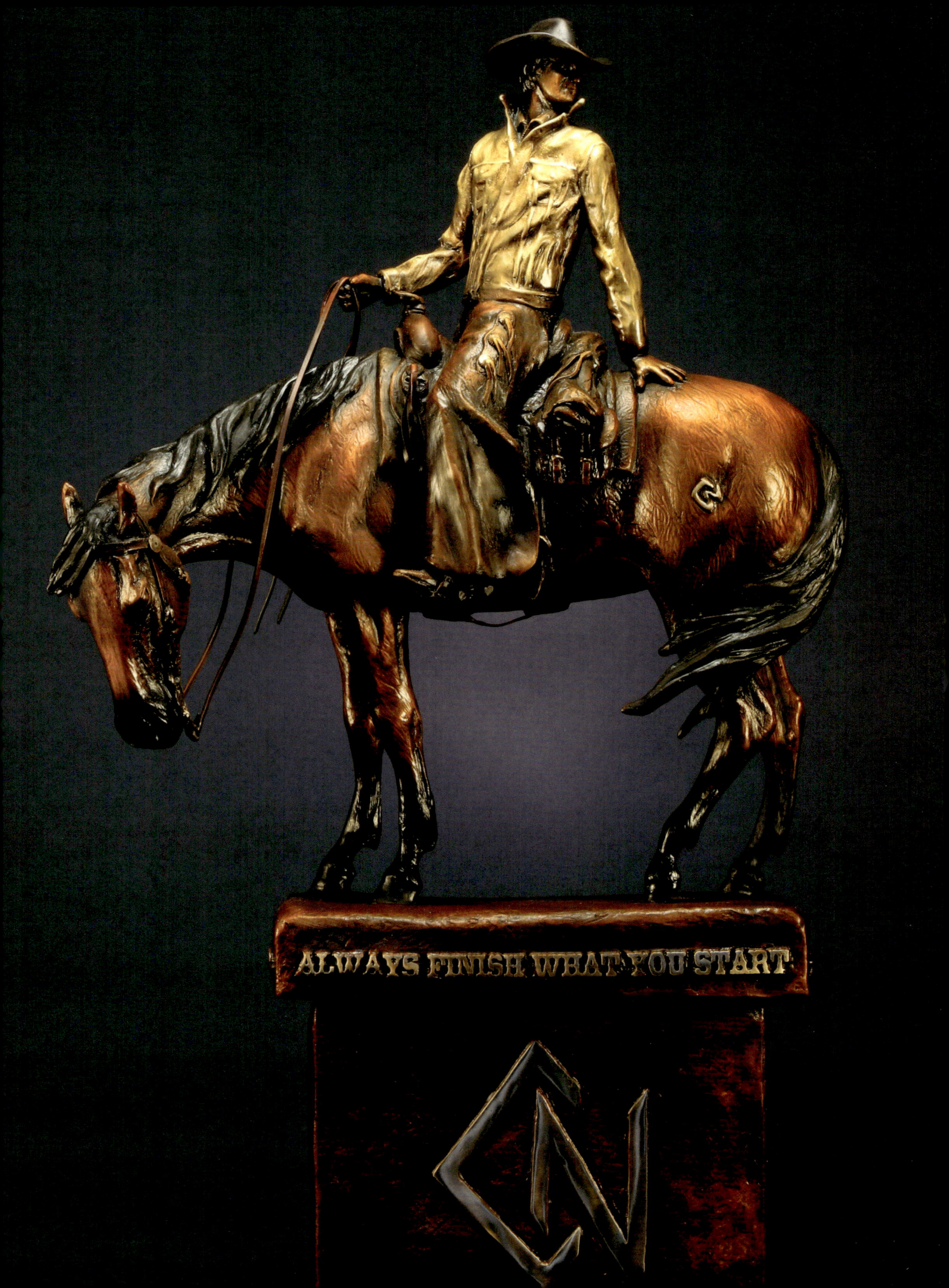
ALWAYS FINISH WHAT YOU START

PEOPLE MAY DOUBT WHAT YOU SAY, BUT THEY WILL BELIEVE WHAT YOU DO.
—LEWIS CASS

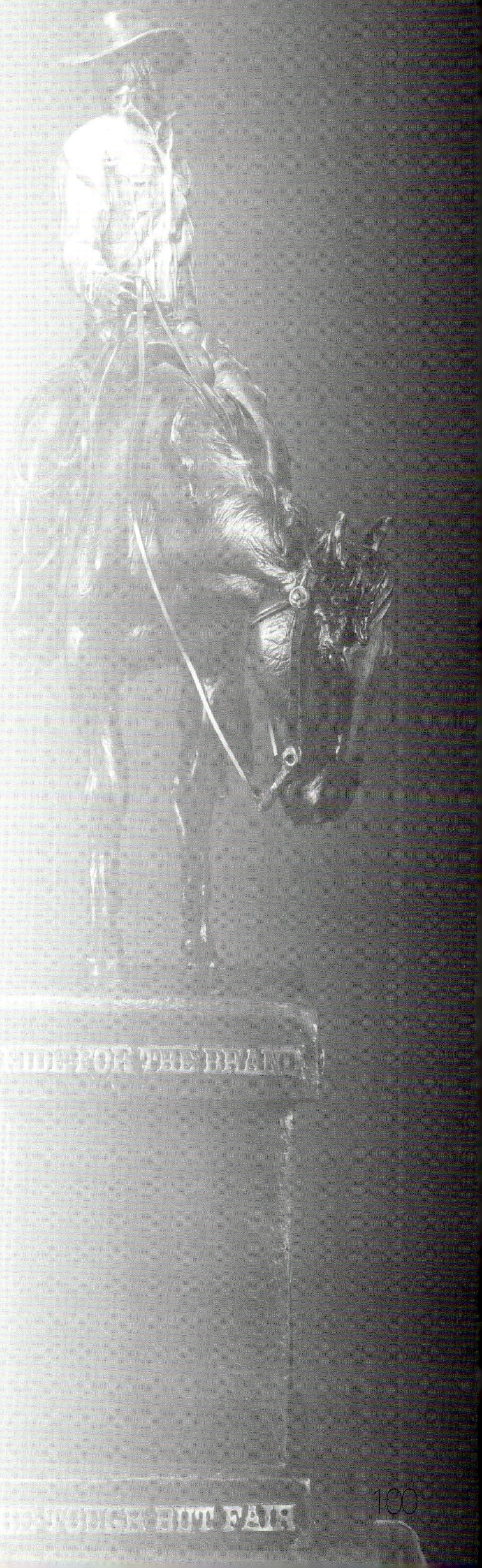

COWBOY CODE (2009)

Bronze, 19" x 10" x 5.5"

Respectable men who lived in the West were bound by unwritten rules that centered on hospitality, fair play, loyalty, and respect for the land. There was no law on the range back in the days when the cowman with his herds carved out a new frontier. Lack of written law made it necessary to develop a rule of behavior, which became known as the "Code of the West." These laws were a socially-agreed-upon code of conduct that helped shape the cowboy culture of the Old West and were respected everywhere on the range.

The sculpture's forward facing horses symbolize the future and what lies ahead. Both of them standing still express the present. The cowboy turning in the saddle, looking back over the trail, represents the past. The brand in the middle of the base stands for the mark and pride he puts on the work he finishes. Surrounding the base are some of the Cowboy Codes of the West. You can't go wrong practicing these principles in your own life:

1. Ride for the brand.
2. Your word is your bond.
3. Be tough but fair.
4. Do what has to be done.
5. Protect and help the weak.
6. Always finish what you start.
7. Take pride in your work.
8. Live each day with courage.

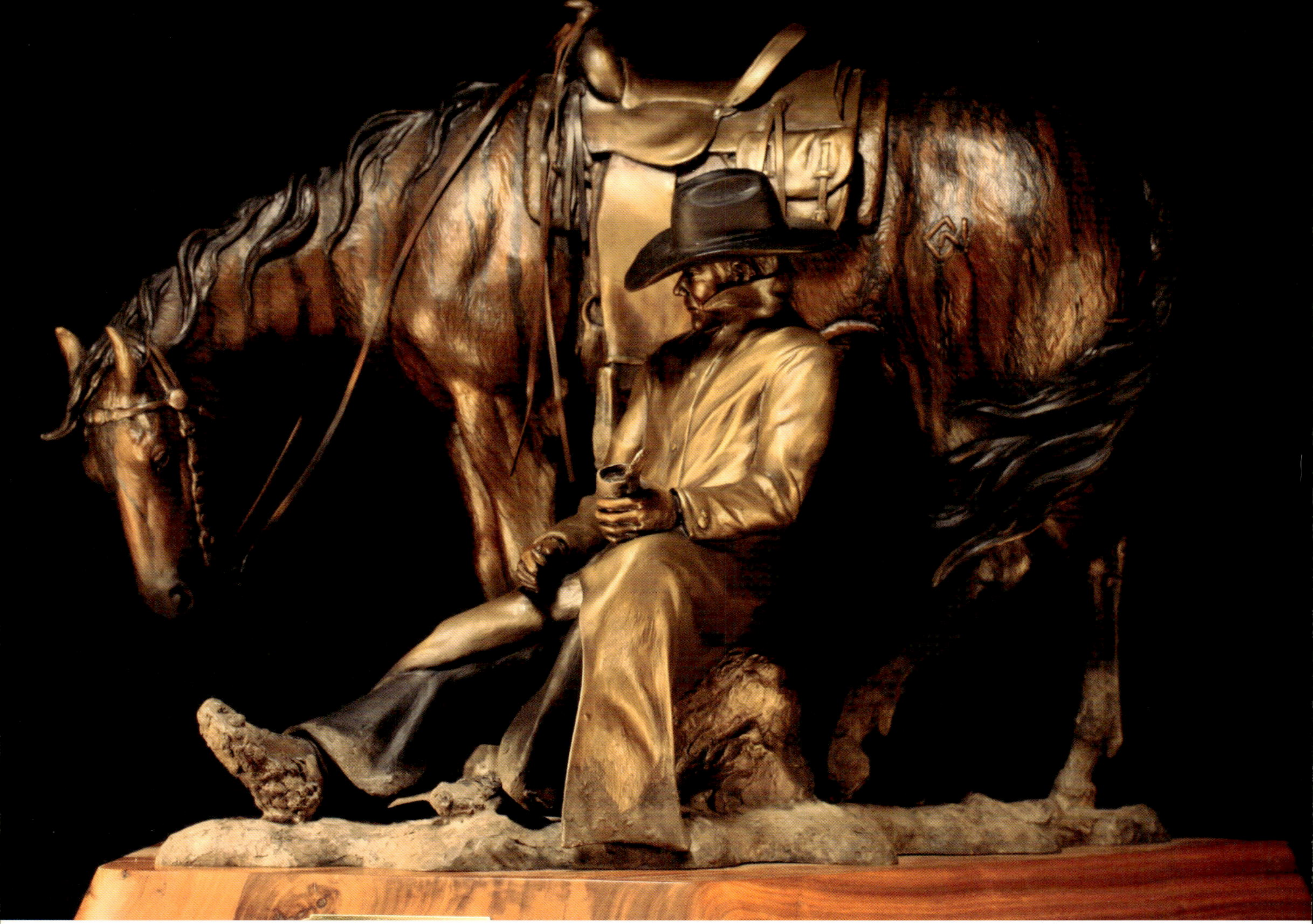

BEING A COWBOY MEANS GRITTING YOUR TEETH STEPPING UP AND DOING WHATEVER IT TAKES TO OVERCOME WHATEVER GETS IN YOUR WAY.
–TY MURRAY

COLD BEANS AND A WET SADDLE (2004)

Bronze, 18.5" x 24" x 19.5"

This sculpture depicts the unglamorous side of being a cowboy – working outside in miserable weather and pushing through to finish a job. It has been pouring cold rain all day long. The cowboy and his horse are covered with mud when they stop for a bite to eat. With no shelter from the rain, the cowboy knows it is too wet to start a fire, so he reaches into his saddlebags for a can of beans. Sitting on a rock, he makes the best of what he has. With cold beans in his belly, he'll swing back into his wet saddle and finish the job he has set out to do. That is the cowboy way.

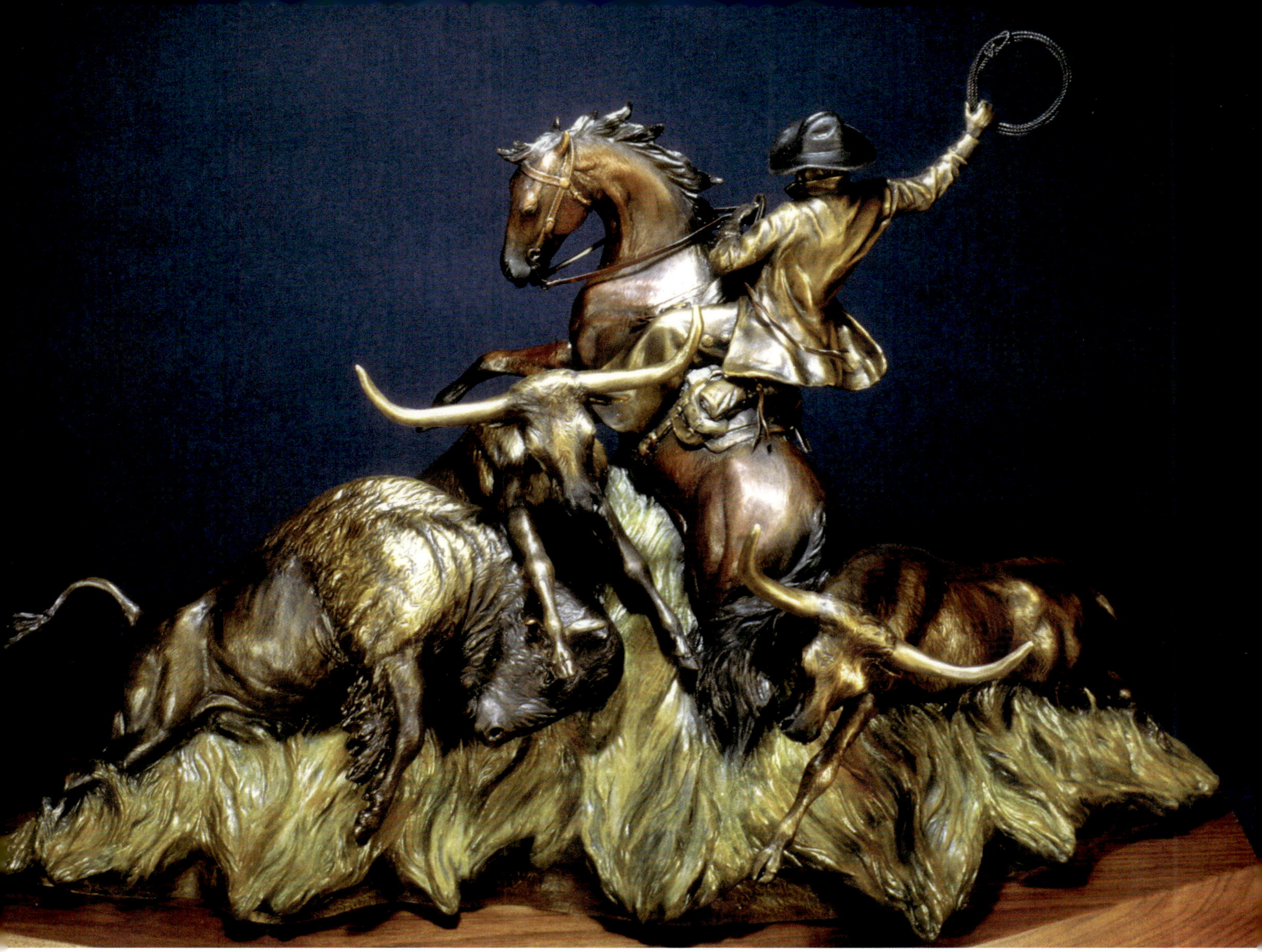

RANGE RIGHTS (1999)

Bronze, 17.5" x 27" x 12"

A lone cowboy is driving two longhorn bulls that have wandered off from the herd. They are on the trail when they come upon an old buffalo bull that challenges them for the right-of-way. The buffalo has no intention of allowing the others to cross into his range without a fight.

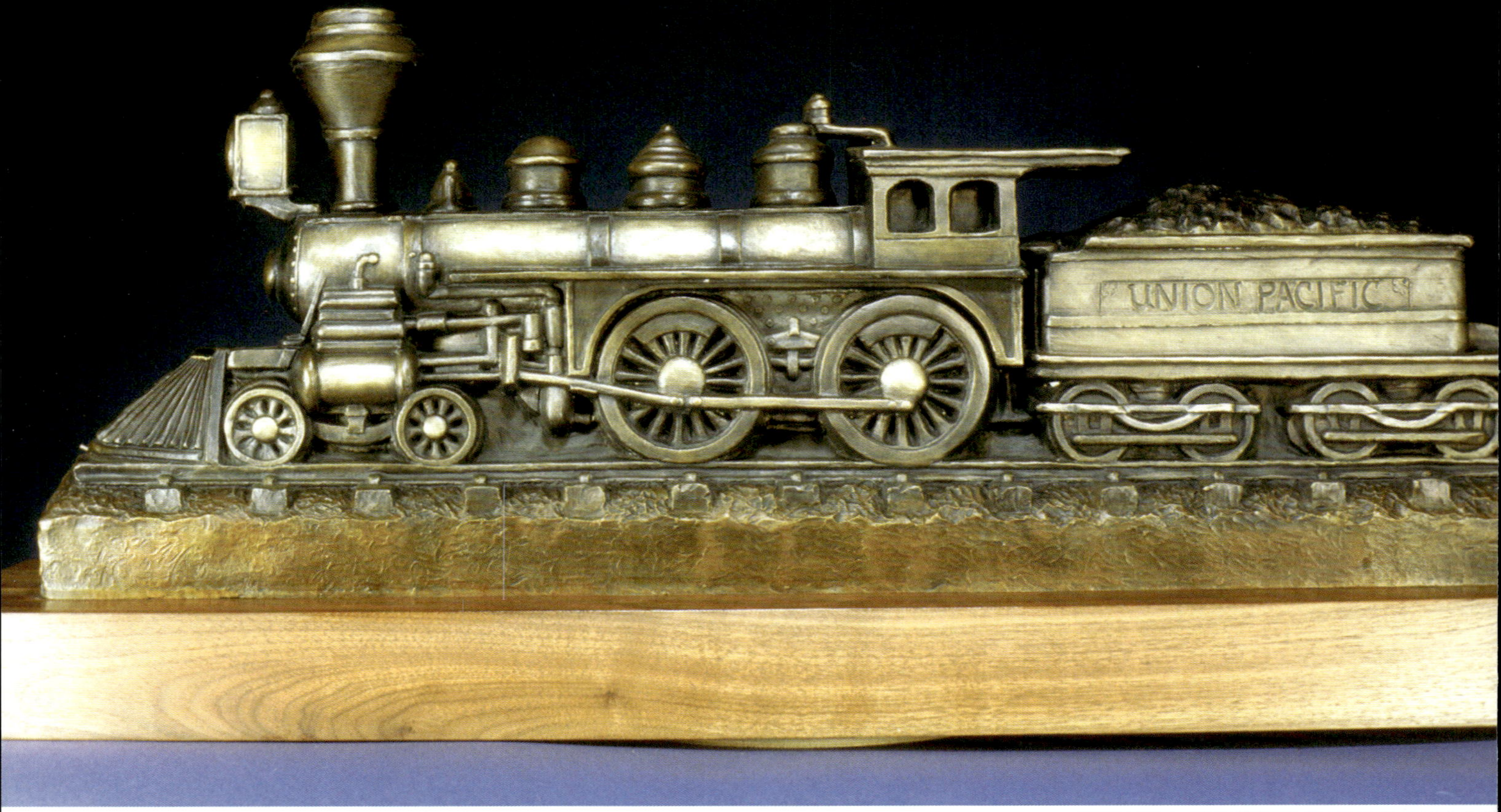
UNION PACIFIC

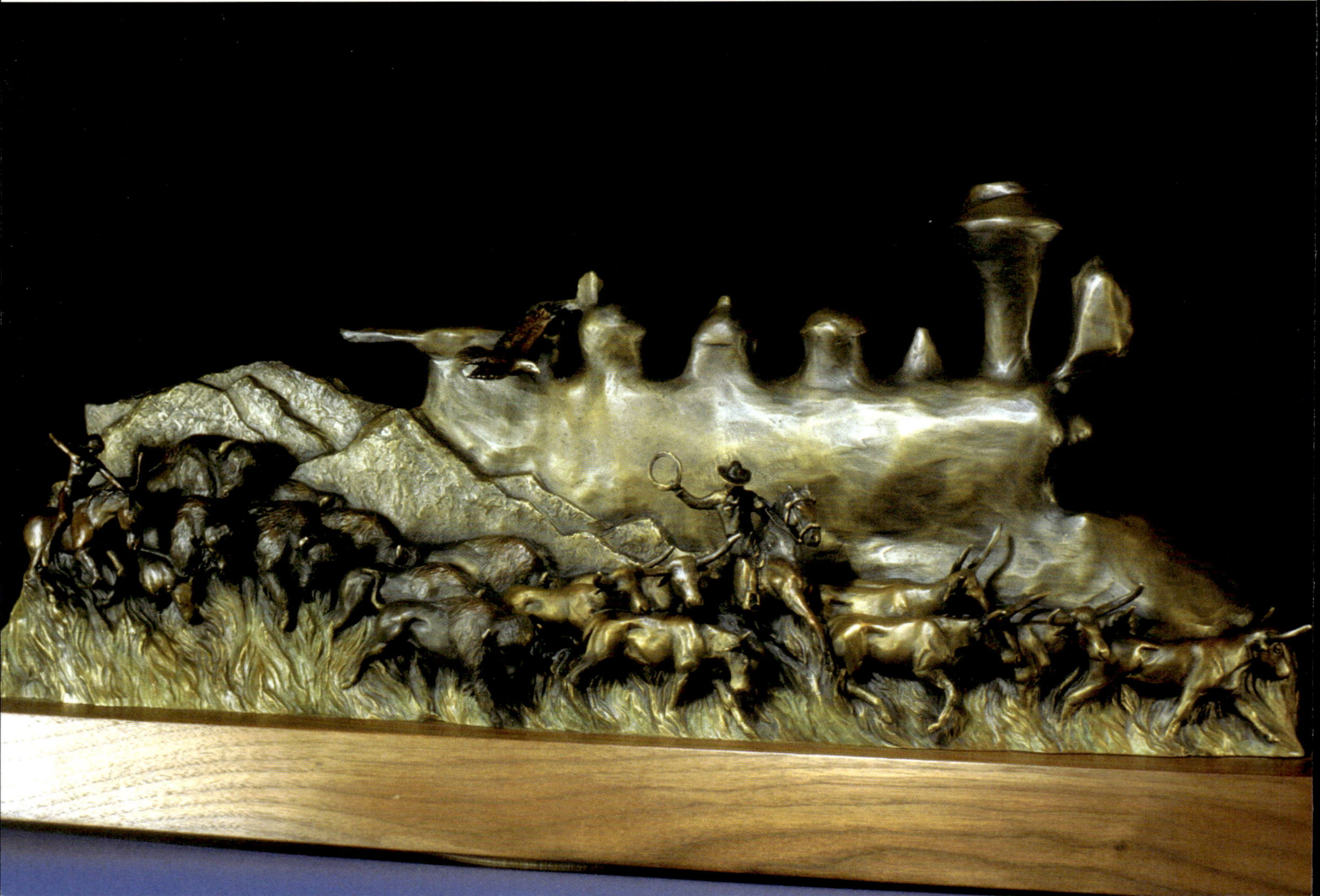

THE ROAD MUST BE BUILT, AND YOU ARE THE MAN TO DO IT. TAKE HOLD OF IT YOURSELF. BY BUILDING THE UNION PACIFIC, YOU WILL BE THE REMEMBERED MAN OF YOUR GENERATION.
–PRESIDENT ABRAHAM LINCOLN

IRON TRACKS THROUGH THE WEST (2005)

Bronze, 12" x 28" x 8.5"

This sculpture of the "iron horse" tells the story of America's Westward Expansion by merging the forces and figures that transformed the continent. Like a stream flowing to a river, the iron tracks of the railroad brought change and accelerated the development and progress of America. The railroad connected the people of the Atlantic and Pacific, helping join a diverse nation. The large steam engine and coal car, in a partial relief, symbolize the American drive to forge ahead through industry and technology. The right side of the sculpture shows a Plains Indian on a swift pony pursuing running buffalo; they represent the Native Peoples and animals of the untamed West. As the running buffalo move through the sculpture, they merge into longhorn cattle, which soon replaced the buffalo that grazed the open grasslands of the prairie. A cowboy on horseback, which is one of the most distinct images of the West, drives this herd of longhorns. Behind these figures, sculpted in relief, rise the Rocky Mountains. An eagle flies through the sky, which is silhouetted in the shape of the locomotive. The eagle's soaring flight symbolizes the freedom and hope of our great nation.

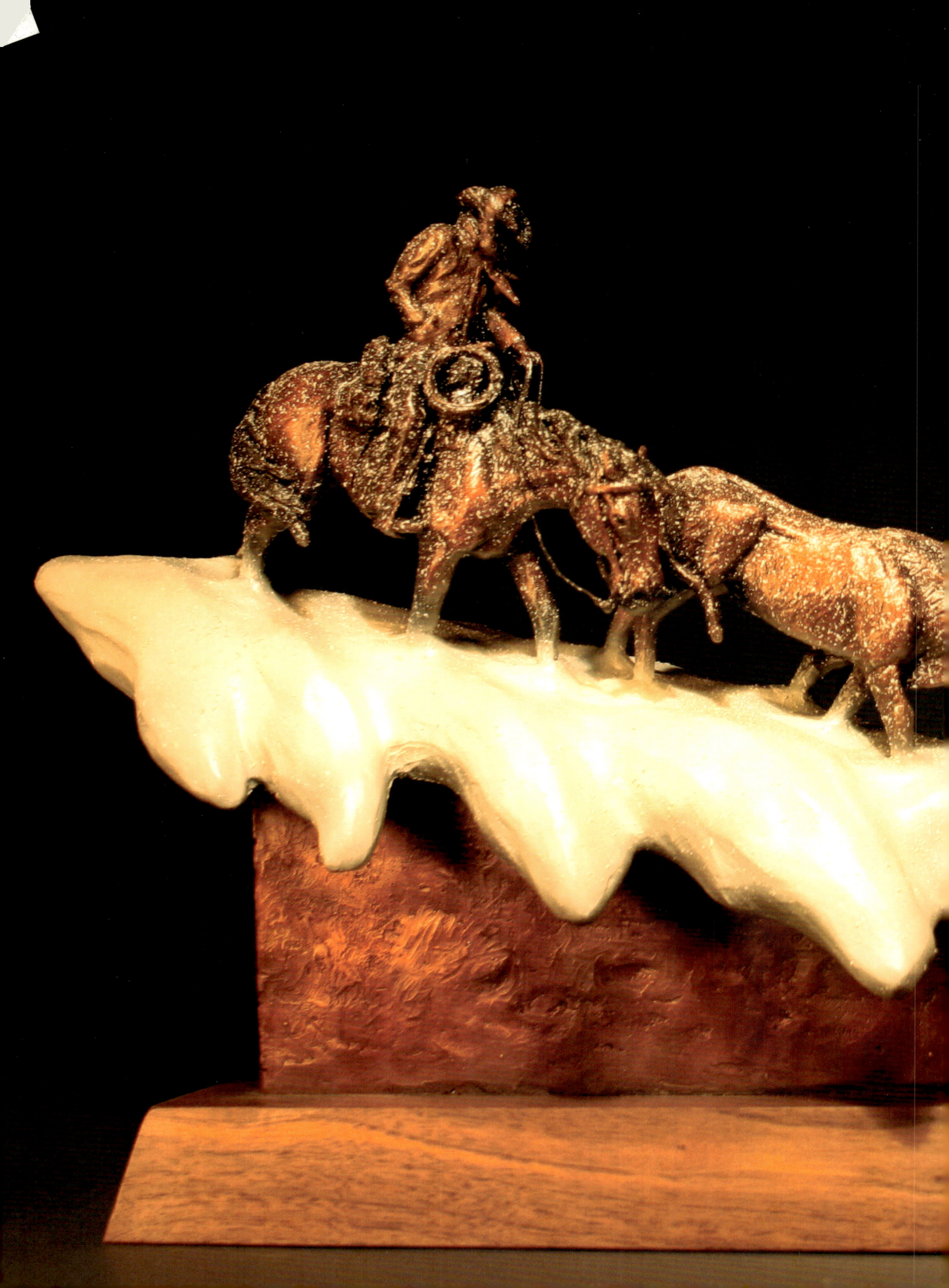

SNOWIN' AND BLOWIN' AT 10 BELOW (2007)

Bronze, 11.5'' x 21'' x 5.5''

I had to help my rancher friend, Guy Robinett, move a bunch of cows that had gotten out through a downed fence. I was working in my studio when he called to ask if I could get on horseback and help him move the cows back to his ranch. "It's 10 below zero outside!" I said. And he replied, "I know, I wouldn't be asking for your help if I didn't need it." I told him I would be there early the next morning. It took us all day to round up the cattle and move them back to the ranch. It was so cold that the horses and cattle had ice sticking to them. We pushed the animals with ropes and horses to get them to move. It was a long, cold, miserable day – one that I will always remember. I used it for inspiration and was able to get a new sculpture from that experience.

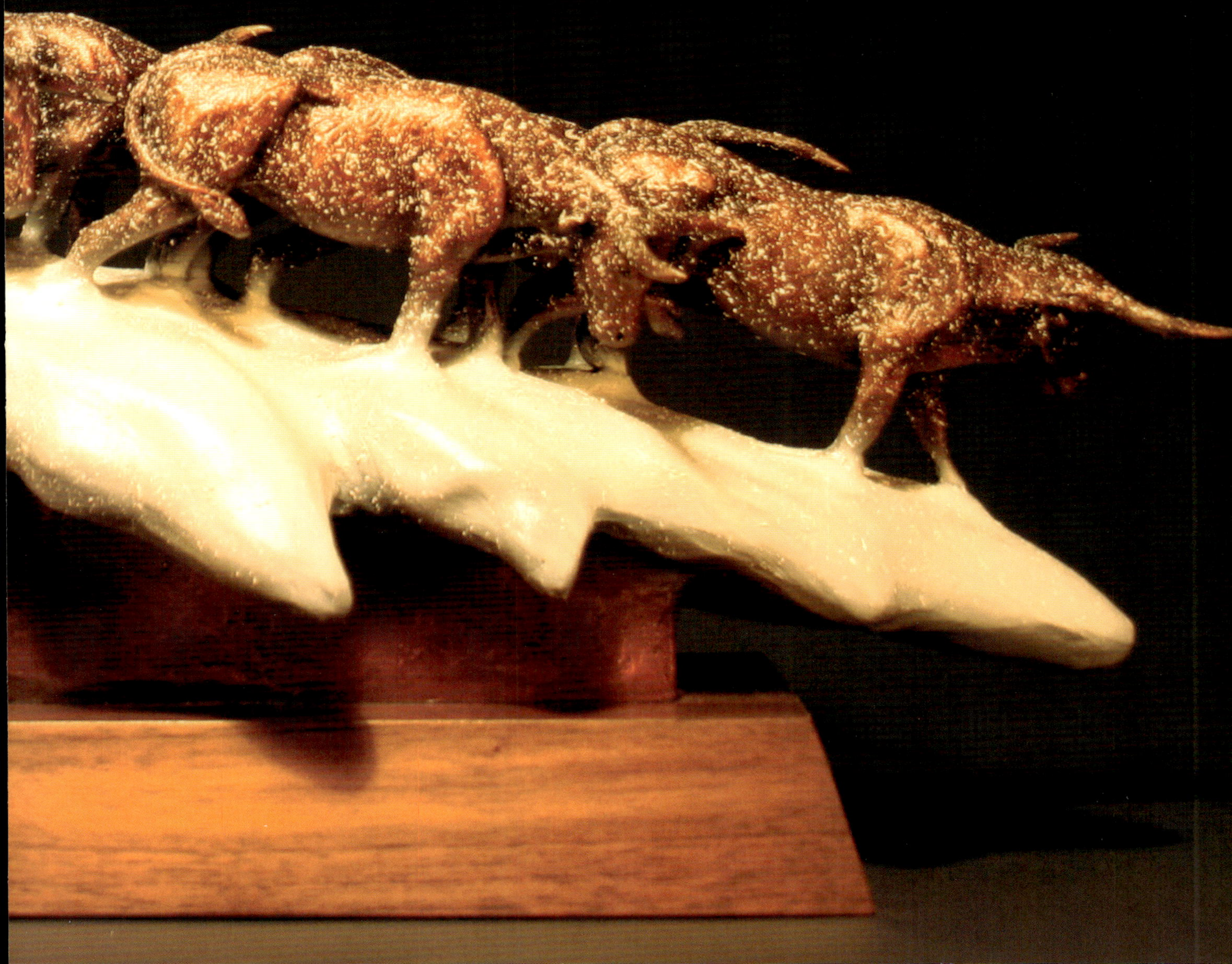

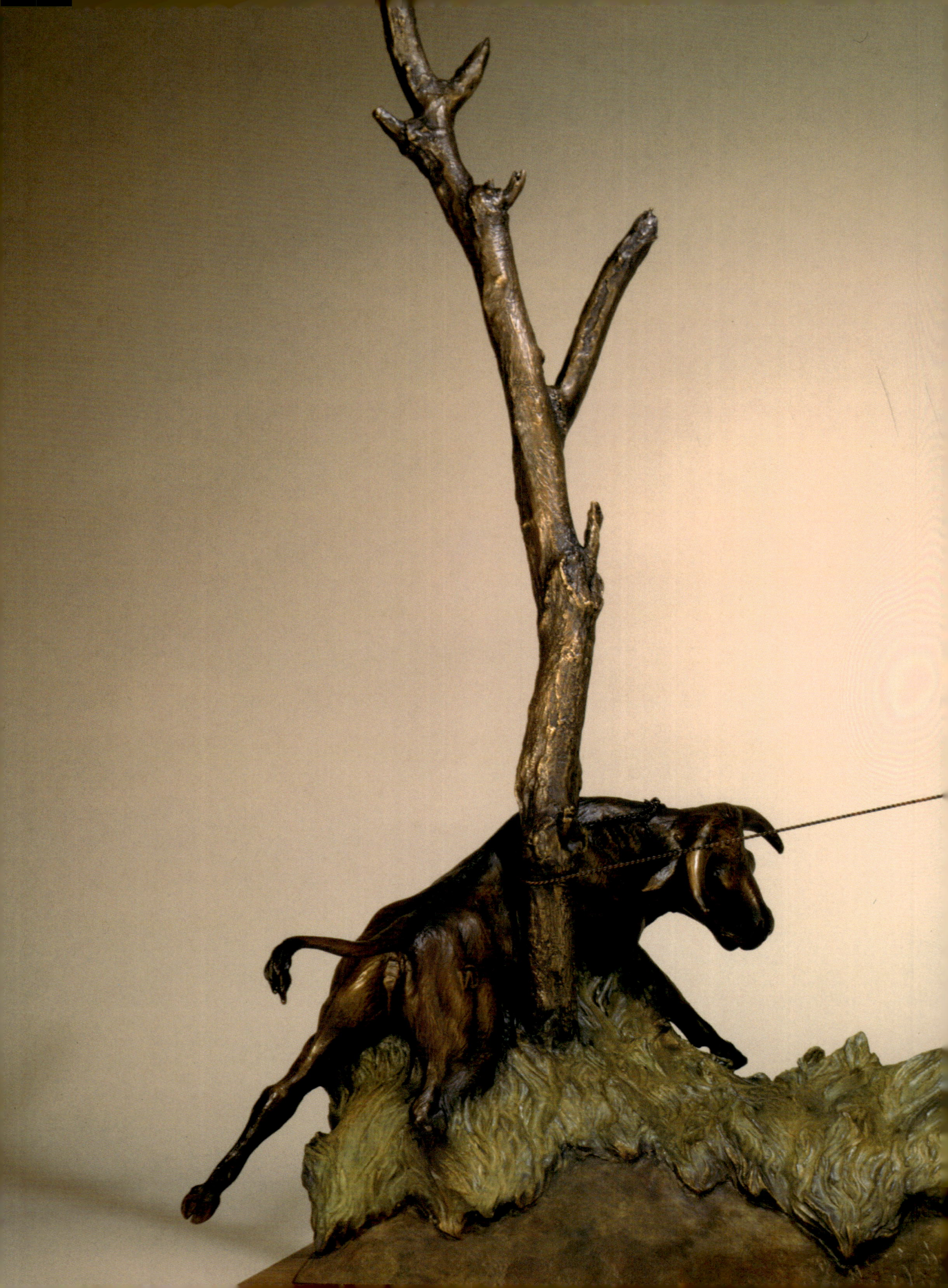

WHAT GOES AROUND COMES AROUND (2001)

Bronze, 25" x 24" x 9"

Roping is my favorite pastime. I use a well-known saying to depict what every cowboy knows from experience: "What goes around comes around." This cowboy is roping a rangy, crossbred, banana horn bull that has gotten in with his cows. The bull is fighting the rope and coming around the trunk of a tree, heading straight for the horse and cowboy. With his saddle starting to slip, he must decide whether to hold his dallies or let go. Either way, there's going to be a big wreck!

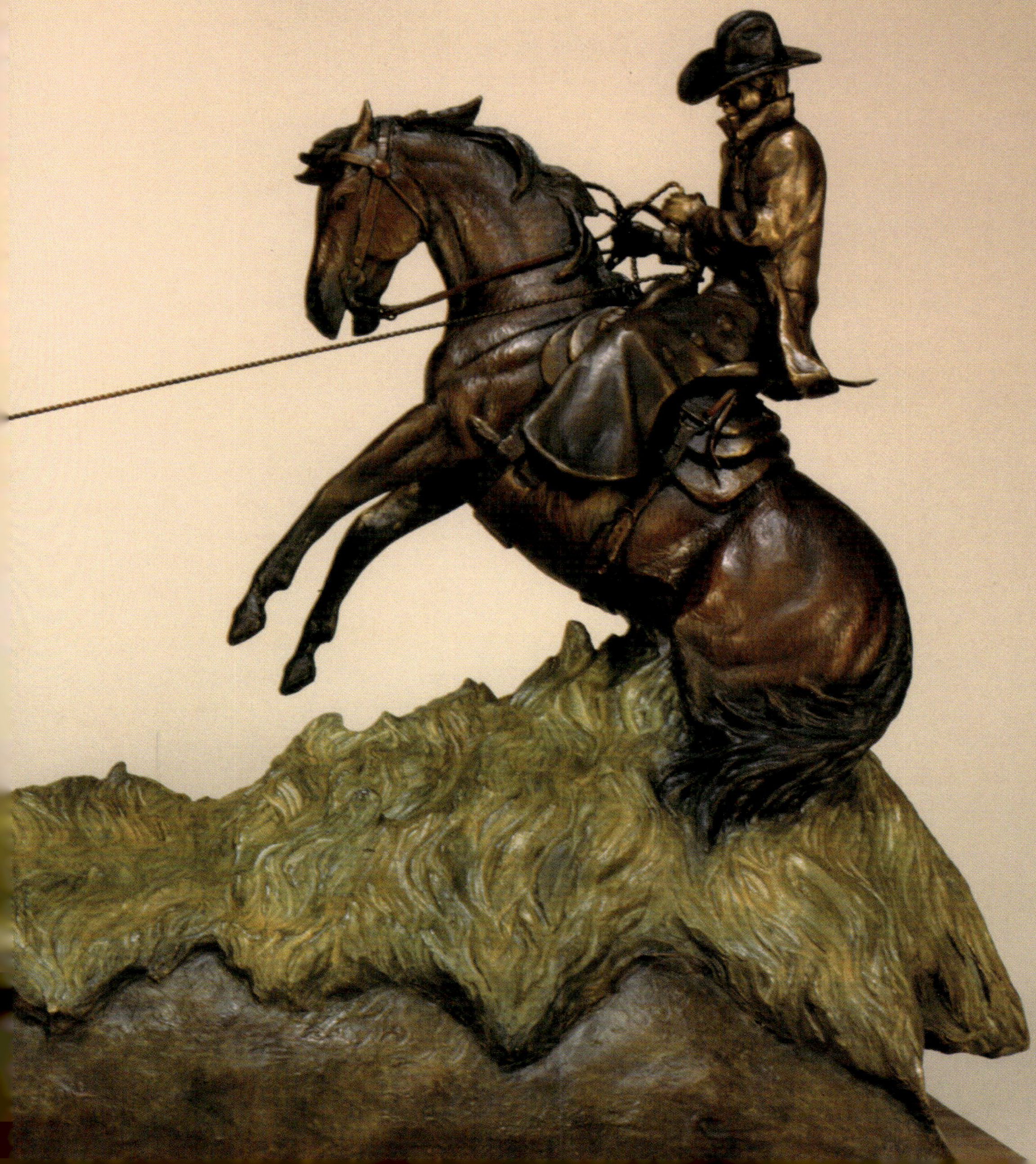

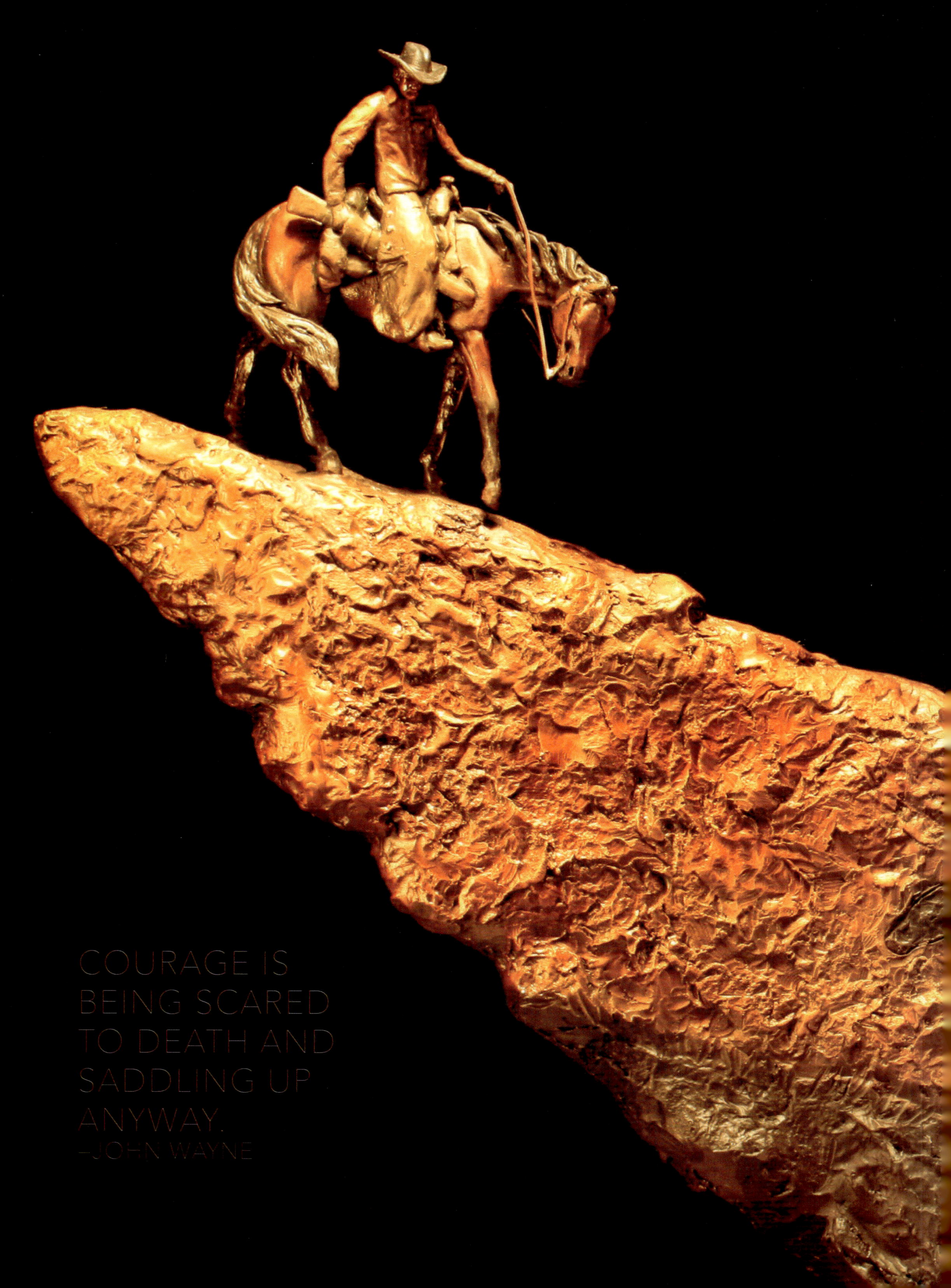

COURAGE IS
BEING SCARED
TO DEATH AND
SADDLING UP
ANYWAY.
–JOHN WAYNE

WHEN SHADOWS SPEAK OF DANGER (2006)

Bronze, 15.5" x 20" x 6"

It's always exciting to tell a good story. *When Shadows Speak of Danger* depicts a lone cowboy riding his horse down a steep ridge. His eyes are focused on the skyline of the next ridge, and he sees three warriors on horseback dressed for battle. The setting sun casts their shadows on the rocks below–a foretelling of what is to come.

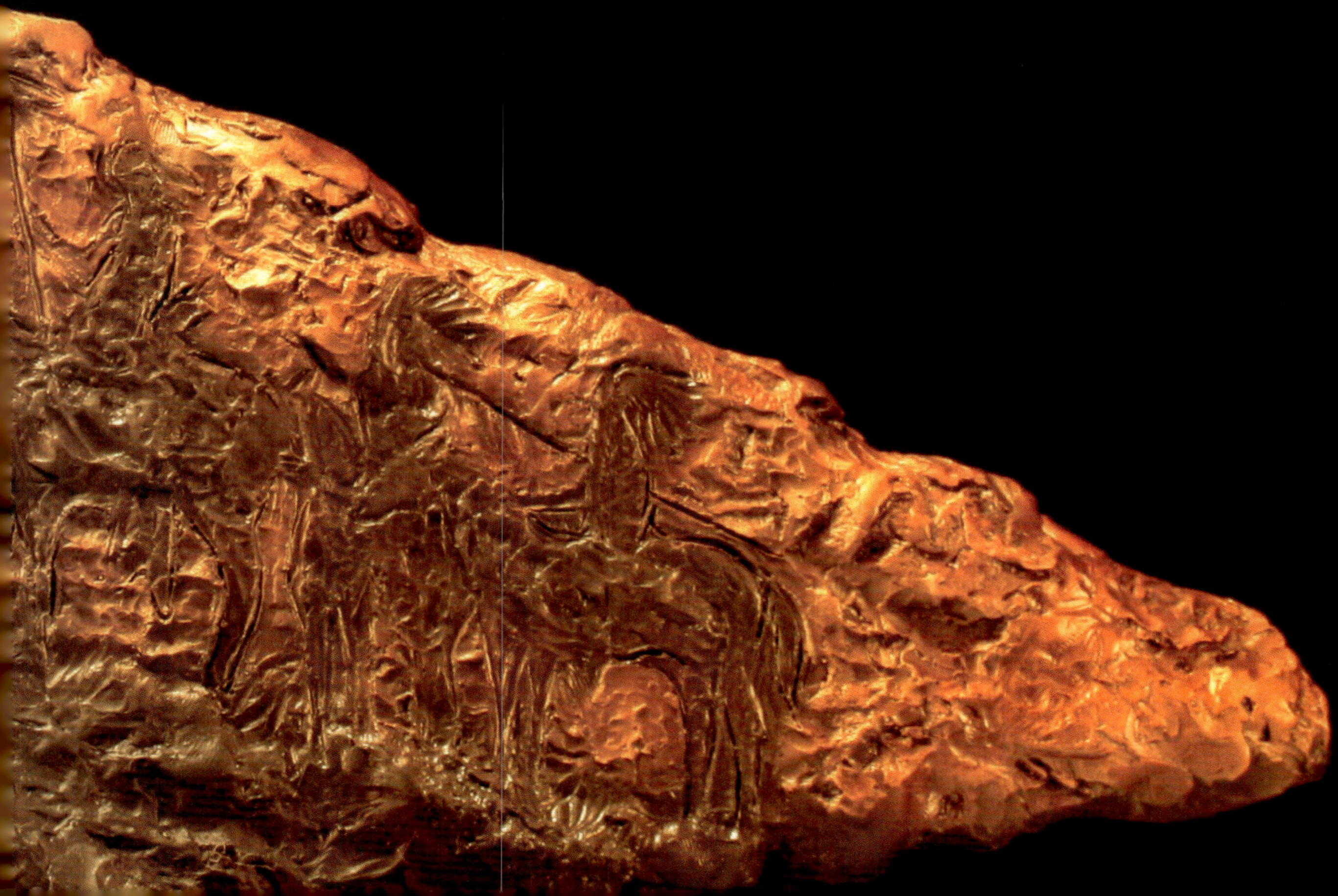

INSPIRATIONAL

THE BIGGEST INFLUENCES IN YOUR LIFE WILL BE THE PEOPLE YOU MEET AND THE BOOKS YOU READ. FILL YOUR MIND WITH POSITIVE THOUGHTS AND FEELINGS.
–CHRIS NAVARRO

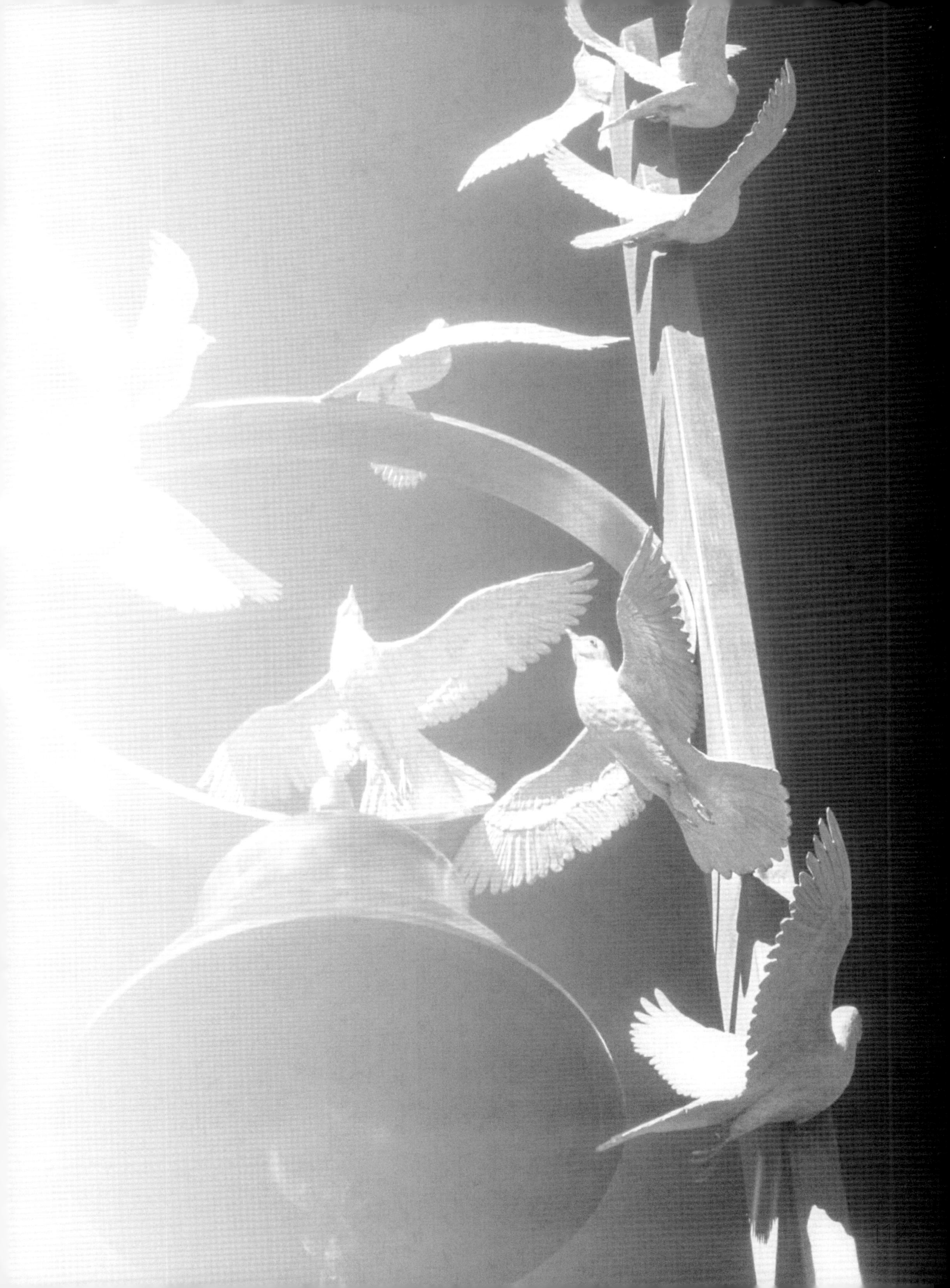

DARE TO DREAM BIG (2013)

Bronze, 15" x 19" x 10"

A cat sitting on a couple of books gazes into a mirror and sees his reflection as a lion. A mouse peeking around the mirror thinks, "Just what I need, a cat who thinks he is a lion!" It is all about the power of belief. The way to become a lion is to think and believe you are lion. My own cat, Grey-boy, modeled for this sculpture.

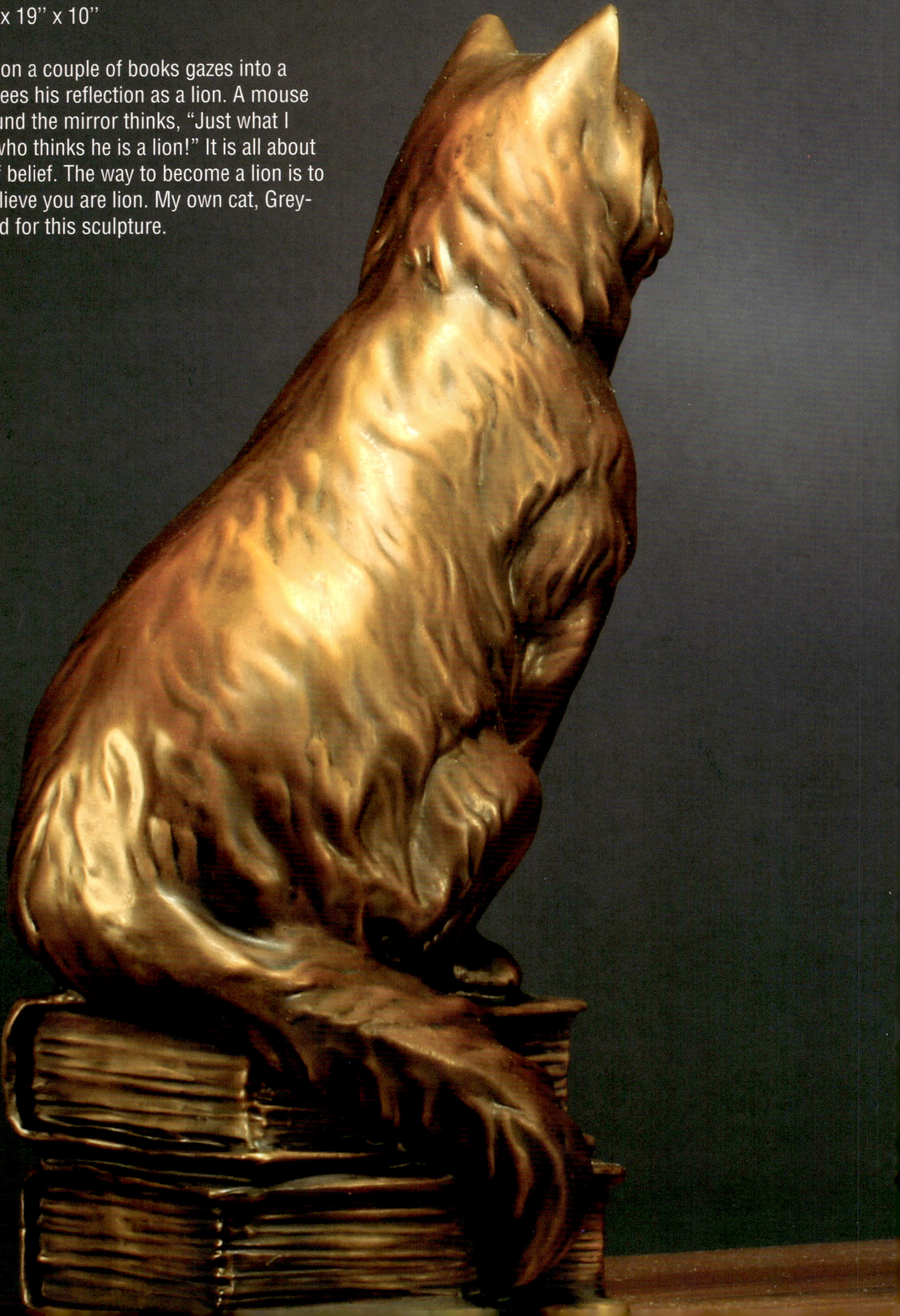

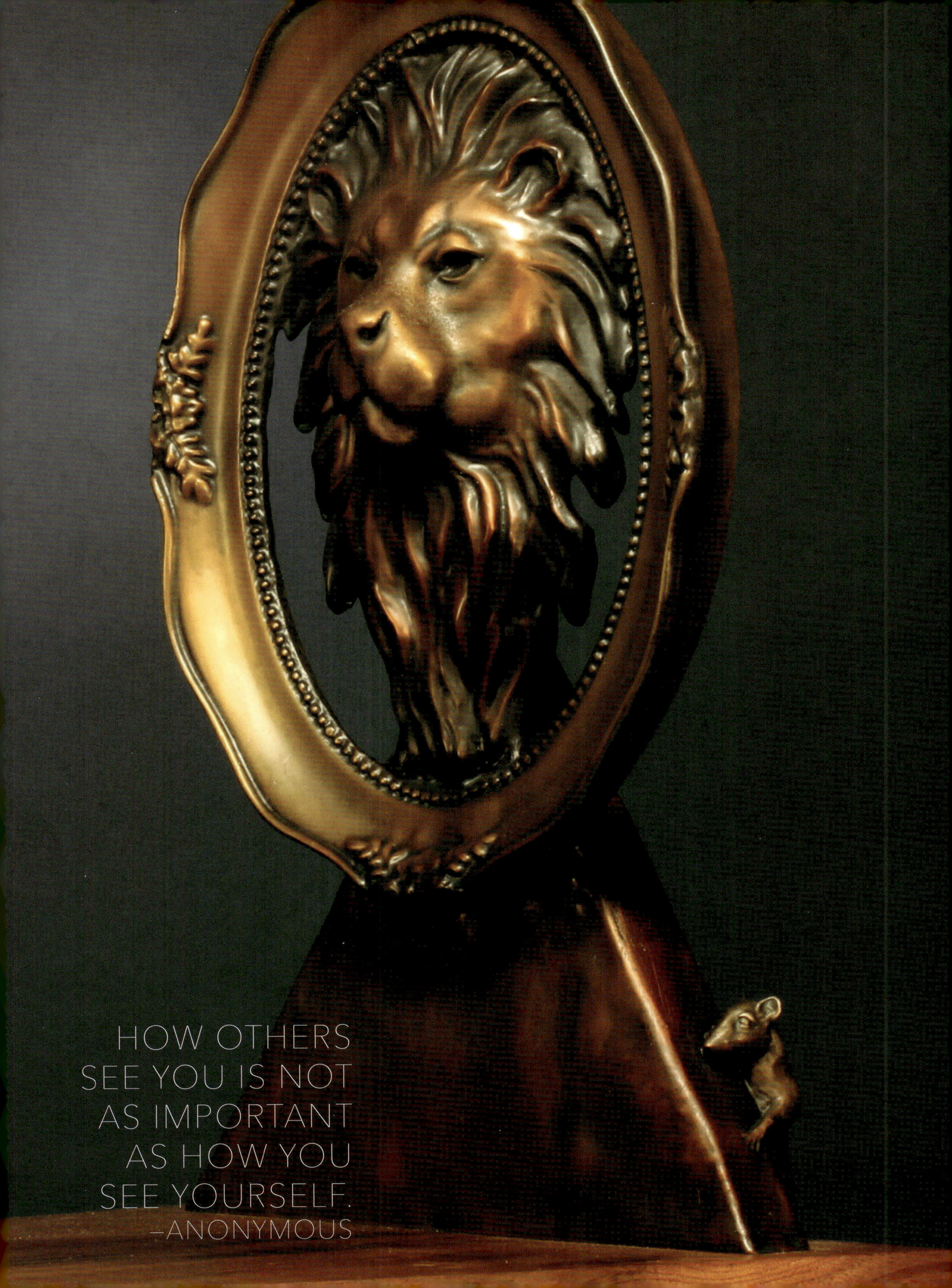

HOW OTHERS
SEE YOU IS NOT
AS IMPORTANT
AS HOW YOU
SEE YOURSELF.
–ANONYMOUS

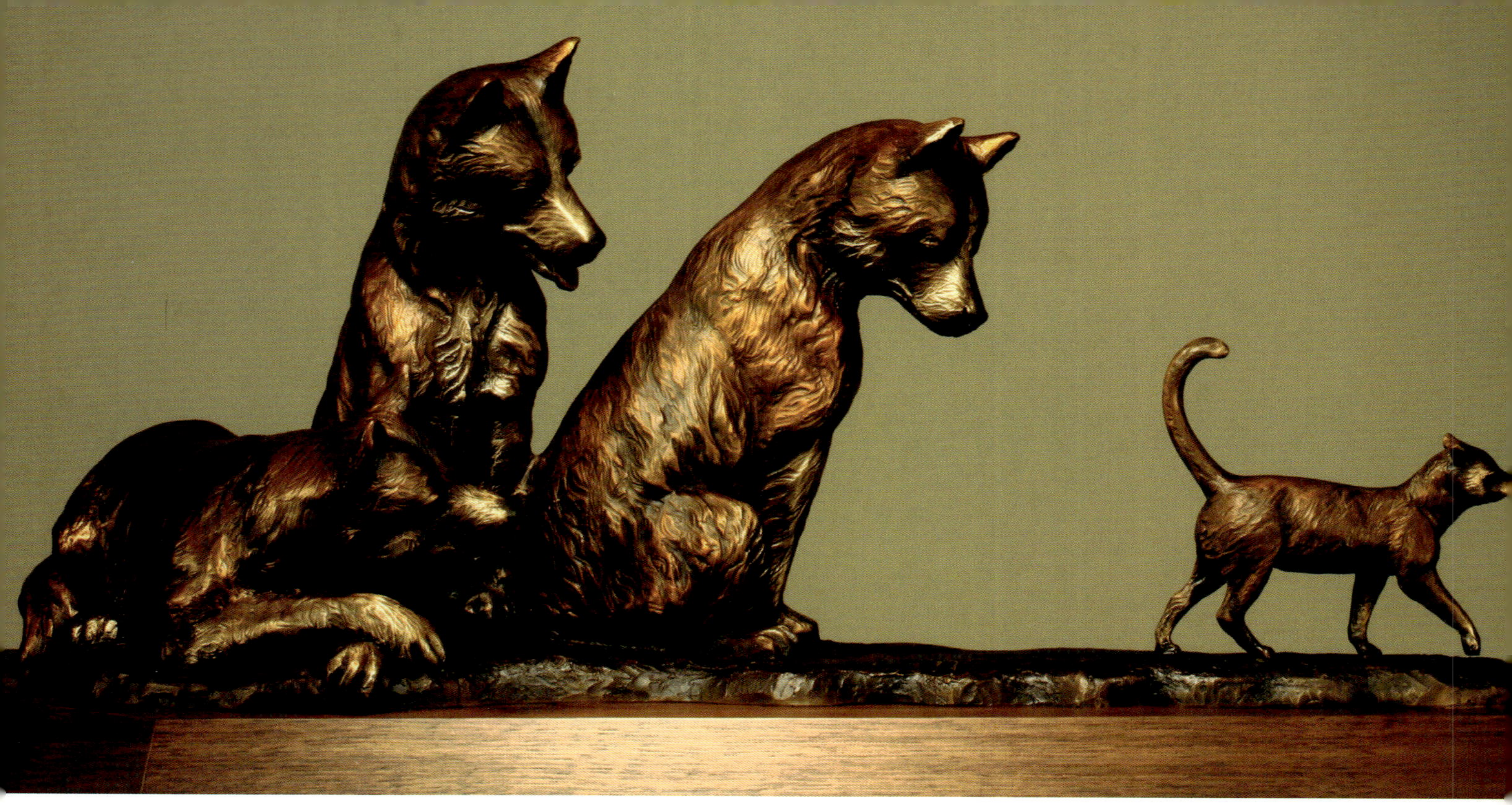

NO ONE CAN MAKE YOU FEEL INFERIOR WITHOUT YOUR CONSENT.
–ELEANOR ROOSEVELT

I SHALL FEAR NO EVIL (2012)

Bronze, 12" x 26.5" x 10"

Three Siberian Huskies watch as this little cat, with a fearless attitude, walks right past them. How you carry yourself in this world will influence many of the things that happen to you. I have always believed that you should try to live with as little fear as possible. Don't blame others or a circumstance for what happens to you. Accept the hand you're dealt and make the most of it. Where you come from does not have to be a limit on where you end up.

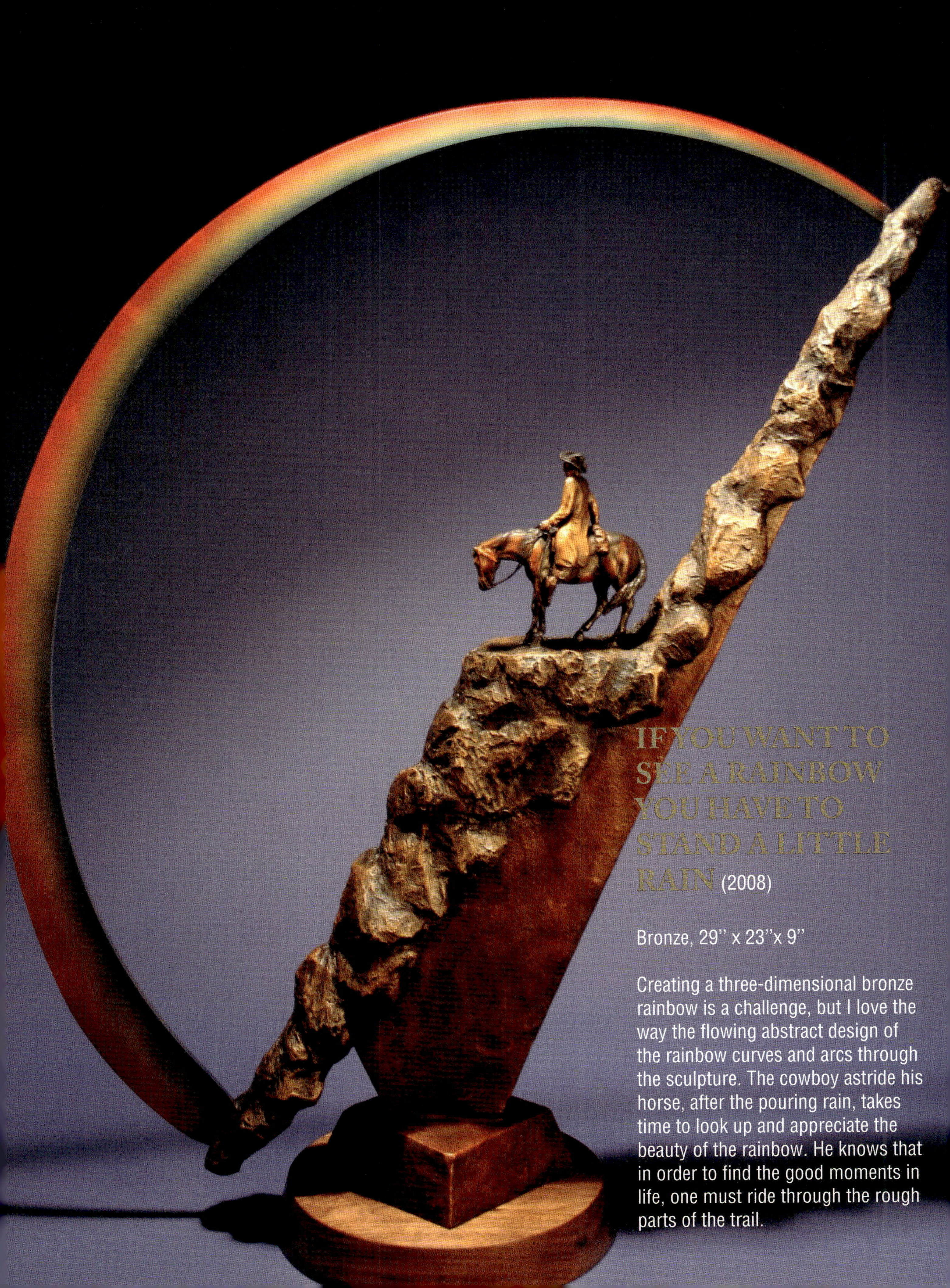

IF YOU WANT TO SEE A RAINBOW YOU HAVE TO STAND A LITTLE RAIN (2008)

Bronze, 29" x 23"x 9"

Creating a three-dimensional bronze rainbow is a challenge, but I love the way the flowing abstract design of the rainbow curves and arcs through the sculpture. The cowboy astride his horse, after the pouring rain, takes time to look up and appreciate the beauty of the rainbow. He knows that in order to find the good moments in life, one must ride through the rough parts of the trail.

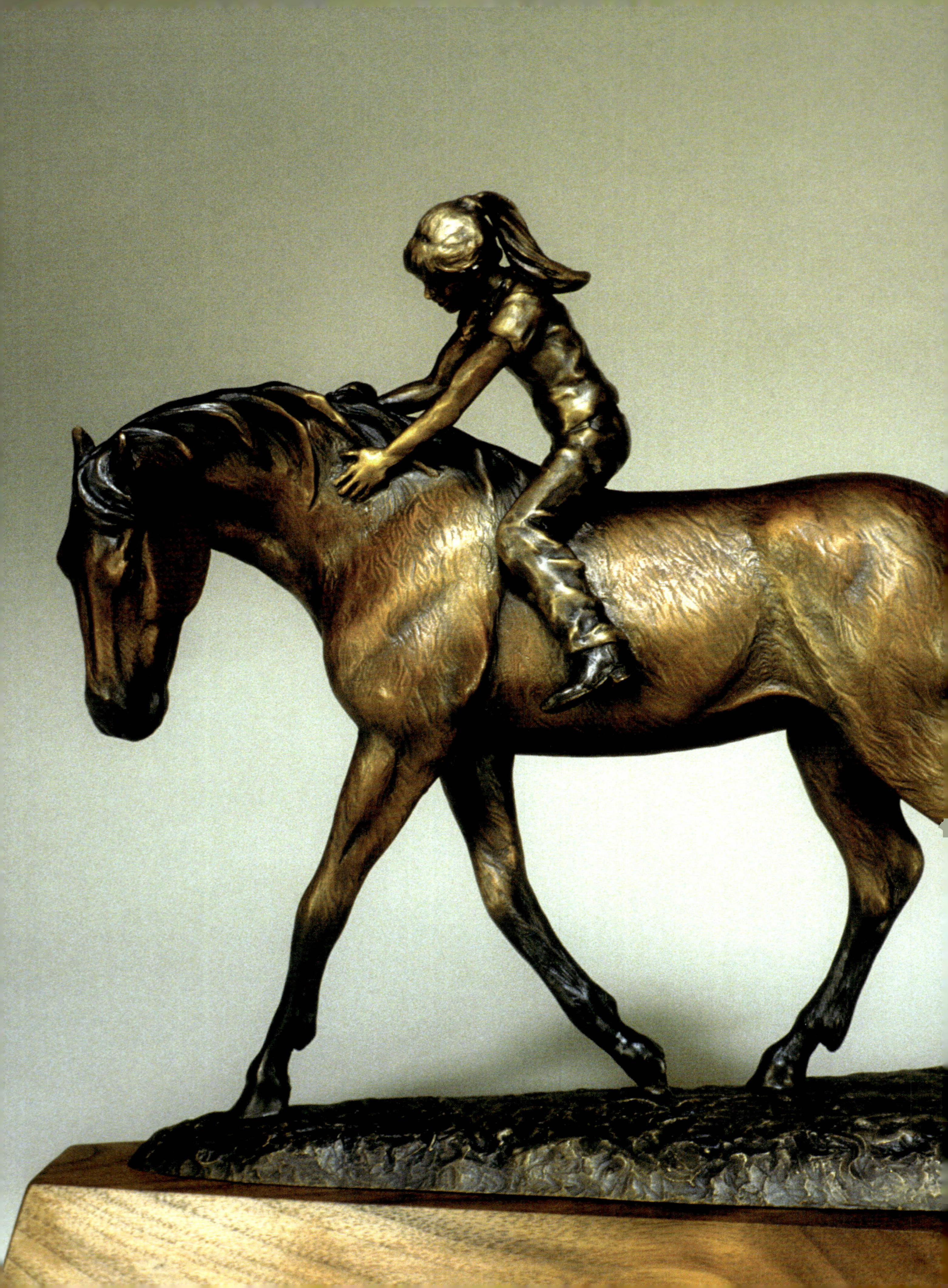

LIBERATION (2005)

Bronze, 11" x 20" x 7"

I created this bronze sculpture for Reach 4A Star Riding Academy, a therapeutic riding center in Casper, Wyoming. I can think of no better cause than using horses to enrich the lives of physically challenged children and adults. The natural motion and height of the horse helps to simulate the feeling of walking and also stimulates the rider's muscles. The rider learns balance and coordination, while gaining an increased sense of confidence with every new accomplishment. The base of the bronze is shaped as an abstract diamond, symbolizing that freedom is the jewel of life. Sitting on the young mare's back, the girl has abandoned the confinement of her wheelchair. She's riding free and easy without saddle or bridle – liberated and moving forward as one with the horse.

I believe that doing good things for others in this life increases happiness for both the giver and the receiver. The old adage, "What goes around comes around," is a motto by which I live.

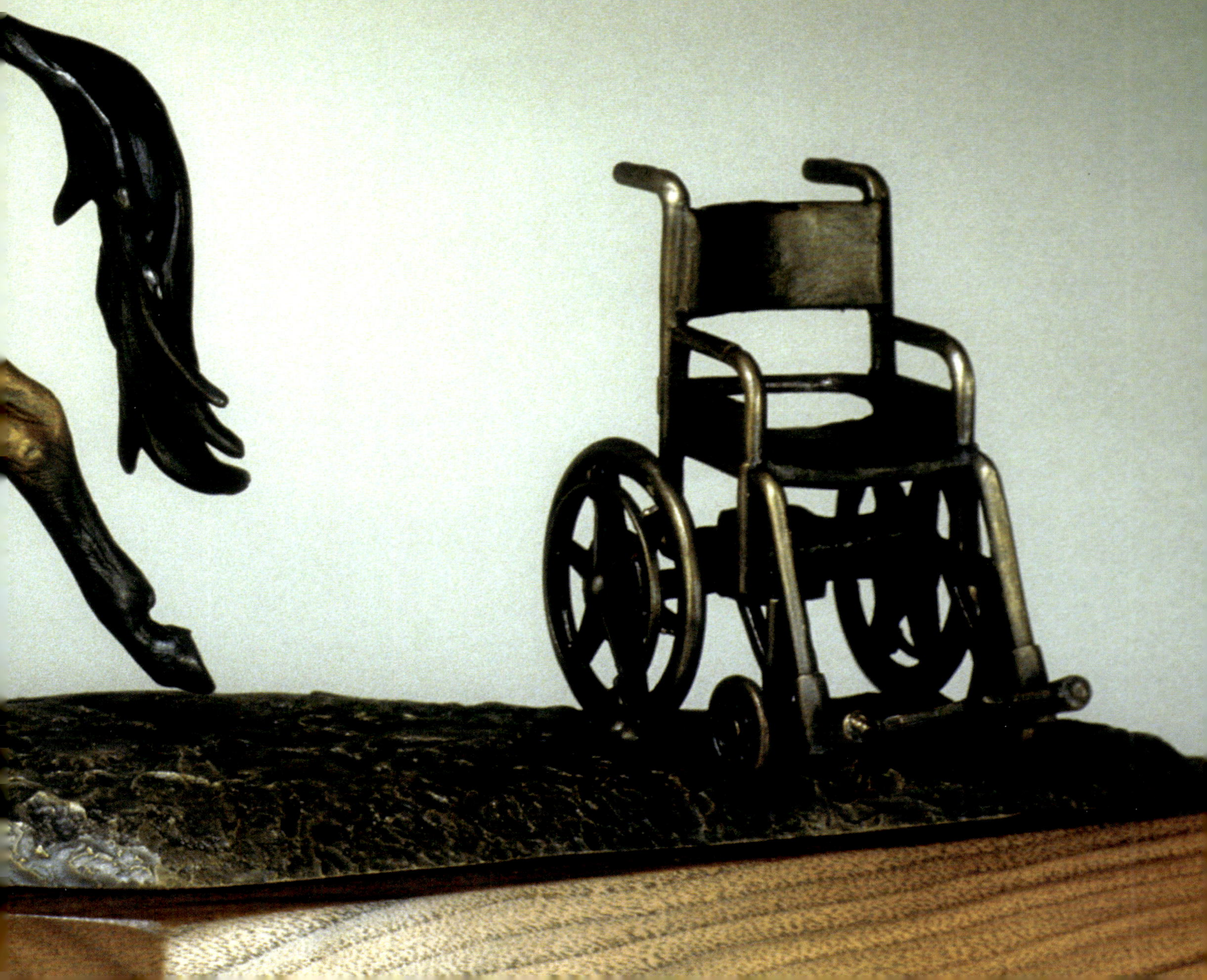

MONUMENTAL & LIFE SIZE WORKS

Title	Size	Description	Material	Location	Year
10TH MOUNTAIN	14'	World War II ski trooper	Bronze	Aspen, CO	1997
20% CHANCE OF FLURRIES	15'	Rancher on horseback with calf	Bronze	Fort Collins, CO & Casper, WY	2005
AUTUMN'S CHALLENGE	9'	Bull elk	Bronze	Vail, CO	2004
BEST FRIENDS	4'	Boy with dog on bench	Bronze	Casper, WY	1997
BOLT FROM THE BLUE	6'	Falcon	Bronze	Air Force Academy, CO	2015
BUFFALO SOLDIER	10'	Cavalry soldier	Bronze	Cheyenne, WY	2007
CAT PLAY	2'	Cat	Bronze	Denver, CO	2001
CHAMPION LANE FROST	15'	Bull rider	Bronze	Cheyenne, WY	1993
CLIMB AS HIGH AS YOUR DREAMS	9'	Rock Climber	Bronze	Mesa, AZ	2006
COLUMBIAN MAMMOTH	10'	Columbian mammoth	Bronze	Worland, WY	2010
COWBOY TOUGH	5'	Cowboy bucking on horse	Bronze	University of Wyoming, Laramie, WY	2004
EAGLE AGAINST THE SUN	10'	Eagle	Bronze & Stainless Steel	Casper, WY	1994
EDITORIAL WITHOUT WORDS	7'	Shriner with child	Bronze	Evansville, IN	2003
ESSENCE OF REX	13.5'	Tyrannosaurus rex	Bronze	Casper, WY	2014
FAMILY TIES	3.5'	Boy with girl	Bronze	Casper, WY	2003
FOUNTAIN OF HOPE	9'	Fountain with doves	Bronze & Stainless Steel	Sedona, AZ	2001
MUSTANG PRIDE	12'	Wild horses	Bronze	Casper, WY	2003
PRIDE OF THE ROCKIES	6'9"	Bighorn ram	Bronze	Tulsa, OK & Glenrock, WY	2014
PRINCE OF THE FOREST	5'	Whitetail buck	Bronze	Scottsdale, AZ	2001
RUFF & TUFF	3.5'	Brother & sister grizzly cubs	Bronze	Casper, WY	1997

Monumental & life size works cont.

Title	Size	Description	Material	Location	Year
SAINT ANTHONY'S JOY	8'	Saint Anthony	Bronze	Casper, WY	2011
SALMON DREAMS	2.5'	Two life-size grizzly bears	Bronze	Jackson, WY	2006
SO THAT'S A DUCK	2'	Labrador retriever puppies	Bronze	Denver, CO	2001
SPIRIT OF THE THUNDERBIRD	15'	Eagle dancer	Bronze	Casper, WY	1995
THE BIG BULL	9'	Bugling bull elk	Bronze	Vail, CO	1992
THE JOY OF LIFE	9'	Mare & colt	Bronze	Scottsdale, AZ & Casper, WY	2004
THE RING OF PEACE	19'	Bell with doves	Bronze & Stainless Steel	Casper, WY	2004
TREE OF LIFE	9'	Doves & tree	Bronze	Casper, WY	2005
WHEN CHAMPIONS MEET	15'	Saddle bronc rider	Bronze	Greeley, CO	1997
WILD SONG	8'	Coyote	Bronze	Cal State University, San Bernardino, CA	2016
WYOMING COWBOY	16'	Cowboy on bucking horse	Bronze	University of Wyoming, Laramie, WY	2014

AWARDS

Buffalo Bill Art Show & Sale, Cody, WY

Invitational 1991-2015

Peoples Choice Award for Quick Draw

2008, 2011 & 2013

Calgary Stampede Art Show, Calgary, Alberta

Invitational 2012-2013

Best of Show for New Artist 2012

Buffalo Bill Art Show & Sale, Cody, WY

2015 Honorary Artist

Wyoming Arts Council, Cheyenne, WY

2015 Governor's Art Award recipient

MUSEUM COLLECTION

Buffalo Bill Center of the West
Cody, WY

National Cowboy Hall of Fame
Oklahoma City, Ok

Pro Rodeo Hall of Fame
Colorado Springs, CO

Old West Museum
Cheyenne, WY

Pioneer Museum
Douglas, WY

Booth Western Art Museum
Cartersville, Georgia

Washakie Museum
Worland, WY

Tate Museum
Casper, WY

Bull Riding Hall of Fame
Fort Worth, TX

CONTACT

For information on sales, consultations, speaking opportunities, and bookings contact:

Navarro Studio
5231 Squaw Creek Road
Casper, WY 82604
307-259-7305
chrisnavarrostudio@gmail.com
chrisnavarro.com & cnavarroart.com

Navarro Gallery and Sculpture Garden
Tlaquepaque Suite D103
336 SR 179
Sedona, AZ 86336
928-204-1144
navarrogallery@gmail.com